THE THINGS

OUR

FATHERS SAW

THE UNTOLD STORIES OF THE WORLD WAR II GENERATION FROM HOMETOWN, USA

VOLUME VIII:
ON TO TOKYO

Matthew A. Rozell

WOODCHUCK HOLLOW PRESS

Hartford · New York

Information at matthewrozellbooks.com.

Maps by Susan Winchell.

Front Cover: "U.S. Marines in Landing Craft head for the beach at Iwo Jima on Feb. 19, 1945, during the initial landings." U.S. Marine Corps Historical Center. Public Domain Photographs, National Archives.

Back Cover: "Marine Aiming at a Japanese Sniper on Okinawa, 1945." National Archives, public domain.

Any additional photographs and descriptions sourced at Wikimedia Commons within terms of use, unless otherwise noted.

Publisher's Cataloging-in-Publication Data

Names: Rozell, Matthew A., 1961- author.
Title: On to tokyo: the things our fathers saw : the untold stories of the World War II generation, volume VIII / Matthew A. Rozell.
Description: Hartford, NY : Matthew A. Rozell, 2022. | Series: The things our fathers saw, vol. 8. | Also available in audiobook format.
Identifiers: LCCN 2022913755 | ISBN 978-1-948155-29-8 [hardcover] | ISBN 978-1-948155-27-4 [paperback] | ISBN 978-1-948155-30-4 [ebook]
Subjects: LCSH: World War, 1939-1945--Personal narratives, American. | World War, 1939-1945--Campaigns--Pacific Ocean. | United States. Marine Corps--Biography. | Military history, Modern--20th century. | Veterans--United States--Biography. | Military history, Modern--20th century. | BISAC: HISTORY / Military / World War II. | HISTORY / Military / Veterans. | BIOGRAPHY & AUTOBIOGRAPHY / Military.

matthewrozellbooks.com.

Created in the United States of America

To the memory of
~The World War II Generation~
and
~Thomas B. Vesey~

1930-2022
Korea Vet and Beloved Gentleman

"So much of war depends on ordinary soldiers, sailors, Marines, and airmen. Yes, you need brilliant people to lead them, but God, when I think of some of the things that happened because ordinary people just did the impossible, or the near impossible..."
—US ARMY RADIOMAN, PACIFIC, WORLD WAR II

THE THINGS OUR FATHERS SAW VIII:

ON TO TOKYO

THE STORYTELLERS

FRANK J. CASTRONOVO

CHARLES M. JACOBS

PAUL ELISHA

JAMES A. SMITH, JR.

SAMUEL R. DINOVA

ALBERT J. HARRIS

UNKNOWN JAPANESE SOLDIER

JOHN H. KOLECKI

HENRY C. HUNEKEN

STEVE T. JORDAN

MITCHELL MORSE

THE THINGS OUR FATHERS SAW VIII:

ON TO TOKYO

TABLE OF CONTENTS

AUTHOR'S NOTE   15

PART ONE/THE HARD ROAD BACK   21

THE PEARL HARBOR SURVIVOR   31

HAWAII   34
'WE WERE GOING TO GO TO WAR WITH JAPAN'   35
'SMOKE, FLAMES, EXPLOSIONS, SIRENS'   36
GUADALCANAL   39
THE GRENADE   40
'IT DIDN'T TAKE US LONG'   41
DOG TAGS   42
'JUST KEEP GOING'   43
HOME   44
'I HAVE NEVER TALKED MUCH ABOUT IT'   46

THE MARINE RIFLEMAN   49

'I FEEL LIKE I HAVE TO DO SOMETHING'   50
'A GUY WHO WANTED TO KILL SOMEBODY'   52
JIM CROW   53
SHIPPING OUT   55

'ISLAND PARADISE'   55

'HE GOT KILLED LAST NIGHT'   56

THE PATROLS   58

'DON'T WORRY ABOUT THE WORMS'   59

THE BEACH   60

'I WOULD FOLLOW HIM INTO HELL'   62

'THIS GUY'S DEAD'   63

'I WAS IN VERY BAD SHAPE'   64

THE BOXER   68

CAPE GLOUCESTER   70

STATESIDE   71

'HE HAD TO KISS IT'   72

'I THOUGHT THEY WERE ANIMALS'   73

'IT'S NOT YOUR JOB TO DIE FOR YOUR COUNTRY'   74

THE INVASION RADIOMAN I   **77**

RADIO SCHOOL   79

THE JOINT ASSAULT SIGNAL COMPANY   80

COMMANDO TRAINING   81

ATTACK IN THE ALEUTIANS   83

THE SCR-284   85

ATTU AND KISKA   87

'SURVIVING YOUR FIRST COMBAT'   88

LIBERTY   89

THE GILBERTS-MAKIN AND TARAWA   90

LANDING AT MAKIN   92

'I'LL SEE YOU ON THE BEACHES'   93

THE TIDES   95

'THE ONLY THING THAT SAVED ME'   96

THE 165TH IN ACTION 97

MAKIN MARY 98

KWAJALEIN 101

THE RATS OF TOBRUK 103

THE MARINE MECHANIC I 107

THE JAPANESE GENTLEMEN 109

'WHERE'S PEARL HARBOR?' 110

'I WANT YOU!' 111

PARRIS ISLAND 115

LEARNING THE ENGINES 116

MUD MARINES 118

THE EARLY LANDINGS 119

JUNGLE ROT 120

BOUGAINVILLE 121

THE SEABEES 123

KEEPING THE TANKS IN ORDER 124

GUAM 127

THE FEVER 130

ZEROES 131

PART TWO/BANZAI 135

THE RUNNER 137

'WE'RE GOING FOR A YEAR'S VACATION' 138

JUNGLE TRAINING 141

SHIPPING OUT 143

THE LANDING   145

WOUNDED   152

'THEY HAD BAKER PROPPED UP AGAINST THE TREE'   153

'HE SWUNG THE SWORD'   155

THE REPLACEMENT   156

HOME   159

THE MARINE GUNNER I   161

'YOUR ASS BELONGS TO THE MARINE CORPS'   163

TRAINING TO BE A MARINE   163

'AWED BY THE DESTRUCTION'   165

THE MARSHALLS   166

'LOSE IT AND IT'S YOUR ASS'   167

THE 'INSTRUMENT CORPORAL'   168

SAIPAN   169

'THE MOST HORRIBLE MOMENT OF MY LIFE'   170

'THE PLACE WAS FULL OF BODIES'   171

RUNNING INTO THE 27TH DIVISION   172

MARPI POINT   174

THE LITTLE GIRL   175

TINIAN   175

'NOBODY KNEW WHO THE GUY WAS'   177

'REVENGE FOR THE DEAD'   179

THE AMERICAN LANDINGS   180

MOVING THE PATIENTS   182

PREPARING FOR BANZAI   183

'Sadness, Pity and Anger' 184

'My Foxhole is My Grave' 186

'Please Cut Skillfully' 188

'The End Has Come' 189

PART THREE/'I HAVE RETURNED' 193

THE INVASION RADIOMAN II 195

Leyte 196

Abandoned 197

Kamikazes 198

'You Don't Want to Get Stuck Here' 200

The Luzon Campaign 201

The Baby 202

'I Have Returned' 203

THE MARINE MECHANIC II 205

Iwo Jima 206

Tank Retrieval Under Fire 208

Hit on Iwo 210

Going Home 211

'It saved A Lot of American Lives' 214

The Truck Accident 216

'He Hugged Me, And He Started to Cry' 217

'So Many Stories' 219

THE BAR MAN 221

'I HAD A PREMONITION' 222
'YOU WON'T HAVE A SCAR' 223
'THE HORRORS OF WAR' 226
'A DEAD COMPANION FOR THE NIGHT' 226
THE EXPLOSION IN THE CAVE 228
FRIENDLY FIRE 229
'DROWNING IN HIS OWN BLOOD' 230
GOING HOME 231
'PEOPLE WHO DETEST WAR' 234

THE MARINE GUNNER II 235

IWO JIMA 235
'SOMEBODY MADE A BIG MISTAKE' 236
'THAT WAS MY LAST VISIT TO A CAVE' 237
'I HOPE IT'S OUR GUYS!' 238
'YOU DIDN'T GET A CAKE' 239
'I NEVER SAW A HERO' 240
'MY TEN MINUTES OF FAME' 241

THE B-29 RADIOMAN 243

FLIGHT TRAINING 245
A PIONEER CREW 248
'WE GOT CLOBBERED' 249
OVER THE TARGET 251
THE INCENDIARY BLITZ 251

'KOBE IS BURNING!'   252
SAVING THE CREW   256
CLOSE CALLS   257
'I KISSED THE GROUND'   260

PART FOUR/OKINAWA AND BEYOND   263

HACKSAW RIDGE   265

'GREETINGS FROM UNCLE SAM'   268
THE 77TH DIVISION   269
LEYTE   270
THE RUN-UP TO OKINAWA   270
THE KAMIKAZES   271
HACKSAW RIDGE-THE MAEDA ESCARPMENT   272
'HELP ME!'   273
JAPANESE INFILTRATORS   274
'BURN THEM OUT'   275
'FIX BAYONETS, NO ROUND IN THE CHAMBER'   277
DESMOND DOSS   277
MORE LOSSES ON THE ESCARPMENT   281
'OLD PEOPLE AND CHILDREN'   282
ERNIE PYLE   283
RETURN TO OKINAWA   284

THE NAVY CORPSMAN   287

HOSPITAL CORPS SCHOOL   288
THE INVASION OF GUAM   291

OKINAWA   295
'HE WAS LEFT THERE TO DIE'   295
'A LONG TRIP HOME'   297
THE RESERVES   298
ON TO KOREA   299
THE CHOSEN RESERVOIR   301
CHESTY   303
THE STOLEN CIGARS   304
THE GREEK AIR FORCE   305
THE CHINESE ON THE MOUNTAIN   307
BLOOD   308
'THE CHOSIN FEW'   309
'YOU PLAY THE HAND YOU'RE DEALT'   309

THE INVASION RADIOMAN III   311

OKINAWA   311
MEETING ERNIE PYLE   312
GI REPORTER   315
PUSHING THE ODDS   316

PART FIVE/FINAL THOUGHTS   319

OCCUPATION DUTY   321

TRAINING TO BE AN OFFICER   324
'AN EDUCATION BEYOND BELIEF'   324
'THEY THOUGHT I WAS SENT FROM HEAVEN'   325
THE JAPANESE HOUSEBOY   327

AN EXTENDED STAY   328
TRANSITIONING TO HOME   329
'FROM SMART-ASS BOY TO A MAN'   331
REUNION   331

THE INVASION RADIOMAN IV   335

'THE STYLE OF THE TIMES'   337
HOME   339
ADJUSTING TO CIVILIAN LIFE   340
'I'M NOT GOING TO BE A PART OF IT'   343
LESSONS OF WAR   344
'YOU HAVE TO HAVE BEEN THERE'   345
THE 'GREATEST GENERATION'   346

THE RESTING PLACE   349

ACKNOWLEDGEMENTS   363

Author's Note

I landed at Albany International Airport just as the evening was getting underway, returning from a trip to Toronto to re-interview an old Holocaust survivor friend of mine. It was a great trip, sitting with her in her living room, with the film director, cameraman, and one of Ariela's daughters. It was so good to see her after several years of meeting her at our soldier-survivor reunions, the last of which was in 2015 for the 70th anniversary of the liberation of the Train Near Magdeburg. But it was also good, given the extra stress of pandemic-era flight, to return home to upstate New York.

I still had an hour's drive north to the homestead where I pen these books. Two of my children currently share an apartment across the Hudson River from the state capital at Albany, in Troy, New York, so I decided to pay them an unannounced visit, but they already had plans, of course—they are young people, after all, and it was a beautiful Friday night.

I went up the hill to the old state highway that runs for fifty miles north and brings me almost to my door. City kids were out riding bikes in the street of their working-class neighborhood down by the river, others sitting comfortably on their stoops, watching the world go by. Troy, New York, is the home of Uncle Sam.[1] Also

---

[1] *the home of Uncle Sam* - "Uncle Sam is based on Samuel Wilson, who resided in Troy from 1789 until his death in 1854. Wilson and his brother owned and managed a meat packing business in Troy. They supplied a contractor, Elbert Anderson, for the federal government with beef, pork, whiskey and salt, which were sent to troops stationed nearby. Wilson, who also

known as the Collar City, a hundred plus years ago it hosted over two dozen shirt and collar factories. Irish and Italian men and women emigrated to work the industries, organize labor, build their churches, create their neighborhoods. Irish labor leader and future revolutionary James Connolly, executed by the British for his role in the famed 1916 Dublin 'Easter Rising,' even lived here for two years during the turn of the last century. Today, modern-day film crews flock here to use the spectacular architecture of that day as the backdrop for their turn-of-the-century dramas, such as *The Gilded Age* and *The Age of Innocence*. But there is another story, from this town, that needs to be told—the story of the sons who went off to fight the war as part of a federalized National Guard unit, drawn from the good stock at Troy and surrounding communities.

As I took my time leaving the heart of the city, I once again passed by St. Peter's Cemetery—rolling hillocks, beautiful trees and shrubbery, groomed pathways, the memorials adorned with mostly Irish surnames. I had never stopped here before, but then I noticed a historical marker. I turned around and entered the cemetery.

---

worked as an Army inspector, stamped on every barrel of goods he approved the letters, 'US/EA.' Following the death of Wilson, who was affectionately known as 'Uncle Sam,' a legend began. Dock workers joked that the 'US' of 'US/EA' stamped on inspected barrels stood for 'Uncle Sam.' Many of the men who worked in Troy and shipped the barrels became soldiers during the War of 1812, and ate the beef they had packed. They continued to spread the joke to other soldiers. The story grew until Uncle Sam and the United States became synonymous.

In 1961, the U.S. House of Representatives and Senate unanimously passed a law which proclaimed that Samuel Wilson of Troy, New York, was the progenitor of the nation's symbol, Uncle Sam, and that Troy is the official home of Uncle Sam. The bill was signed by President John F. Kennedy." Source: The City of Troy, New York - Home of Uncle Sam. Library of Congress, American Folklife Center. memory.loc.gov/diglib/legacies/loc.afc.afc-legacies.200003395/

So, this was where LTC O'Brien was buried. I knew I had to find him.

The sun was now about to set. I was the only person I could see in the cemetery; I drove and walked around for a good time, looking for the grave of a man I had learned of in writing my first volume on the Pacific, a posthumous Medal of Honor recipient killed in Saipan defending his men.

No luck. His burial site was just not standing out. So why is it that, aside from the roadside marker, this man who so heroically gave all for his comrades in arms, his country, is now seemingly a footnote to history for everyday Americans?

*

In this eighth volume in The Things Our Fathers Saw series, we return to the Pacific with the soldiers, sailors, airmen, and Marines who offer up their remembrances of comrades and friends, of baptisms by fire, of comraderies and sorrows from a generation we were lucky enough to get to know, who returned to tell us what they experienced, not so long ago. It has been my honor and privilege to observe and coalesce their interviews into the book you hold in your hands. The New York State Military Museum's Veterans Oral History Project came into being shortly after our own high school oral history project began; we gave our 200+ interviews to them and gleaned more from the recordings found there that were conducted at the same time we were doing our work. I have spent many days getting reacquainted, editing, researching, and writing to bring them back to life in the form of their own words, recorded for posterity by forward thinkers and questioners. So take these voices, pause, if you will, after each story, and think about what they did, what they went through, for future generations of freedom-loving peoples.

Matthew Rozell

July 7, 2022

The 78th anniversary of the banzai charge at Saipan

Washington County, NY

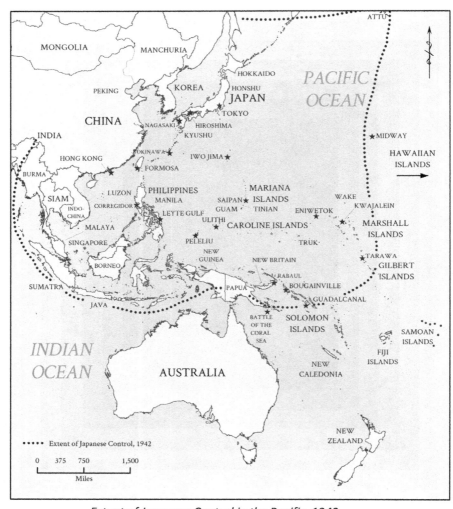

Extent of Japanese Control in the Pacific, 1942,
featuring battles and locations in the book.
Drafted by Susan Winchell,
after Donald L. Miller.

PART ONE

THE HARD ROAD BACK

'I'm going simply because there's a war on and I'm part of it and I've known all the time I was going back. I'm going simply because I've got to —and I hate it.

This time it will be the Pacific.'

—EXCERPT FROM ERNIE PYLE'S COLUMN, 'BACK AGAIN,' FEB. 6, 1945

Ernie Pyle shares a cigarette break with a U.S. Marine patrol on Okinawa during the Pacific campaign in World War II, April 8, 1945, ten days before his death. U.S. Marine Corps Photo, public domain.

CHAPTER ONE

The Pacific

There's nothing nice about the prospect of going back to war again. Anybody who has been in war and wants to go back is a plain damn fool, in my book.

I'm certainly not going because I've got itchy feet again, or because I can't stand America, or because there's any mystic fascination about war that is drawing me back.

I'm going simply because there's a war on and I'm part of it and I've known all the time I was going back. I'm going simply because I've got to —and I hate it.

This time it will be the Pacific.[1]

—*excerpt from Ernie Pyle's column, 'Back Again,' Feb. 6, 1945*

In 1949, a grave was opened on the tiny island of Ie Shima just off the northwest coast of Okinawa. Like many hasty wartime burials for men killed in action, this grave was one of many, side by side. It was time to bring the remains back home, time for a proper burial.

Ernie Pyle had seen a lot in his forty-four years, enough so that anyone looking at his photograph would guess they were looking at a man at least twenty years older. He was tired, haggard, and by the spring of 1945, looking thinner and gaunt. He suffered from bouts of depression.

He began his wartime correspondence career by visiting London during the Blitz in 1940. He was impressed with the resilience of the people, and wanted to know more, how everyday folks were coping, even thriving amidst the chaos of war. He was hooked, and so were his readers back in the States, who looked forward to more. His work led to his first book, and by the time he returned home, he was a household name. This surprised him. After all, he was writing about ordinary people. But then again, they were doing extraordinary things.

After a rest, he expressed an interest in going on an Asian tour, but the attack on Pearl Harbor put an end to that. Rejected by the Navy for being too small of frame, in November 1942 he packed his bags and headed to North Africa to cover the Allied landings. He was always close to the front lines, talking with soldiers, getting their names and stories right with little notetaking. At times, he witnessed the men he had been talking with subsequently killed in battle.

He followed the soldiers through the invasion of Sicily, then came back home to rest. His work took a personal toll, yet he found he was once again celebrated almost as a national hero, which led to the release of his second book, *Here Is Your War*. Uncomfortable with the acclaim and itching to be back with the men, he returned to the battlefront later in 1943, following the GIs as they slugged it out 'up the bloody boot' in the brutal Italian campaign.

Returning to England to cover the buildup to D-Day, he was tired but could not turn down an invitation to be present onboard General Omar Bradley's flagship *Augusta* to witness the Normandy landings firsthand, the greatest land-sea-air invasion in the history of the world. He followed the troops ashore, and at his peak, he was filing six columns a week. By now, he had also been awarded the Pulitzer Prize for his reporting, though no one seemed to know if he was ever even formally nominated. In the fall of 1944, he returned home again, utterly exhausted by what he had witnessed and had been attempting to process through his columns.

By the 1944 holiday season, he once again felt restless. By January he had made up his mind to go to the Pacific Theater. Although he did not really want to go, he felt that he owed something to the men fighting there. He told his now-estranged wife, 'I promise you that if I come through this one, I will never go on another one.'[2] In private, he confided to friends that he was not sure he would survive the war.

*

On Wednesday, April 18, 1945, Pyle accompanied a contingent of 77th Infantry Division soldiers as they were midway through operations to secure Ie Shima's airfield. A Japanese machine gun position opened up; he and his party jumped out of the jeep and scrambled into a roadside ditch. When Pyle lifted his head, he was struck in the left temple by a Japanese bullet and killed instantly. He was buried two days later alongside fourteen other men.

Ernie Pyle's death came just six days after the death of President Roosevelt. To the American public, both losses were sudden, and both were shocking, a double blow to a nation reeling from four years of war. Three weeks later, Nazi Germany formally surrendered, but the men fighting on Okinawa barely noticed. It was still all-out war in the Pacific.

Pyle had gone to the Pacific partially out of the nagging feeling that the soldiers, sailors, Marines, and airmen had been really overlooked, almost neglected in the big picture of what was really happening in World War II, by himself and the press in general. For some, this general attitude was symbolic of America's understanding of the war, even though World War II had started in the Pacific. It would now have to end there against a foe that was so fanatical, and so formidable, that it boggled the imagination, but as it began, the United States would be essentially engaging in two full-blown wars at the same time, taxing America's resources and families to the hilt. The sheer expanse of the Pacific Theater encompassed one-third of the Earth's surface; new methods and materials would have to be invented to drive the Japanese back.

Still, it was as if the fighting man in the Pacific was the proverbial red-headed stepchild of the American war. Only one quarter of the United States' sixty-six Army infantry divisions raised during World War II, coupled with six Marine Corps divisions, were committed to the Pacific. American fighting men were abandoned in the Philippines, suffering terribly at the hands of the conquerors. These forsaken soldiers, without hope, bitterly recited verses created by another war correspondent:

Battling Bastards of Bataan

We're the battling bastards of Bataan;
No mama, no papa, no Uncle Sam.
No aunts, no uncles, no cousins, no nieces,
No pills, no planes, no artillery pieces
And nobody gives a damn
Nobody gives a damn.[3]

The road back was rocky, and rough. It took seven months after Pearl Harbor to engage the Japanese on land at Guadalcanal, after the Japanese succeeded in almost total domination of the Pacific region. Late 1943 brought new amphibious landings where unforgivable mistakes were made, and hard lessons learned, but then more of a centralized island-hopping strategy began to crystallize. The summer of 1944 in the Central Pacific brought joint Army-Navy thrusts to within air-striking distance of the imperial Japanese homeland with attacks in the Marianas at Guam, Saipan, and Tinian, with horrific battles on the horizon for the reconquest of the Philippines, Iwo Jima, and Okinawa, not to mention the planning for the bloodletting in the event of the invasion of Japan itself.

Still, we need to keep in mind that there was no crystal ball, and our veterans' fears and anxiety, as well as their determination and resolve, is telegraphed in their own words after fifty or sixty-plus years in a way that is a frank testament to the times. Never before had Americans encountered an enemy like this. The ravenous Japanese war machine had to be stopped, pushed back, made to cry uncle, but even though they were reeling by 1944, they seemed to welcome death in battle as one of life's great honors. *Who crawls on their belly for a thousand yards in the dark, armed only with a knife? Who rushes a blazing machine gun nest with a sword or a stick, screaming at the top of his lungs? Who deliberately crashes their aircraft into a moving ship?*

What made people do this? How does the war-weary GI, Marine, or sailor fight *that* foe?

It has been seven months since I heard my last shot in the European War. Now I am as far away from it as it is possible to get on this globe.

This is written on a little ship lying off the coast of the Island of Okinawa, just south of Japan, on the other side of the world from the Ardennes…

For the companionship of two and a half years, death and misery is a spouse that tolerates no divorce. Such companionship finally becomes a part of one's soul, and it cannot be obliterated...

Last summer I wrote that I hoped the end of the war could be a gigantic relief, but not an elation. In the joyousness of high spirits it is so easy for us to forget the dead. Those who are gone would not wish themselves to be a millstone of gloom around our necks.

But there are so many of the living who have had burned into their brains forever the unnatural sight of cold dead men scattered over the hillsides and in the ditches along the high rows of hedge throughout the world.

Dead men by mass production—in one country after another—month after month, and year after year. Dead men in winter, and dead men in summer.

Dead men in such familiar promiscuity that they become monotonous.

Dead men in such monstrous infinity that you come almost to hate them.

Those are the things that you at home need not even try to understand. To you at home they are columns of figures, or he is a near one who went away and just didn't come back. You didn't see him lying so grotesque and pasty beside the gravel road in France.

We saw him, saw him by the multiple thousands. That's the difference.

We hope above all things that Japan won't make the same stubborn mistake that Germany did. You must credit Germany for her courage in adversity, but you can doubt her good common sense in fighting blindly on long after there was any doubt whatever about the outcome.[4]

—excerpts of the draft of Ernie Pyle's final column, found in his pocket upon his death [April 18, 1945]

On July 19, 1949, the National Memorial Cemetery of the Pacific in Honolulu, Hawaii, conducted its first five interments. One of them, lying now next to the men he had written about so well, was Ernest Taylor Pyle, 1900-1945.[5]

CHAPTER TWO

The Pearl Harbor Survivor

At age 82, Frank J. Castronovo sits in a chair at an armory on Long Island, New York, near his home of fifty-plus years, holding photographs and newspaper clippings, reminders of the things he saw, the experiences he had that he can't forget, the friends that he lost. He feels the need to speak up, to keep the memory alive. He wears a special medal around his neck.

"This medal was given to us at the 50th anniversary of Pearl Harbor. It was a Congressional medal only given to Pearl Harbor survivors. I wear this to every meeting and every parade. It shows Pearl Harbor and has President Roosevelt's famous words: 'This day shall live in infamy.'

This is from the local newspaper a few years ago, my picture and the speech I made, [titled 'A Salute to Veterans']"

"Frank Castronovo is a Pearl Harbor survivor and a veteran of Guadalcanal in the Solomon Islands. He enlisted in the Army July 11, 1940, and was discharged December 12, 1944. His words say it best: 'I shall never forget December 7, 1941, when the Japanese sneak attacked Pearl Harbor at five minutes to eight in the morning. Those gallant men on those ships never had a chance to defend themselves. I will live with this memory for the rest of my life.

At Guadalcanal we battled the Japanese until we secured the island. In my company alone, 35th Infantry, Company E, we lost nine men and about twenty-eight wounded. I am proud to write this in memory of my comrades.'"

*

Frank turns over more photographs in his hands.

"This is at Oyster Bay where we Pearl Harbor Survivors meet every December 7, and it was cold there, right by the bay. There are only a few of us left. The Elmont Memorial Day parade is coming up and we are the grand marshals at that parade. And this one, let me show you another one here—this is a month or two after the Pearl Harbor attack, when we got our first leave.

This is my friend Denman, then Ruggerio, and myself. Denman was later machine-gunned on Guadalcanal. Ruggerio died of natural causes just recently."

He gave this interview in May 2001 at the age of 82.

Frank J. Castronovo

I was born November 29, 1918, in the Bronx, New York. I can't tell you about my father because, as you might have read about, at that time in 1918 there was an epidemic going around called the Spanish influenza. My mom told me people were dying like flies, they couldn't bury them fast enough. People were lying on the sidewalk waiting to be buried, that's how bad it was. My father died eight days after I was born. My mother said he got to touch my fingers as a baby. That's the only thing I know about him. But my mom, she was the greatest person in the world. She raised six kids without a husband after that.

In 1929 the stock market fell, and I was about ten years old. I grew up during the Depression, from 1929 until 1940 when I went into the Army. People were helping one another. We had nothing, but whatever we had, we shared. It wasn't like today with the drugs and everything; it was about helping one another. If you had a dime, you were lucky. If you had a quarter, you were rich. If you had a dollar, you could yell it out and do whatever you wanted. A Coca-Cola was a nickel, White Castle burgers were six for a quarter, and all that kind of stuff. It was beautiful. The milk wagon came around and you'd steal a bottle of milk if you could get it. [*Chuckles*] I remember going shopping with my mother and for ten dollars we had three full bags of food, meat and everything. I think we ate better then than we do today. It was really nice as we helped one another and stuck together.

So 1939 came, and my mother got cancer, and a year later I lost her and she was the best part of my life. She was a great mom. What she did, women today should know. There were no refrigerators, no washing machines, no laundromats. Everything my mom did was by hand on the tub. She kept us clean as a whistle. She cooked, cleaned, and fed us kids.

Anyway, there was nothing around and I was 19, almost 20. My brothers were all married and one of my brothers was living in Pennsylvania. My brother Al took me to Pennsylvania and put me to work in a factory just to make a few dollars, but I didn't like it. Also, he had two children, and I felt I was in the way. I decided I wanted to enlist in the Army because I will never get this opportunity again to travel, and see what the rest of the world was about. I did the right thing and I'm glad I did it. I'm not sorry.

I enlisted in the Army on July 11, 1940. When I enlisted, they asked me where I wanted to go. The choices were Hawaii, Panama, or the Philippines. Well, I remembered all about the hula girls so I said I'll take Hawaii. [*Chuckles*] I'm glad I did, because of what happened in the Philippines [later after the Japanese invaded and many U.S. soldiers were taken prisoner], and so we went through the Panama Canal going to Hawaii.

I first went to Fort Slocum in New York City. I stayed there until they were ready to ship us to California. While I was there, waiting for the ship to come in, they sent us to Camp Drum, New York, way up next to the Canadian border, on maneuvers.

Our ship finally came in and took us to California. We got to California and spent a couple months there, waiting for our ship to take us to Hawaii. When we arrived, we had to stop at Alcatraz Island, where we helped unload supplies. Eventually our ship came in again and we were able to sail for Hawaii.

Hawaii

In Hawaii I went through basic training and I was there from November 1940 until they hit us in December 1941. If I'd had another six months I'd have been sent back to the States, as my two years would have been up. Then the Japanese bombed us, and that was the end of that.

[Training as a unit], we just learned how to march, how to respect the flag, how to get up in the morning. The first detail you had was on the 'honey wagon,' taking care of the garbage. You learned how to use a gun and how to dismantle it and put it back together. You learned how to dress, how to respect officers, and how to salute them. We respected [the soldiers who had been there a long time] a lot at first, but within a month or two you were one of them. As a matter of fact, pretty soon I had a buddy here and a buddy there. You are all away from home, so you become a family. They were from Pennsylvania, Carolina, Tennessee, New York, etc. But coming from New York you had to be careful because right away you had a bad name. [*Chuckles*] Oh yes, I [took some heat], I must admit. Some were very nice. But being a nineteen-year-old kid, I didn't realize that they would be still fighting the Civil War! I didn't believe in that; I didn't even remember who General Grant or General Lee was. But some of those guys had that embedded in their minds, like I do Pearl Harbor. If you were from New York, you were a Yankee. Luckily, I was able to handle myself because there was a lot of fighting going on. I said we were all GIs, and a lot of them were my buddies, but there were a few who resented you. We eventually got it sorted out and got along with each other.

The sergeants were like our fathers. The officers gave commands to the sergeants and the sergeants controlled us. If we went on maneuvers there would be a 1st lieutenant, a 2nd lieutenant, and maybe a captain.

'We were Going to Go To War With Japan'

Honolulu [before the attack on Pearl Harbor] was beautiful. You could go to town, have a drink. We only got $20 a month at that time and a Springfield rifle. From that $20 they took out for your haircuts and laundry, so there wasn't much left. So with what we had left we would go into Honolulu, if the Navy wasn't in. If the Navy was there, we didn't go because they took over the town. It was their time. When we went to town, we would have a few drinks and a good meal. we met people and some even invited us to their house. We met a lot of people that way. It was wonderful.

Before the war, a couple of months before they bombed us, they told us that we were going to be at war with Japan. They didn't say when or where it would start. They started giving us fixed bayonets and camouflage stuff. We were patrolling in trucks in 4-hour shifts looking for sabotage or anything that shouldn't be there, because they knew we were going to have war with Japan, and Hawaii would be one of the first places they would want to take. Once you conquer Hawaii, you are on your way to California.

We were looking for anything that shouldn't be there, like any kind of weapons or positions they were building, for anything suspicious. But we didn't see anything like that. Oh yes, it was nice. It was a beautiful climate. We in the military didn't mingle too much with the civilians. We made friends with people here and there but we had to keep our distance and be careful about what we said and who we mingled with. The natives didn't like us too much. There was jealousy about some of their women liking GIs. We had a few drinks, we had good dinners, and we met people. We played tennis once in a while or went to Waikiki Beach.

The night before the attack me and two buddies decided to go into town to have a little fun. Then we remembered the Navy was in. There was only one hotel, the Royal Hawaiian, and it was maybe three stories high. It was booked for the weekend. Every place was crowded. You had to fight your way to get a beer. I suggested to the guys that we should just go back to camp. So, we took the bus back to Schofield Barracks about ten o'clock that night. It was a good thing that so many of those Navy guys stayed in town that night. Otherwise, there would have been a lot more casualties during the attack.

After Pearl Harbor there was no more life; it was just 'go'. Everything was in blackout. It was at least a year after that before I saw lights again.

'Smoke, Flames, Explosions, Sirens'

It was December 7, 1941. It was a beautiful morning, early Sunday morning, when it was always very quiet there. There was nothing suspicious about it. Most were getting up to go enjoy the day off. We used to have lunch with Navy guys. They would come to our barracks or we would be invited to have lunch on their ships.

Where I slept in the Schofield Barracks was near the kitchen and I could smell the bacon, pancakes, sausage, and coffee. On Sundays you could sleep all day if you wanted to, but not me. I wasn't missing breakfast. That was the best meal of the day. I jumped up, grabbed my toilet articles, and headed up to the third floor to take a shower.

Just as I was about to shower, I heard this roar of planes coming over. It kept getting louder and louder, and closer and closer. All of a sudden it was right on me. I dropped everything and ran to the window. At that time the Schofield Barracks was like an island. There were no other buildings, no roads, no nothing. About a mile or two away was Wheeler Field and that's where the first bombs were dropped; they hit Wheeler Field. They hit the planes and the hangars. The Air Force men were running every which way, trying to get to the planes, trying to get out of the way, because you couldn't just stay there.

From there the Japanese went right into Pearl Harbor and dropped bombs. Then the next wave came over—I think they were four abreast—and the next wave and the next wave. For I don't know how long, a half hour or three quarters of an hour, it went from a beautiful morning to nothing but smoke, flames, explosions, sirens.

When those planes on the field were blowing up all over the place and the hangars were blowing up, I knew it had to be the Japanese; I was surprised and shocked, but I knew it had to be the Japanese.

I was out on the quadrangle outside the barracks, looking up at them. Each company, A through G, had its barracks and they surrounded a quadrangle. I was standing there like a dummy looking up at them; I was using some profanity, seeing one of the pilots smiling, and then he opened up with his machine gun and I hit the deck and was falling all over the place. Like a fool I had been just standing there looking up at him. I couldn't shoot at him because I had no ammunition. Our supply sergeant was in town. He was married. We were stuck without any ammunition. Even if I could, what are you going to do with a rifle anyway? These guys are coming over fast. You would have to be pretty good to hit one of them. Some who had ammunition did try.

We ran inside because we got the alert call. We all got together and the sergeant came and the captain was there. They told us to get ready to ship out. So we grabbed our stuff, lined up, and got ready to go to our positions. We went to the beaches. The artillery went up and the headquarters went up and so on, but you couldn't see much because of all the smoke. Though it was daytime it looked like night time, there wasn't much to see. When those battleships were hit and went up, it was nothing but flames and black smoke, huge clouds of black smoke. With explosions going off that was all you could see. There were bodies all over the place. We heard the ambulances, but our job was to get to the beaches and get to work. The next day we got equipment and materials and we started building and took our positions right away without the barbed wire. Every hundred feet was a machine gun position. We figured they were coming right back.

We set up the machine gun positions. They got their heads together pretty quickly. The sergeants and the officers did very good. They positioned us well. I give them credit. They knew what they were doing; it was a case of 'let's just do it.' I wasn't worrying about whether I was going to die. I was afraid, but I just put it out of my mind.

After that was cleaned up some, the next day the artillery was sent to positions and the coast artillery was set up in their positions, etc. The rest of us, the 19th, 21st, and 25th Infantry, had the job of stringing barbed wire along the beaches from one end to the other.

It took us a couple months—we expected the Japanese to invade us. Anyway, maybe every one hundred feet we had machine gun positions. I had mine and then the next, and on and on all over the island.

The Japanese did their job but they didn't follow through. If they had followed through, they would have wiped us out. We had a peacetime army, and we didn't have all of the equipment that we needed. We didn't have that many men. We could have held out a few days maybe. Later on, we started to get information about Japanese landings on Wake Island and others. Even when we were on the ship, we continued to get information on actions going on.

The worst part of the attack on Pearl Harbor was [what happened to those] gallant Navy men. The courage they had; they didn't have time to put their shoes on. They tried to get up on deck to man the guns. But it was too late, though they tried anyway. And it happened at five minutes to eight. I got up at ten to eight and in five minutes it all happened. Guys were getting ready to go enjoy the day playing golf or tennis, picnic, [or whatever]. Some were getting ready to go to eight o'clock Mass. That's when they hit. Many weren't just killed, they were murdered in their sleep. That's how I address it. It was cold-blooded murder, and I shall never forget it. We survivors will never forget it. It was a dirty sneak attack.

Guadalcanal

We expected an invasion, but that never happened. After we secured the island, they shipped new troops to the Hawaiian Islands, and we were sent on to other islands. Some went to Bougainville, some to New Caledonia, Guadalcanal, New Hebrides. My outfit ended up in Guadalcanal in the Solomon Islands. It took us 23 days to get there from Hawaii, because every eight minutes we had to change course because of submarines.

So we got to Guadalcanal, and there we had our hands full with the Japanese. They were positioned, ready, willing, and waiting for us. In those jungles you don't see anything. You just hope you are throwing grenades where they are supposed to be. Almost nothing was hand-to-hand. They had snipers tied in the trees. You had to be in their line of sight before they could fire. It was very still in the jungle so we watched for anything that moved. We would hear voices, and when we did, we threw grenades or fired mortars. We also had BARs and flame throwers. We weren't trained for jungle warfare; in Hawaii we were trained for open warfare, not jungle warfare. We learned the hard way. When we got there, it was do or die.

The Grenade

On Guadalcanal, before dark, we had to dig foxholes. There were two men to a foxhole. We were ordered to not move after dark no matter what. Anything that moved was the enemy. We couldn't smoke a cigarette. You couldn't even cough because it would give your position away—you had to put your face to the ground and cover your head to cough. And it rained every night there.

In the next foxhole a guy heard a noise and he panicked. He threw a grenade, which is what you are supposed to do, but not at night. The grenade flew up, hit a tree limb above them, and fell back into their foxhole. A fella [I knew], George Ferrara from California, lost both of his hands and had many shrapnel wounds. They couldn't move him, so the medics came and put a tent over him to treat him. They moved him out the next morning and got him to a hospital. I heard later that he survived but lost both hands and part of his leg. It was all because his foxhole buddy panicked and threw that grenade.

At night you used your rifle. The Japanese strategy was to fight at night, which was stupid. You can't see in the jungle to begin with so you can imagine what it is like at night. Our strategy was to stay quiet and don't move. If anything moved in front of you, you let 'em have it. Once when one of them came at us, there was just enough light to make him out and one of our guys opened up with a BAR and got him. But nobody moved. At night it was like fighting with your eyes closed. I don't know why they did it.

It was all up in the hills in the jungle. The hill we were on was Hill 27, [not far from Henderson Field]. We were in very heavy jungle. We had artillery and mortars; the artillery would blast away to clear the way for us to advance. The artillery guys knew where we were and we could tell approximately where the Japanese were. Sometimes we could even hear their voices. We also had mortars, which were very effective. Another thing was that our weapons were more powerful than what the Japanese had. Our grenades packed 48 steel fragments and exploded like a bomb. Thank God our weapons were more powerful. Even the rifles; if they didn't hit you in a vital spot, you could survive. It was the same with their grenades. If one didn't hit you directly, you could survive.

'It Didn't Take Us Long'

The Japanese were seasoned troops and knew how to handle it. But I am proud of us Americans. It didn't take us long to learn how to fight in the jungle. We had the Fiji natives who came to help us out. We didn't call them mountains, we called them hills. We were on Hill 27. Every night it rained up in those hills and it ran down the hills. It took us a day to get from the bottom to the top. Half of the guys couldn't make it because they had full field packs, ammunition belts, and rifles, and you had to crawl on your stomach. The Fiji natives led us and showed us how to get to the top. We finally got to the top and continued into the jungle. It took us between five and seven months to secure the island.

My company lost seven to ten men killed and 18 to 25 wounded. Three of my buddies, Nick, Denman, and Reynolds, were machine gunned right next to me. I was the target because Nick asked me to go down and fill our canteens and bring up more grenades. I said okay, and as I got up, the Japanese sprayed them. Don't ask me how I didn't get hit because I don't know! To this day I still don't know, but they got machine gunned and they all died. When I came home, I went to visit a couple of the parents because I knew where they lived.

Dog Tags

One day there were two Americans killed out ahead of our position that we couldn't get to. After four days we finally got clearance to move. The sergeant tells me to go up there and get their dog tags. For every guy that died you had to get his dog tag to verify that he was deceased. So I said a 'Hail Mary' and went up there, hoping they were still there. I got up there, and after four days, I don't want to tell you what that was like. I got their dog tags. There were two dead Japanese and the two guys from our regiment.

Then we just kept going day after day. The Air Force would bomb and we would advance, day by day. As a matter of fact, one of our Marines had found a diary on a dead Japanese. It was translated into English and it told the same story about how they were going day by day.

'Just Keep Going'

You don't think. You just do. You're young and gung-ho. What I was thinking, [I suppose], was that I just wanted to get this over with and get out of there. So, you just followed orders and the orders were to just keep going. Just when we were exhausted and trying to get a couple hours of sleep at night, 'Washing Machine Charlie' would fly over and wake us up. His plane sounded like a washing machine. Nobody knew where he came from. I remember passing out after four days without sleep.

When I got malaria, I was taken down off Hill 27 to the Red Cross medical tents. They were marked with red crosses so they would not be bombed. There I was, with a high fever, shaking like a leaf, with five blankets over me and an IV in my arm, when a couple Japanese planes came over and dropped bombs on that area. Everybody ran for shelter, but there I was, lying there hoping they wouldn't hit my tent. They weren't supposed to do that, but the Japanese did it anyway.

For food, we had K-rations, but I couldn't stand that. Once we had secured some of the island, I met this native. He was a wonderful person and I called him friend. The native men fish at night. They put out their nets, and in the morning, they pull them in with all the fish. Then they pick whatever fruits and vegetables they have, so I ate what they ate. That's why I survived those seven months before I got malaria. I was getting the vitamins that I needed that I wasn't getting from those rations. I lived with the natives, who loved us and hated the Japanese, who took their food and raped their women. With one of the natives, I used to go 'shopping.' By that I mean finding the local fresh fruits, vegetables, and fish, so I was getting a lot of vitamins and held up longer than a lot of others. But then finally I got the malaria very bad. My mind was not affected but my whole body was shaking like a leaf. They eventually flew me to a hospital in New Hebrides. That was much better than what we had at Guadalcanal.

*

We kept pushing them back toward Japan. MacArthur returned to the Philippines where the Japanese had done bad things. It was no wonder that the Filipinos hated the Japanese. When I was in Tennessee there were POW camps where the Italian and German prisoners were treated as well as we were treated. We hung around with them, had dinner with them, and treated them like human beings. Not the Japanese. On Bataan, they made the Americans march until they dropped dead. They raped and plundered the Philippine people. They were vicious and treacherous. They were good fighters and hard to kill, but they were bad. A lot of guys took souvenirs, and yes, I knew of a few who took gold teeth. What I really wanted to get was one of the officer's swords, but I didn't. They were really nice, but I was not interested in taking souvenirs as much as I was anxious to keep moving and get out of there. I have a diary that was given to me by a Marine, written by one of the Japanese telling about their day-to-day life on Guadalcanal.

Home

At New Hebrides, Mrs. Roosevelt came to visit the troops. We had lunch with her, and I sat right across the way from her. She interviewed me and she was a pleasure to talk to. She had a great sense of humor. She asked what she could do for me, like mail some letters, etc. I said if she could put me in an envelope, I could go with her. [Laughs]

From New Hebrides they sent me to a better hospital in Auckland, New Zealand. I was there for a couple of months. It was a beautiful country. They finally had to send me back to the U.S. to try to cure my malaria. I was sent to the Kennedy Hospital in

Memphis, Tennessee. There they asked for volunteers for a malaria study, and I volunteered. They drew blood every day for testing, and I was there for seven months. The reason I did that was that it relieved me from duty. I gave blood each day and was then free to go. From there they sent me to North Carolina. I don't remember how long I was there. They finally decided to discharge me, so they sent me back to Camp Upton in New York. I was discharged and came back home, December 12, 1944.

A couple months before I was discharged, I married my sweetheart whom I had met on the beach in 1939. We were just kids when we met. I was nineteen and she was sixteen. We kept in touch and fell in love through the mail.

My first job after I was discharged was working for the Port Authority of New York at the Holland Tunnel. I did that for about two years. But there wasn't much money in that, and we were raising a family. I left that and went to work in construction for about thirty years. Thank goodness for the GI Bill. With that you had a choice of going to college or buying a home. Having a family, I bought a home. We have that home today and I appreciate that. I still get a small pension since I was discharged, and we've been in that home for over fifty years. I appreciate what the government did for us. Without them I would never have been able to buy a home.

My wife's brother knew someone in real estate on Long Island who was selling these homes for the GI Bill. He suggested we look into it. So he took me out to Elmont to see the realtor. He showed us a home and we took it. All we needed was $800. I had $500 and a couple of my brothers loaned me the rest and we put the $800 down and bought the home and I was happy. The home cost $11,000 then. It is worth probably $150,000 today. We were moving to the country. There was nothing out there back then. I told my wife I was going to go hunting for small game. It was all woods around us. Pretty soon there were bulldozers and fast development.

I went from the bottom to the top. We adjusted to it and enjoyed it. We had a wonderful family. We had six children, three boys and three girls. They are all out there now, of course, though I lost one boy six years ago. I've had a wonderful life and now I'm enjoying my golden years.

'I Have Never Talked Much About It'

I had almost five years in. It was a great experience, a powerful experience, and one that I will never forget. I'm 82 now and I could still tell you what happened. I like to give speeches. I have given a couple speeches to the American Legion and to schools to enlighten them. I wanted them to know not what I did but what the ones who died did. I want the world to never forget, especially the newer generations, what all of those soldiers, sailors, and Marines did in places like Iwo Jima, et cetera. We risked and sacrificed our lives so that we could all be here today in this beautiful country of ours. I have belonged to the American Legion for twelve years now. I belong to the Pearl Harbor Survivors, and we meet every month. I keep in touch with everybody. And I have made the speeches to schoolchildren, and they were great. They surprised me. They would ask questions and I had to have the answers; they were sixth graders. When I talked about the natives, they asked how I could talk to the natives because they didn't speak English? I told them about Guadalcanal being controlled by England and how the English would send natives to school in England where they would learn the language. They spoke better than I did. You had to be on the alert. It was a great experience. I have never talked much about the war but when asked a question I have answered. But when I talk to these younger people, I want them to know what those men did, losing their lives for their country. I always speak for them.

Well, [my service] made a man out of me. I became a good family man because of my experiences. I was a kid who came from the Bronx and saw what life was all about. The people I met, the things I'd seen, the people I lost. It was a great experience. It really made a man out of me. I grew up overnight.

Frank J. Castronovo passed on July 6, 2014 at the age of 95.

CHAPTER THREE

The Marine Rifleman

A working-class kid from Troy, New York, Chuckie Jacobs became a United States Marine and a recipient of the Purple Heart after being wounded on Guadalcanal in the opening days of America's engagement with the Japanese on land. He went from high school to being schooled hard into how to kill. Unfortunately, being of Jewish descent, he was no stranger to discrimination, but like many of our men from the North Country, training in the Jim Crow-era South came as a rude awakening. He shared many stories about fighting across the South Pacific in the early days of the war as he gave this interview in the summer of 2001 when he was nearly 79 years old.

Charles M. Jacobs

I was born in Troy, New York, on December 29, 1922. I went to public school in Troy, and I went to high school in Troy, and I played football and basketball there. And I got into this war because I had to get into it. I enlisted on January 21, 1942, in Albany, New York. I lived in Troy and there was no Marine station in Troy, and I had to come to Albany to enlist. The way I got into this thing—I was a member of a Greek fraternity in high school that had chapters in Albany, Troy, Schenectady, and Hudson, New York. On

December 7 my group from Troy—six of us—went down to Hudson for a joint meeting with the Hudson, New York, boys. On the way back I was driving the car—it was my friend's 1931 Plymouth—and on the way back one of the fellas said, 'Turn the radio on.'

I turned the radio on, and we heard a little of what today they call elevator music, Benny Goodman and so forth. The program was interrupted, and the announcement came through that the Japanese had just bombed Pearl Harbor, there were many casualties, our Navy was shot up pretty badly, and the next day the president was going to declare war on the Japanese. To make matters worse, one of the boys with us had a brother and the brother was stationed at Pearl Harbor. Of course, he was beside himself with fear and anxiety over what had happened to his brother, and it was about three weeks before he found out that his brother was uninjured.

'I Feel Like I Have to Do Something'

I went home that night, and my folks were still up, and they asked me if I heard the news, and I said, 'Yes,' and they said, 'What are you going to do?'

I said, 'Well, I feel like I have to do something.'

I was taking a PG course at Troy High School to try to get a scholarship, which I never got, and I said to my folks that I would probably just end school right now and sign up at the Marine Corps. Do you know the reason for the Marines? Okay, I'll take you back to the eighteenth century. Back in the eighteenth century, they had sailing ships, and the idea when you had a sailing ship was to grapple them with these grappling hooks and pull them together and board them and kill everybody on board and take the ship and win the battle. The Marines were up in the crow's nest, up in the sails on the bars. The Marines were the sharpshooters and they used to shoot the officers of the enemy, so they had no leadership. That was their first purpose. Their second purpose was to go ashore and fight shore battles for the Navy. That's why the Marines were started back in the eighteenth century. I wanted to go into an outfit that I thought was a good tough outfit.

My mother said, 'Why do you want to join the Marines?' Because she knew what kind of an outfit it was, because her brother had run away from home and joined the Marines when he was a young man. He went from an enlisted man—he became a captain in WWII. He was practically blind, and he was running the officers' mess in Quantico, Virginia.

I wrote him a letter and I said, 'I'm thinking of joining the Marines now that the war has started.' I much admired him and his integrity and his honor and he came from being a private and became a captain. And it was a prestigious outfit, and I just wanted to be a Marine; I didn't want to be a soldier.

He wrote me back and said, 'I can't do anything for you.' I wasn't really interested in him doing anything for me; I was just interested in what his opinion was, and no matter what it was, I went down to Albany and I signed up at the Marine Corps Recruitment Office in Albany, New York. It was on probably the 10th or the 12th of January. As time went on, we passed the time of day—I left school, I told my coach and my teachers that I was all through. I had my diploma from June, and I was going into the Marines.

On the 21st of January my family—my brother, my mother, my father—got on a bus and we went from Troy to Albany. It was a very, very sad day because I left my family, and I didn't see them again for over two years. You know, I had been down to New York for a long weekend. But I had never been away from home before; when I left home, I was nineteen years old.

They put me on a train. I had a ticket that they gave me, and they sent me down to Parris Island, South Carolina, for boot camp. Now, I was in very good physical condition, but I was completely unprepared for boot camp. I was never subjected to harsh discipline by my parents; I never had any harsh discipline from any of my teachers because I usually did what they told me to do.

When I got to the Marine Corps it didn't make any difference what you were, or who you were, or how they felt—they really busted you up pretty good. I realized later the reason for this—the reason they worked on us like this—was so that we would be an army that was disciplined that could go in and fight a battle, because they no longer did battles where they had masses of soldiers trying to knock somebody out. It was a little more finessed. And you have to have people who will obey officers—who will obey non-commissioned officers—so this is the reason for that harsh treatment. We had to say 'sir' to everybody, everybody, on the base at Parris Island and Platoon 122—even the guy that did the cooking, or anybody. 'Yes, sir,' 'No, sir,' we had to say, and salute. But that got us ready for what came later.

'A Guy Who Wanted to Kill Somebody'

Well, we did our stint at Parris Island. We were there five weeks—they taught us close-order drill, they taught us bayonetting, they taught us weaponry, they gave us a rifle and wouldn't give us any ammunition yet, but they gave us a rifle. We had to know how to field strip it, we had to learn how to fight with bayonets, and they taught us how to kill people with our bare hands or with a knife. It was all things that I wasn't used to—this kind of thing. I was brought up in a decent home and there was never any talk of killing anybody, and all of a sudden from a nice young man I became a guy who wanted to kill somebody. And this is what I was taught in the Marines and that was what I had to do. At the time I was a little shocked. But I realized that this was what I had to do, because I did sign up, I am a Marine, and if the Marines have to do the fighting this way, this is the way I'm going to do it. And so we trained at Parris Island for that five weeks and about three days before Easter in April 1942, they told us to pack our gear; we were going to be transferred and we were going down to join a regiment.

They sent us to Camp Lejeune in North Carolina. They assigned me to A Company, 1st Battalion, 7th Regiment, 1st Marine Division, Fleet Marine Force—the United States now being in a state of war. And I finally had my assignment. I must mention I tried to get into the Marine Air Corps, but I wasn't accepted. I had to become a grunt, just a regular mud Marine.

Once we left Parris Island, we saluted everybody we saw, and everybody we saw, except the officers, said, 'It's not necessary to salute—only officers—you don't have to salute enlisted men.' We felt more like Marines then. They do tell you in the Marine Corps that you're the toughest guy on the street. Of course, it's not true, but we thought it was. We got to Camp Lejeune and there we started some real serious training—boat landings, invasions, jujitsu. We did a lot of hiking; we did a lot of squabbling amongst each other, and we finally figured we turned out probably halfway decent Marines. Then after a couple of months or a little bit less, one officer came into our tent and said, 'Pack up your gear, we're leaving.'

'Where are we going, sir?'

'I can't tell you that because I don't know either. Pack up your gear. We're leaving in twenty-four hours.'

Jim Crow

Twenty-four hours later we were down in Norfolk, Virginia, waiting to get on a boat. It was there that I saw one of my first signs of Jim Crowism, which really set me to thinking as good as this country is, there's some things wrong with it. I had a buddy who was from Georgia, and we got on the ship, and then we were given twelve hours' leave. We had to be back by midnight because we were going to sail. So we got on a streetcar, my friend Hig and I, and I got on the car first and there was a big heavy black man sitting in a seat all by himself and there was a very, very drop-dead gorgeous black girl sitting right in front of him. Of course, they weren't blacks then, they were Negroes.

I sat down next to the black guy. I pointed to the other seat, [near the black girl]. 'Here, Hig, sit there.' He had a funny look on his face, like he was ready to kill me.

Finally we got off the trolley car, and he says, 'Don't you ever have me sit next to a black girl like that, ever!' Only he didn't say 'black girl'; I never heard that 'N' word in my house. He finally got over his anger, though, but that was the first taste I had of Jim Crow. I thought it stunk, if you want to know the truth. It's not a way to treat people—very bad. I grew up playing basketball on a high school team, and football too, with a bunch of black guys and we smoked cigarettes with each other. They were all good guys. I had nothing against them. We weren't social friends, but I wasn't social friends with some other guys.

There was another Jim Crow incident [that I remember]. I was going on a train, and we had to stop in Washington. When I got off the train, everybody on it was white. And I got on the other train—because we had to change trains—I remembered my ditty bag was on the first train, so I ran back and [now] the other train was all black—all black people. I looked around and I said, 'I left something here,' and some guy said, 'Is that it right there?'

I said, 'Yeah, thank you very much, sir.' And he looked at me as if I said something wrong. I was just being polite. He was a guy. He was a black guy, but he was a guy. I never discriminated against people in any way.

Anyway, we got off the trolley car and we had a few beers. They weren't supposed to serve us, but they did. There were no girls around because there were so many sailors and Marines, so we went back to the ship, and we boarded the ship.

Shipping Out

The next day the ship took off around Cape Hatteras—one of the roughest pieces of water I ever saw. Guys were losing their breakfast and I think their lunch from the day before. It was pretty rough. Fortunately, it didn't bother me too much. I was able to eat and control everything. We went down through the Panama Canal and that was an interesting experience because you go on one level and the boat comes up and then you are talking to people on the dock. It was very, very nice. The food on board the ship wasn't too great. I walked into my bunk that was right on the water line and all I could think of was if a torpedo comes through this boat I am going to be blown to smithereens. And I figured to myself later, 'What am I worrying about because I'll never know the difference.'

'Island Paradise'

We got to where we were going—we were going to British Samoa. British Samoa was the next place that the Japanese were going to hit, according to what the brass thought, so we were there to defend British Samoa. And we got there and we trained, and we trained, and we trained, and they had a rifle range and we learned how to use our rifles better, we learned how to field strip them blind, we learned machine gunnery, we learned as many aspects of the war as they could teach us, and of course foxhole digging was my number one preference. We were pretty good at that.

At that time I was a rifleman. On Guadalcanal I had a rifle grenade, if you know what a rifle grenade is, and many people don't know. It's a rifle with a groove you put on the top and you put the grenade in and you put it on the ground and you pull the trigger and the thing comes out and goes over the hill and kills everybody on the other side theoretically. I never did get to fire it, but I did have it, and I did know how to use it. I used it, but I never fired it in combat.

British Samoa was like forty years behind the times. We went into a department store once—of course there wasn't much to buy. There were natives there—they wore the lava-lavas around them. They had some very strange toilet habits, but we put up with that. But they were okay; we didn't have any problem with them.

We did have one captain we had a lot of problems with, though. He was allegedly part of the Vitol Oil Company—I don't know if he was or not. He was about six foot seven and he had a stride that was very, very wide, and going up the hill the fellas at the bottom, at the back, they just couldn't keep up. And he gave us a bad time because we were doing this. I had the privilege of serving under a man by the name of Lewis B. 'Chesty' Puller, who was a Marine Corps legend, and this guy wasn't even in the war yet. [2] While this guy was berating us, Chesty came down and berated him. He let him have both barrels. When it came time to leave this island paradise, this captain was gone—he was sent someplace else.

'He Got Killed Last Night'

When we left that island, we were going into combat. In August we were on British Samoa. You see, we had been 1st Division, but when we came to Samoa we were detached, and we became the 3rd Marine Brigade. That was what we operated under with the whole

---

[2] Lewis B. 'Chesty' Puller (1898-1971) was a career Marine Corps officer and is the most decorated Marine in history, having been awarded five Navy Crosses, a Silver Star, and one Distinguished Service Cross, second only to the Medal of Honor.

regiment—called the 3rd Marine Brigade—because we had other people attached to us. We got put on ships and we didn't know where we were going, but we had a pretty good idea because we heard the rest of the division had invaded Guadalcanal because that's where the Japanese were and that was their stronghold. And I remember going on the ship and going over the ladder and we hit the beach. And of course, there wasn't anybody shooting at us because the Marines had a little base there and I can remember very distinctly, and I have to digress now. My father ran a dress factory in Troy and he had a lady working for him by the name of Mrs. Mulhalick, a very lovely old lady, and she brought her grandson up. Her grandson joined the Marines, and he was a sergeant. I never knew him, never met him, never knew what he looked like. As we were marching up to the lines, there was another group coming out. They hollered to us, 'Where are you guys from? What are you?'

We said, 'We're A17. What are you?'

'We're D25.' Whatever they were.

And I hollered out, 'Do you know a guy by the name of Bill Mulhalick?'

Some guy hollers, 'Yeah, he got killed last night!' That was the first real meaning of what a war is.

*

We went up and they gave us the airport to guard. I guess they didn't trust us on the line yet. So we guarded the airport and we asked, 'What's out there?'

'Well, nothing.'

'What do you mean nothing? Japs out there?'

'Of course. If anybody's out there, shoot him!'

Fortunately, nothing happened. The next day we were put in another position, moved up to the lines, and we were told to dig holes. So we dug our foxholes and I thought I had a foxhole about four feet deep. About two o'clock in the morning, we hear a 'putt,

putt, putt, putt, putt.' It was the Japanese version of a Piper Cub, but we called them 'Washing Machine Charlies.' Washing Machine Charlie came over and he would drop flares and light the place up like daylight and he would drop two or three of those, and then he would drop a few little bombs and then he'd go away. He was harmless. He didn't hurt anybody, or not too many. But the bad thing was, out in the bay, ten miles or nine miles out, was a Japanese cruiser, and he was throwing shells at us and that was the first time in my life that I was ever petrified. I was so scared my knees were knocking.

This is something that you get over. So I dug my hole deeper; I thought I had it about eight feet deep. I woke up the next morning—it was only [about a foot!] If a shell had landed near me, I would have been gone.

The Patrols

The next day, we started on patrols. We had various ones, sometimes we were just on a reconnaissance patrol, sometimes we were on a combat patrol, we did all kinds of patrols, and we got into firefights and guys got hurt, a lot of people got killed.

And after a while, you know, you get used to it. One of the first Marines that I knew that got killed was a guy by the name of Beamer. I don't know where he was from, but he went out in the woods to take care of some business, out into the jungle not far from our lines, and one of the guys saw movement out there, one of the Marines, and shot him. He died; he was dead. The war was beginning to come home to me now—that people have to die.

And on this one patrol, we went out—it was a combat patrol—of course we ran into problems. We ran into trouble, we ran into the Japanese, and we were having quite a fight and fortunately we kicked them out, we got them to run. My friend Higginbotham got shot, he didn't get killed, he got shot, but he left Guadalcanal. Strangely, I never heard from him again, he never wrote a letter; I never saw him again. Yet, we were pretty good friends.

After the fight I went around to see who got hurt. They had a little sort of a field hospital for the guys that got hurt and weren't dead. So I went over. There was this friend of mine, a guy by the name of Roe. He was lying on his stomach. I said, 'Where did you get hit?'

He said, 'I got hit in the butt.'

I said, 'Oh, that's good, you'll get to go home!'

He looked at me kind of funny, quizzically, and said, 'Yeah.'

So I went to sleep that night and it was quiet after that. I woke up the next morning to see how Roe was, and somebody said he died during the night.

I said, 'What did he die from?'

The corpsman told me, 'He wasn't only shot in the rear end, he had three bullet holes in his stomach, and he died.'

So friends of mine were beginning to have some problems. Higginbotham left, he was gone. I made friends with other people. As time went on, we started to get illnesses—jaundice, malaria, dysentery—we all got it. We all got malaria. This is the scourge that makes you practically useless while you have it, but when they manage to bring your fever down and break it, you're okay.

'Don't Worry About the Worms'

Living conditions on Guadalcanal were pretty rugged; there were no tents. We slept on the ground or in pup tents if we had a chance; most of the time we just slept on the ground. The food was abominable. We had no line of communication to get food or ammunition. It was very weak, the line was, and the food that we ate was sometimes Japanese rice and that was wormy, but somebody said, 'Don't worry about the worms—they're protein.' Living conditions were not good, but, hey, we didn't think anything of it—this was a war.

But I will tell you about the big fiasco. I said I served under Colonel—he became a colonel; he finally became a lieutenant general—Chesty Puller. At that time, he was a lieutenant colonel. He was our battalion commander, and he was away at a divisional meeting with whoever—I don't know. So, the man in charge was a fella by the name of Major Rogers. He was from Washington, D.C. He was in the reserve. In my mind, he wasn't too bright, because when he went into combat, he had his major's insignia on; he had shiny boots and a clean uniform.

The Beach

Anyhow, we were back in R&R coming off some patrol and the word came down that the Japanese were coming up the beach and at company strength—somebody go stop them. So who got it? A Company got it. So we all—they put us on Higgins boats and we went out and made the landing. Now this is significant to the story because when Higgins boats wait for you out in the bay, they go in a circle, and when one breaks off, all the others follow. We made our landing, we took the high ground; we didn't dig holes because there wasn't time. The Japanese were coming up; we're taking shots at them, and we discovered that there's not a company down there, there's a whole battalion! And we're a company of probably only 120 of us left. We were in big trouble. So we called for some artillery fire. Of course, the artillery was 75 mm, they only go three or four miles. The shells were landing among the Marines and not among the Japanese! We were getting it from our own men, from our own artillery, and we were getting it from the Japanese! So, somebody said, 'We better get the hell out of here! We're in trouble.' The first one to get killed was this major. He was walking around with those fancy boots on and the insignia; he took a shot right away. There was a young guy—I don't know from what company, he was a signalman—he got up on a stump and signaled the boats in the bay with the wigwag and they wouldn't come in! They stayed out there. I think he got a Navy Cross, because they were shooting at him, but nobody hit him. On the way down, we were all scared now; not scared to the point of panic, but we were trapped, we were going to get annihilated. There were just too many of them.

I was running down towards the beach and there was this Marine off to my left. I don't know who he was—he was probably with a machine gun company. I was here and a hand grenade went off and blew up. It hit me in the leg and knocked me—just like somebody threw a body block on me, and knocked me right off my feet and on my face. I crawled over and looked at him and he was gone. He was dead.

I figured I had to get to the beach. I did the best I could. I looked down at my leg and I said, 'I wonder if it's still there.' So I pulled up my pant leg and there was a little tiny hole in my leg and there was one hole in my pants. I figured it's a small piece. I got up to try to run, and I couldn't. I had to crawl and hop and everything else. I finally got to the beach, and we set up a perimeter. Meanwhile, those boats were still circling around in the harbor.

We had the perimeter up. The Japanese were attacking us lightly. I don't know why; we must have been holding them off pretty good. A young fellow by the name of Hittit—I don't know where he was from—stripped bare naked and swam out to the boats. They pulled him on board, and he said, 'Thanks for picking me up. Now go in and get the rest of the guys.'

I swear this is the truth. They said, 'No, there's too much shooting going on there!'

This was a war. He picked up a pipe wrench and he said to the coxswain on that boat, 'If you don't go in and get those men, you're going to get killed!' The boats went around and came in [to pick us up].

'I Would Follow Him into Hell'

One of my worst enemies, yet one of the best soldiers I ever knew, was a man by the name of Anthony P. Malinowski. He was my platoon sergeant. For one reason or another which I don't want to go into, he and I didn't like each other. Well, the truth is he didn't like me because of my religion, and I didn't like him because he didn't like me. So I got all the 'good' details—digging the trenches, desk duty, and everything bad he could give me. But I would follow him into hell because he was a good soldier, so I figure I got a better chance of living. He was a hero. He came down to the beach and he had a BAR, which is a Browning Automatic Rifle, which shoots a lot of bullets. He was shooting that, fighting the Japanese, and he got hit in the chest kind of hard. Before he fell down, he gave the BAR to somebody else. Another kid from New Mexico, we called him Tex-Mex, he was one of these dark-skinned guys, probably Indian descent from New Mexico, real nice guy, good-looking guy, good kid, nice boy, had a lot of fun. He got shot in the legs. He got beat up pretty badly. He said, 'Give me a BAR and give me some ammo and I'll hold them back.' And I guess he did, because then we got out. I never saw this guy again, so we assumed that he got killed too.

Once we got in the water, I was having trouble. My leg was numb. I finally got myself pulled up and into the Higgins boat. My company commander crawls up on the Higgins boat and he's got his .45 in his hand, and puts his hands up on the gunnel of the boat.

And, 'boom,' his pistol went off and he shoots himself in the hand! I thought that was pretty sad, but that wasn't the saddest part. He got onto the boat by himself, and he goes and he sits down over on the opposite side from me. There was a BAR sitting there and it had been shot, fired. It was hot and he sat on it with wet clothes. He jumped two feet up in the air. I laughed. He said he was going to court martial me.

I said, 'Well, there's no charge,' and I didn't worry about it, and he never did.

'This Guy's Dead'

They took us back to the base, and I said, 'Hey, this is great! I'm alive! Maybe I'll go home!' They took me back to the base. I couldn't get off the boat. I couldn't walk, so a couple of corpsmen came up and took me under the arms and brought me and put me down on a stretcher. I had given my jacket to somebody because he was cold. Now it's dark so I'm getting cold. I said to the corpsman, 'Can you get a blanket? I'm cold.'

And he says, 'Yeah.' So he went and got a blanket, and he threw it over me. I was lying there under the blanket. Some guy came over and kicked the stretcher and said, 'This guy's dead.'

'No, I'm not.' I sat up. 'I'm not dead.'

'Oh, go to the hospital.' So they took me to the hospital. The doctor examined me and looked at my leg and he said, 'Well, that doesn't look like much.'

I said, 'It hurts!'

He said, 'We'll give you something for the pain.' And he said, 'Nothing in there now.'

I said, 'When did it come out?'

He said, 'Well it bounced out.'

And I said, 'It bounced out where?'

And, well, he said, 'It went out the same hole.'

I knew he was lying to me. They were so hard up for men, they had to keep me there.

I couldn't walk. They kept me in the hospital about ten days. Ten days later I got out and my legs were swollen up and I could hardly walk from the sulfur drugs. And I went back to duty. And I missed out on one of the best shoots I ever missed out on, it was a wonderful shoot. The boys sat on the side of the hill and shot all the Japs who were trying to get out. We had them trapped. I wasn't even there. I couldn't walk. My captain told me to stay home, back at the base.

'I Was in Very Bad Shape'

After that I went from bad to worse. I got malaria, I got jaundice, and my leg started to get infected. I had a knot in my groin as big as your fist. Come December, I couldn't even stand up. I couldn't even sit up. I went from 175 pounds to about 125 and I was in very bad shape. So they said to me, 'You're relieved of duty. We'll take you down to the beach.' They took me down to the beach. I don't know what I was waiting for. And I woke up one morning and there out in the bay was a beautiful big white ship. It was a hospital ship. Some corpsmen came down and said, 'Do you need some help?'

I said, 'Yes, I can't walk.' So they took me and brought me right into the sick bay on the hospital ship and they unwrapped my wound. I had gauze around my wound, and I swear as they pulled the gauze off it stuck to the scab, which wasn't really scabbed over, it was just a little scabby. They pulled it and the blood shot twenty feet across the room. He said, 'My God, what happened to you?'

I said, 'I got hit with a piece of something—hand grenade.'

He said, 'Why didn't they take it out?'

'They told me it bounced out.'

He said, 'That's ridiculous. We'll fix you up.'

So that night on the ship I got another attack of malaria. I had 104.5; at 108 you're probably dead. But they broke the fever, and I was okay the next day. I was weak but I was all right. They started a [transfer] and they sent me to a hospital in Wellington, New Zealand. Nice country, nice people.

I was in the hospital, and I started to get better because they had taken the shrapnel out of my leg. The sinews and tendons were all wrapped around it. It was only a little piece but once they took that out, about ten days later, the bump in my groin, that went down, and I was feeling pretty good. So I was walking on the base one day. This was the Naval Hospital, of course, because everybody knows the Marines are part of the Navy; even our corpsmen are sailors. They didn't like it, but they were ours. I noticed on the bulletin board was a sign—'any Jewish serviceman who wanted to spend the Passover holiday with some New Zealand people, report to the chaplain.' So I reported to the chaplain. I think he was a Baptist. He said, 'I will send you to a rabbi who will assign you to a family.'

I said, 'Okay.' So I got my pass and everything, and I went down to see this rabbi, and I knocked on the door of the address he gave me and a man comes up—a big, tall man—and he had his collar on backwards. I looked at him and said. 'Gee, Father, I'm sorry, I must be in the wrong house.'

He said, 'No, I'm Rabbi 'So and so'; you're in the right house.'

I said, 'Why the collar?'

He said, 'In the British Isles, the British possessions, all clergymen wear their collar this way.'

I said, 'Okay, I can live with that. So we got talking and the second thing he said to me after my name is, 'Where are you from?'

'Well, I'm from a small town in upstate New York. You probably never heard of it.' This is down in Wellington, New Zealand.

He said, 'Where?'

I said, 'Troy.'

'Oh,' he said, 'Troy, New York,' and his eyes lit up.

He said, 'Do you know Rabbi Geffen?'

I said, 'Sure, he was my rabbi. He prepared me for my bar mitzvah.'

He said, 'I'm the man who talked him into becoming a rabbi. I'm going to give you a good home to go to.'

I said, 'Great.' So he sent me over to #6 Park Street, Thorndon, Wellington, New Zealand, to a man by the name of Jack Meltzer. He was a barrister—a lawyer—he was a lawyer for all the policeman in the country of New Zealand when they got into civil trouble. And he had a very nice home. It was 1942. He had a nice home; he had a wife, he had a sister-in-law and a mother-in-law and a daughter. Very nice people.

The first thing he said to me was, 'Do you want a shot of Dewars?'

I said, 'What's Dewars?'

He said, 'Scotch.'

So we had Passover—very nice—we had a Passover service. I went down to breakfast the next morning. I sat down and they gave me some toast and they gave me an egg and I knew that eggs were impossible to get—very, very difficult. They got maybe one egg a week a person, maybe, if they could get them.

I said, 'Gee, I don't want this egg, I get eggs all the time. Please, somebody else eat it.'

'You're our guest, you eat it.' I choked it down; believe me it was hard going down. And it was very nice.

They said, 'Why don't you come back next week—the end of the holiday.'

They were so nice to me I decided that there was something I had to do for them. I knew, because they had told me, that canned fruit was absolutely impossible to obtain in New Zealand in 1942.

They just couldn't get any canned pineapple, peaches, pears, anything, it was just unavailable. So I went back to the base and said I got to figure out a way to get them some canned fruit. And I really didn't know how to go about it because it involved theft.

I went down to the commissary, and I looked around and nobody's around, and there's a whole case of pineapple sitting there, canned pineapple, So I took that and I ran with it under my arms back to where my sea bag was, my duffle bag, and I threw it in my duffle bag. If I ever got an inspection, I would probably have gotten imprisoned or something. But it didn't happen that way. When I took that to them, they thought that I had given them a bar of gold. They were so happy.

Now, being Jewish has never affected me to any great extent. I always knew that we, the Jews, are a minority in this country and we have to give up some of the things that we cherish—not all of them, just some of them—to be able to get along in this country as human beings, and most of us do this. It hasn't affected me at all— only in two instances, the one with my platoon sergeant and then there was another instance; no sense in even going through it because this guy was a vicious guy, and he was also a coward. Malinowski, on the other hand, was a hero. I didn't like him, but he was a hero. There were a lot of guys that didn't like me, but most never really showed it, and a lot of guys did like me. It really wasn't a factor. Oh, I'm sure there was discrimination, but I found that out when I was going to school, that you've got to be what you are and just do the best you can. I got along with 98% of the people that I came in contact with, because that's the way I was trained. My father said, 'Don't insult anybody.' I only do it when I have to.

The Boxer

We had some recreation. At one time over on New Zealand the Marines had a football team. There was a guy by the name of 'Crazy Legs' Hirsch—he used to play for Notre Dame, I think. We used to go down and watch that, we used to play softball. Over on Samoa, we boxed. We put the gloves on with the Samoan guys and this guy kept telling me he's a champion, he's a champion. He kept coming at me. He said, 'Take it easy, take it easy. I'm taking it easy on you.' He hit me. I was never a boxer, but I knew a little bit about it, so I hauled off and I feinted him one way and he took the feint and I hit him in the jaw and knocked him right on his [ass]. He got up and ran away. That was the end of that fight.

There was a guy by the name of Flynn. Another guy and I were fooling around in the tent. We were wrestling; we knocked his rifle over. In the Marine Corps, the rifle is your god. You keep it clean at all times. It's the first thing you clean when you come off the field before you even clean yourself. This is an important thing—you've got to keep it working.

So, I knocked his rifle off on the ground. This guy Flynn said, 'Clean it.'

So I said, 'Okay,' and I picked it up and wiped it off. I said, 'That's good enough.'

He said, 'No, it's not.'

I said, 'Yes, it is.' So we started fooling around again, this other guy and myself, and knocked the rifle off again.

'Now pick it up and clean it and take it apart.'

I said, 'No, I won't take it apart! You want to make something out of it, come on outside!'

He was only a little guy about 135 pounds. I was 170. I [figured I] could kill him.

He said, 'No, no.' I thought he was scared of me. I felt pretty good, went back to my tent.

A couple of days later I'm reading *Ring Magazine*. You know what *Ring Magazine* is? I'm thumbing through the pages and there he is, 'Irish Frankie Flynn,' Number 7 welterweight in the country! I'm going to take him? So I ran over to his tent.

I said, 'Is that you?'

He said, 'Yeah.'

I said, 'Why didn't you take me outside? You would have killed me!'

He said, 'No, I can't. If a fighter hits somebody—these [fists] are weapons—and they hurt him, they are in big trouble. That's why I didn't go out with you.'

I said, 'Now I know! Thanks for not going out.'

So a couple of days later we were putting the gloves on, and he said, 'You want to put them on with me?'

I said, 'Yeah, under conditions,' and he said, 'What are the conditions?'

I said, 'That you don't get too cute.'

He said, 'Don't worry; I just want to practice bobbing and weaving.'

So we put them on, and I was swinging at him and I was missing like crazy, and all of a sudden he bobbed when he should have weaved, and I caught him with a left hook. He came at me and then he stopped, and he smiled and he said it was a good shot.

On Guadalcanal he was out on patrol, and he got shot in the back and he lost the use of his legs. And I felt so sad for Frankie Flynn. He was from Buffalo, New York, a nice guy; we were good friends after a while.

Cape Gloucester

A short time later, I was sent back to my outfit on an LST to Melbourne, Australia, and it was a different outfit. I was sent back to the same company, I was in the same platoon, I was in the same squad, but I didn't know anybody—maybe three guys—it had turned over so much with illness, disease, killed, wounded. But I made some new friends, and we made the Cape Gloucester landing and it was much the same as Guadalcanal; there was fighting and there was killing and there was dying. Everybody knows that this is what happens in a war.

In Cape Gloucester we were much more organized: we had backup, we had people to bring in food, people to bring in ammunition, they brought fresh troops in. And when we went to Guadalcanal, the Marines were—I wouldn't say we saved them—but they were in very tough shape because we were reinforcements. We were a whole regiment. In Cape Gloucester we went in as a big unit. We had lots of help. It was a much easier combat, the food was better, we had more time off because we had more people.

I was a mortarman on Cape Gloucester, I was a BAR man, and I was also a rifle grenadier. I did it all. I did shoot the 60-millimeter mortar. That was pretty interesting because you could lay back behind the lines a little bit. Of course, they could always break in through, too. I remember one incident; we had a spotter. There are things in the back of the mortar called increments. And you pull them off if you wanted to go a short distance, and you leave them on if you wanted to go a long distance—so many increments, so many feet. I used to know all that; I don't know it anymore. Our spotter told us what to do, and we did it. I dropped one in; I was the assistant. I dropped one in, and he said, 'Bullseye!' There were three Japanese soldiers running along and we hit right in the middle of them—got them all.

Stateside

After Cape Gloucester they sent us to a place called the Russell Islands. This was a small group of islands. I don't even know much about them. But they had a bulletin board. I'm a man of bulletin boards—the bulletin board got me to the Meltzers and got me two other things. I went to the bulletin board and there's a big notice and it said, 'All Marines with so many points can go back to the United States.'

I thought, 'How many points do I have?' And I read it out, what I had and what was required. I had, I think it was, eighty-six points and the requirement was like sixty, so I was number two on the list.

They put me on another ship and sent me back to San Francisco and Camp Pendleton and back to Albany. Years ago, the city of Troy had a Niagara Mohawk power coke plant—I don't know if anybody remembers it—but there was a smell from that, there was a terrible smell in South Troy, and in that taxicab going home, I smelled it and I knew I was home. So I had thirty days home, I had thirty days' leave. I had a good time. I only got malaria once and put in for an extension of leave. They gave me ten more days.

I reported back to Camp Lejeune, North Carolina. I was checked in by a sergeant who was taking the role and he said, 'Jacobs, Charles Jacobs?'

I said, 'Yes.'

He said, 'Are you Chuckie Jacobs from Troy?'

And I said, 'Yeah.'

He said, 'I'm Ikie Ring.' I didn't even recognize the guy. We played baseball against each other. He played for the tough guys from downtown. I played for the tough guys from up above.

He said, 'I have a good job for you.'

I said, 'Gee, thanks. What is it?'

He said, 'Just report to me every day.'

So every day I reported to him.

He [would then say], 'Get lost.' Great duty. Great duty. [*Chuckles*]

'He Had to Kiss It'

So anyhow, I was scheduled to go back overseas. Now, I'm not a fool—I figure the chances of coming out alive this time are little or none, or slim, or maybe—you know, who knows. But I figured I still wanted to serve my country. I wasn't going to fight it. I was going to go.

I came to a bulletin board. There on the bulletin board, it said, 'Any service personnel, any Marines, who think they want to go to college and become an officer—must be a high school graduate—report to so and so.' I scooted right down there. I told them I'd like to become an officer.

They said, 'You've got to take an IQ test.' I figured this is the end. But I took the IQ test and I failed it.

They said, 'You were so close, you only missed by one point, why don't you take it again?' I took it again and I sailed right through it. I passed it and the Marine Corps sent me to Colgate University and now I'm going to become an officer and a gentleman. And everything went fine at Colgate University. I got a military education. I got a year in.

Then one day we're standing in the chow line waiting to go to chow. We were all in uniform—we're still Marines—and there was a newspaper published that said the atom bomb has been dropped on Japan and mass destruction. So me with my big mouth, I said, 'I'll bet the war's over in ten days.'

One guy up there said, 'I'll kiss your ass if it is!'

I said, 'Huh?' Ten days later the war is over, and I was up in my room getting ready to go to class or doing something. The next thing I know there is a ruckus in the hall and here comes the whole company in and they grabbed me.

I said, 'What do you want?'

'Come on with us.'

They took me downstairs, and they got the guy that said he would kiss and brought him downstairs, and they took my pants off and he had to kiss it. This is a true story. I had a picture of it which I kept, but my mother had a flood in her cellar, and it's all gone.

The war ended. I was glad and I went to Bainbridge, Maryland, and got discharged, and the last thing I remember going through the discharge line—going through all the papers they have, you know the military has nine thousand papers—there was a guy sitting over at a little desk, a Marine all by himself, and he gives me the finger [*indicates index finger*]. 'Come here.'

I walked over and said, 'What can I do for you? I'm getting discharged.'

He said, 'Would you like to join the reserves?'

I said, 'Absolutely not!'

He said, 'Well, if another war erupts?'

I said, 'If another war erupts and my country needs me, I will be the first one to volunteer. I don't want to be in the reserves.' Of course, this is 1946 and in 1950 we had Korea.

'I Thought They Were Animals'

Having come in contact with the Japanese on several occasions, I thought that they were not too bright, some of them, but some of them were very smart. I thought that they were animals in some cases—maybe that's a little harsh term—but they did some awful jobs on some friends of mine and the one guy who was a captive of the Japanese. They actually had him on the block to cut his head off. They didn't, fortunately, but they did a lot of them. We had one

Marine go out on a patrol and he got separated from his group, or separated from his squad or whatever, and the Japanese captured him. We found him on the wire the next day with his hands and his legs cut off. Which I didn't think was very nice. Shoot him, shoot him. Don't do this; don't mutilate a guy. For a long, long time I had a resentment against the Japanese. I wouldn't buy a Japanese car.

Today, things have changed. The people who live in Japan today are not the same people. I figure maybe I killed their grandfather, you know. They're different people. I have even forgiven the Germans because they are not the same people that were so miserable to us. But this country was so good to us, so good to my family. One great-grandfather came over from Germany in 1850 or 1860 or somewhere around there and another one came over in 1880 and we found a haven here and it's been a pretty nice country.

'It's Not Your Job to Die for Your Country'

It was a very memorable war. It was the greatest experience of my life. I was taught early—I realized early, in the beginning, when you go to war, it's not your job to die for your country, it's your job to see that the other guy dies for his country, and we won. We saved democracy; we saved the world.

After the war I came home. I got out in January. The following spring, I met my wife, and the following year in '47, I got married, went to Union College in Schenectady and got my bachelor's degree. The GI Bill was the only way I could get to college. Two things I appreciate about World War II—I was able to get a college education, and I didn't get killed. Those are the two things that I really feel good about. We've had three children and each child has two children of theirs, so I have six grandchildren. I went to work for a liquor wholesaler, and I eventually became a sales manager. I've had a pretty good life. I can't argue too much.

My military career was a career, for me, of necessity. I had to go to war because I felt it was my duty as a citizen and a patriot of this country to go to war, [but] I still think war is not the big answer. I think war is a terrible thing—is it Sherman or somebody who said, '[War is] hell,' but it's more than hell. Hell's nice compared to war. You have to live in a muddy foxhole and dirty clothes and see your friends get shot. It's really a very uncouth, unfair, and undignified way of life, and if we could eliminate wars, I think we would all be better off. But I don't know if there's any way to do it. I don't know how. If I did, I'd make a lot of money.

I hope someday down the line somebody looks at this and sees it and says it did them some good, and they were happy to read it.

Charles Jacobs passed at the age of 87 on January 10, 2010.

CHAPTER FOUR

The Invasion Radioman I

A man of culture and letters, Paul Elisha is a vocal advocate for what he came to call an enlightened army. He speaks with a confidence that comes from first-wave battle experience that ranged from the blizzards and frostbite of the Aleutian Islands to the tropical atolls of the South Pacific and beyond, tempered by fifty-plus years of reflection and contemplation about what it all meant, and the lessons that we have not apparently learned.

He also had a front-row seat to one of the most famous events in that theater, when Douglas MacArthur returned to the Philippines in 1945. A veteran of eight separate amphibious landings, trained by Marine commandos, he is a battle-hardened yet gentle soul, a poet and musician, and an advocate for civil rights and civic responsibility; he even hosted his own classical music show on public radio. He was with war correspondent Ernie Pyle in the days before Pyle was killed; Pyle encouraged his writing and told him to apply to Indiana University, which he followed through with. He gave a series of interviews in 2000 and 2001.

"I stayed close to that sergeant of mine who was a tough guy. He said, 'You can stick with me.' And I did; the problem, of course, was that he really was tough and didn't care about going where it was dangerous. I felt if I stuck with him, I would come out all right. I think he joined the Army

probably in '39 or '40. He came in before Pearl Harbor. He would say,
'Think about the job. Think what you have to do, don't think about any-
thing else, that will get you through.' Now, people who are into yoga say,
'Be in the moment'—that's what he [taught us]."

Paul Elisha

Before I entered the service on September 2, 1942, I was going
to school at night, at the junior college, studying journalism, and
working in the daytime at the Signal Corps Radar Laboratories. It
was an adjunct of Fort Monmouth. They were working on a lot of
hot projects for the war, and I was a telephone emergency procure-
ment person. They would give you a list of suppliers, and a list of
what they needed. You would call three of them that met the specs,
then get the bids, and the low bidder and the guy who could deliver
it fastest got the contract. Then you just fill out the form and go on
to the next one. I was doing that because I was underage, wanted to
join right after Pearl Harbor, but my parents would not let me. As
soon as I was able to convince my father the following September,
he signed the papers, and I enlisted.

The nearest place I could enlist at the time was Fort Dix, so I
went down there and enlisted, and thought I could get back to Fort
Monmouth, for Signal Corps, but I ended up at Camp Crowder,
Missouri. We were the cadre, the first basic trainees at Camp
Crowder. I went in September of '42, and was mustered out literally
within a day, [three years later]. I came on September 24, 1942, and
was mustered out at the same place at Fort Dix, New Jersey, on September 25, 1945. So it was three years. During the first three
months that I was in the service, I got one furlough. I went home
for six days, I think, or something like that. Then after that, I just
kept going west.

Radio School

[The basic training I received] was on par with other soldiers at the time, but it was nothing like the training I got later at Camp Pendleton with the Marines. It was a quick thing, six or eight weeks, I forget which. Close-order drill, hikes, lots of pushups, KP, other things like that, some work details on the camp itself. And you got tested for various things so they could decide where they were going to send you. I was lucky because when I joined, early in the war, you could still ask for a branch of service. So when I asked for Signal Corps, they gave me a number of tests. I was also a musician; I played the violin and the drums. And typical of the Army, 'Aha, musician with good rhythm, good hearing, we'll make him a radio operator.' So they sent me to a civilian radio school, which had been taken over by the military, Coyne Radio School in Chicago. We lived in a hotel, and I went to radio school, and [studied] electronics, technology, and code. I was rated when I graduated as a high-speed radio operator. From the day I joined my unit, I don't think we ever used code. We always used voice. It just wasn't feasible in the field.

In January we graduated, but in December we were visited by a large group of high-level people, brass. They came through school, watched us at work. We were told they would be giving exams, and that those getting the highest scores would be getting a wonderful surprise. The rumors were rife, of course; the Army was going to build—on Top of the Mark, in San Francisco—a worldwide propaganda station.[3] And we were going to man it. I studied very hard,

---

[3] *Top of the Mark*- The InterContinental Mark Hopkins Hotel is a luxury hotel in San Francisco, built in 1939. The Top of the Mark was the nineteenth-floor glass-walled cocktail lounge with 360-degree views of San Francisco. "During WWII, servicemen would buy and leave a bottle in the care of the bartender so that the next soldier from their squadron could enjoy a free drink; the

and I think of the top ten, I came in fifth or sixth in the class. I was immediately assigned to this great surprise. As a going-away present, we received first-class Pullman accommodations to the west coast rather than a troop train. I remember a sergeant saying, 'I don't know about this. If they are giving us this, it must be pretty awful!' [*Laughs*] And it turns out we were the cadre for the 75th Joint Assault Signal Company.

The Joint Assault Signal Company

[The joint assault signal companies] were literally formed for a purpose. After Carlson's Raiders landed on Makin, that operation told them that for amphibious [operations] you needed [better] communications. Out of that raid came the feeling by Navy and Marine and Army people that if they were going to do any large-scale landings, they needed a unit that would coordinate all of the things that went into the landing and send the word back to the commander on the ships. So they knew whether they had to lay down fire, send in planes, send in more supplies, logistics, medical things, whatever they needed. And one of the things that came out of that commando raid was the idea that for full-scale landings, they needed a unit that would go in and coordinate all the needs and get

---

only requirement being whoever had the last sip would buy the next bottle. The soldiers gathered before shipping out for one last toast to the Golden Gate, believing that the bridge was good luck and would bring them home. As they sailed off under the Golden Gate, wives and sweethearts would draw together in the lounge's northwest corner, where they would tearfully gaze out the windows to watch them go. This corner became known as the 'Weepers' Corner.'" Source: www.historichotels.org/us/hotels-resorts/intercontinental-mark-hopkins-hotel/restaurants/top-of-the-mark.php

the word back to the ships, the idea of a joint assault signal company.[4]

They formed the unit, and put us together at Camp Pendleton, where Jimmy Roosevelt and the Raiders were.[5] So they picked a company strength unit, and they took us out to Camp Pendleton, California. I was one of six radio operators assigned to that, and they put us through a month and a half of training with Carlson's guys. At Camp Pendleton, we prepared for amphibious stuff. And then we became the 75th Joint Assault Signal Company—JASCO; that was the first JASCO ever formed. And the idea was that we were going to do a quick thing, go out to the Aleutians, then come back and train all the other JASCOs. It never happened; we got going and kept going across [the Pacific]. [*Laughs*]

Commando Training

We were formed at Fort Ord. The company was mustered, we got our officers, then after several weeks, we loaded onto trucks and went on down to Camp Pendleton, where we began our training. The first guys in 75th JASCO were Field Artillery, Air Force, couple of Navy people, and all the rest were related to the Signal Corps. The idea was that you had to cover all the bases. In an amphibious assault, the Navy is your artillery, and the Air Force is your artillery,

---

[4] *that commando raid-* Less than two weeks after the Guadalcanal campaign got underway in the Solomons, in mid-August 1942, just over 200 Marines of the 2nd Marine Raider Battalion under command of Colonel Evans Carlson and Captain James Roosevelt were landed on Makin in the Gilberts from two American submarines. The Raiders killed over 80 Japanese soldiers, at a cost of 21 killed and nine captured, who were later beheaded. The Japanese then heavily reinforced the Makin garrison. Source: Battle of Makin, en.wikipedia.org/wiki/Battle_of_Makin.

[5] *Jimmy Roosevelt-* James Roosevelt II (1907-1991) was the eldest son of President Franklin D. Roosevelt and Eleanor Roosevelt and was awarded the Navy Cross for his actions in World War II.

you have to handle the air strikes, the offshore shelling, and all communications on the beach and back to the ships. We would do that until the landing phase was secured, then they would pull us out and [have us] do the same thing somewhere else. You have all these Navy and Field Artillery types, it's a pretty unusual organization. And now suddenly you are being trained by Marine Raiders.

We were amazed when we saw what we were about to do, because these guys were typical of the Raiders, at that time, shaved heads, you know, daggers at the hip. They were nothing like the spit-and-polish Marines and soldiers you saw, they were pretty special people and they acted like it. And we lived with them for the next six to eight weeks. They put us through training in hand-to-hand combat. You would go out to the end of a pier with full battle kit, and they would kick you off the pier into the water, and you would have to get to shore with everything on. They had guys in the water in case you didn't make it. As I recall, looking back, it was pretty rough.

I remember the demeaning way which the [Marine Raiders] looked upon the Army. I can understand why there is still a lot of antipathy among the services. They didn't think we were going to make it. They were told to train us, and they did it. They kept saying, 'You guys can't do this.' I think a lot of that was probably by design. Because if you got angry enough, you could damn well do what they said you couldn't. A lot of us did exactly that.

As I recall, there were a number of times they would put you through a lot. We had a lot of hikes on rugged terrain up and down the coast. Our graduation from that course, they landed us at some godforsaken beach some distance from Camp Pendleton. We had to land, go inland to some particular spot, then make our way back, overland, cross-country, without being detected, to get back to a pickup point. You had to use any and all advantages you could create, scrape up, or whatever [to pull through]. Some of us they had to go out and get. I managed to get back. I was with a couple of guys who had come out of the CCC [the Civilian Conservation Corps]. We had a number of labor men, wiremen, who had come in from the CCC. [See], back in the late thirties before the war, if you got in trouble and had to see the judge, you could join the Army, join the CCC, or go to jail, so some of these guys were pretty creative when it came to getting back to camp. [Laughs]

Attack in the Aleutians

The rumors were all over the place. As a matter of fact, the interesting thing was that a lot of us felt sort of cheated after we heard [a rumor] that we were going to go into a couple of actions and then we would come back and be ensconced in California and train everybody else. We never did get to do that, I guess. One story that we heard was that we got so good at it, they couldn't let us go.

For a while, somebody said they were going to send us to Guadalcanal, [that] they were going to do a second landing on Guadalcanal. We had nothing to do with it. There was a lot of pressure to do something in the Pacific to raise the morale of the country. Since the Aleutians were the only piece of American territory that the Japanese had taken, it stood to reason that it would be great if we could take it back. I think that's why the strike was planned.

After Pendleton, we went back to Fort Ord. We did some maneuvers up and down the coast. Then we got on a ship, did some maneuvers, then moved by truck to San Francisco. We were loaded on some ships and went north. We stopped at Adak, [Alaska], I remember. We bivouacked on a tundra hillside for a couple days, and they gave us some equipment. We realized we were going into something.

As usual, there was a foul-up. We were told it was only going to take a week or two. We went in May. The weather was miserable.

We had field jackets, ordinary pants, and combat boots. We did not have heavy boots or anything else. As a result, there were a lot of guys who got bayoneted in their foxholes because they froze, they could not handle their weapons. The Japanese would come down at night and bayonet them in their foxholes, on Attu.

Actually, I landed with a group from the 7th Division, it was like a Ranger company, and our job was to land in a cove on the other side of the island away from the main landings. We were to climb up this mountain, go over the top, and come down to a place where we could actually see what was below. I remember setting up the radio with my buddy at the time, and tuning the radio to various frequencies, and picking up Radio Vladivostok, and hearing them play part of Tchaikovsky's *1812 Overture*. And then the rest of the invasion landed, the main thrust, and then the Rangers, who we had accompanied, came down from the other side.

You never knew, going in, what was there until you got there, despite all the recon, information, and everything else. I went into eight invasions and was literally in the first wave on every one of them. So I just stayed with it.

Radio communications.
US Signal Corps manual, WWII.

The SCR-284

Usually, we used what they called an SCR-284. It was about the size of a suitcase, on two folding legs. The lid would plop down and that'd be your workspace. The set was facing you in the rest of the suitcase. And then you have a cable going to a generator, which you turn; that was the worst job of the lot. We lost several people because the generator let out a squeal whenever you had to transmit and that gave away your position. You'd have one SCR-284, the large one with the generator. You'd have a couple of backpack radios. Then with you, you'd have a few people for fire support if you ran into a hard time supporting your communications setup you had when you dug in.

If it was possible, you might have a jeep with an SCR-284 on it. So you'd have a driver and a guy with him with a submachine gun or something. But they were combat units. Literally a small combat team, we call them. So, usually, we used people who ordinarily were jeep drivers, company clerks, or people like that. When we went ashore, they ended up as generator drivers. And then they didn't like it because they were sitting ducks. You know, we could lie down [a bit], man the radio or do the voice, whichever, but whoever was on the generator was up there cranking away, so that was not an enviable position to be in. The SCR-284 was a workhorse, you couldn't kill it. It had range, out to the ships, you know; it was a good 20 to 40 miles you could go with it.

During the last year and a half of the war, when production really got up to speed, and they were coming out with new things, and you had these walkie-talkies that you could depress the button to talk and listen. I can remember that they would go bad in a minute. But the 284s that we lugged in on our backs, which you worked with a hand crank generator, never broke down, they always worked. It was the later equipment that wasn't as good. They were not as precise as later equipment, but they were extremely rugged; they took tremendous amounts of punishment. I can remember stuff that would be dropped in the bottom of a boat. It would get full of sand.

We were doing many things. We found out that a lot of things that look great on paper don't turn out that way, as you well know. We found that we could not compartmentalize many tasks. We had forward observers who supposedly had their own equipment, and much of the time that stuff didn't work. So what would happen would be you'd get word back from front line positions saying, 'We need this fire immediately...', so we would get on the frequency and pass that along. We literally became a conduit for whatever was necessary.

Attu and Kiska

The landings at Attu were fine, but there was very poor preliminary intelligence for the Attu invasion. They really didn't have an idea of what the terrain we would be fighting on was like. Most of the guys got foot immersion. I remember the beach was not sand at all, it was thousands of little black rocks, and as a matter of fact, those rocks saved my foot. I got, I guess you would call it, frostbite in my right foot. Our lieutenant told a number of us to go down to the beach, see if you can find a quartermaster, get some dry boots.

I had to cut my boot off. There was a medical tent, and I saw a pile of boots outside. I saw guys go in, and they would throw the boot out. Well, very quickly we got the idea that they did not mess around, and someone with bad frostbite or gangrene, they took the foot off. I went down and cut my boot off. I stomped my foot on that beach rock until my foot was raw, but I got my circulation back. I got over to the quartermaster, got myself some boots, and got back up there.

The weather would change almost instantaneously at five-minute intervals. It could be raining one minute, it could be ice pellets the next, the sun would come out, it was incredible weather. It was almost nightmarish, being on top of the world. Visibility was miserable. That was the other thing—we literally were without air support because they could not fly in that weather. Once in a while they would try to get something up from Adak, but we relied on fire support from offshore, destroyers and cruisers. Once you landed, you were there and pretty much on your own.

At Attu, when we came down, once the landings had taken place and we joined the regular forces, the Japanese counter-attacked just about every night. We were behind a bank of tundra, dug in, and they came down. We were not supposed to be fighting, we were the support troops, but when an attack came everybody had to fire, you didn't lie there. I can still remember the lieutenant coming down and saying, 'C'mon, you guys, you're not here for the fun of it, get those damn M1 carbines working!' As a matter of fact, we had gone in with Garands to Adak. They took them away and gave us carbines. It was the first time we had them. I have to confess that I can still remember firing with my eyes shut the first few times I did it. I was with a crusty, tough sergeant, who had come from the logging camps up in Wisconsin, and he was with me through the entire war, and he said, 'You know, your best bet to getting out of this is to fire that thing at as many people as you can!'

The 7th Division, which really was sent into Attu, was hell for the people who went in. We weren't given the right clothes. We didn't have enough ammunition or logistics ashore. I watched a banzai charge come on Attu in which you just prayed that they didn't get to your foxhole because we were in the tundra, which is not like earth. It's this grass and it holds water, and we were frozen in there and the Japanese came down, many of them with bamboo poles with bayonets on them, and you could hear guys yell because they couldn't get to their weapons. They were frozen and they were just bayonetted and gutted in their foxholes by the Japanese who wore heavy clothing.

'Surviving Your First Combat'

I was pretty busy on Attu; most of us who were doing radios were kept very busy. And that was good, because as long as you didn't think about what you were doing, that got you through. It kept your mind on your work, you did as well as you could.

The feeling [of surviving your first combat experience] is incredible. It's top of the world, we can take anything, do anything. That existed until we found out we had to go back, then it was, 'Oh, shit.' [*Laughs*]. First of all, we were ill-equipped for that battle.

Nobody came back with anything; we left it all behind. As I recall, the general in charge of that operation was relieved. General Corlett was the new general in charge for the Kiska operation. After all, somebody had to pay the price.

One of the first things he did was to differentiate the troops who had tasted combat; there were not a lot of troops in the United States Army who had been in combat. He devised something called 'Corlett's Longknives.' All those who had been in the landings got these trench knives, which we were allowed to wear—a sidearm, so to speak. We would swagger around with these, and they gave us a new patch, a special patch, and that differentiated us from everybody else. Of course, everybody made directly for the nearest bar to bask in the glory. My trench knife went by the wayside, as all such things.

All the way there to Kiska, we expected the worst. They went through with the landings. Very quickly, we learned there was nobody there. Very quickly, they put us on a Liberty ship for almost a month, working our way south, all the way to Hawaii. They set us up in a camp behind Fort Shafter, in downtown Honolulu. We had to prepare for the Gilberts.

Liberty

In downtown Honolulu there was King Street, which you must have heard about by now. King Street was several blocks, near the water, which was literally run by the military. There was barbed wire around it, and it was a string of joints, mostly bars. The bars had other adjunct activity with it.

You went in one end; if you indulged in activity with the young ladies there, you got stamped [on the hand]. You did not depart until you cleared the prophylactic [line], which in those days was not a happy one. The military ran it; their object was to keep you fit for duty. They would give you a little tube of something which would burn like hell. You would go in the latrine and squeeze it. It burned like hell. I only did it once and I never did it again.

One guy in our unit, he was working on a PhD when he got drafted. He would locate a library, the Honolulu Public Library, and he would drag me down there. I got to know the library pretty well. We would go down to Waikiki to the restaurants. There was a theater, and inside there were palm trees and blue sky and stars. It was my first introduction to the tropics. It was my first time to see a centipede and a scorpion up close. At night, if you had to go to the latrine, you had to walk on these boards. If you stepped off, you might step on a scorpion; you would know it.

The Gilberts-Makin and Tarawa

The Marshalls and the Gilberts were nothing more than sand and palm trees and some low bushes. The one thing you worried about at night, believe it or not, were these crabs that had a large shell. They would cast a shadow and it would look like a helmet. [*Imitates crawling*] And they would scuttle, and the moon was very bright in the tropics, and you would see [what looked] like a helmet in the brush.

The one impression [of Makin] I carried back afterward was that I wish I had seen it under peaceful circumstances. It was one of the most beautiful settings I had ever seen. The moon was so bright at night you could almost read by it. I remember feeling badly that we'd messed it up. I realized it had to be done. But I thought I'd like to see it again sometime. I would like to go back to the route I took and see what's happened at all those places, and maybe react to it.

We were assigned to the 165th Regiment of the 27th Division, which of course was the old Fighting 69th.[6] It wasn't until the last week or two before the convoy left for the Gilberts when we trained with them. We went to the place, I am trying to remember, it was the other island. We did not join the regiment right away; they would isolate us. No more passes, we would study maps of where we were going. Our job was to provide communications for their training, so they would get used to working with us.

We boarded our ships, did calisthenics, had meetings with our non-coms and officers to go over the maps, to make sure we knew everything. We would not get the code until we were well out. You get to know people. That was my first introduction to [Marine General Holland M.] 'Howlin' Mad' Smith. He came aboard to talk to us. That was a transport; it was not a Liberty ship. I am trying to remember the name, but I can't. We fared pretty well, since we were communications people, we would 'spell' Navy personnel on the bridge. That way we would get the better food, which the Navy people always got. We could spend our time topside, more than down below where the troops were ordered.

I still remember gathering on the fantail. He is standing on a hatch cover, haranguing us about what we had to live up to with the Marines. He was not a very likeable character. He was addressing the Army troops, the 165th. We were going down with people who had done it all, the heroics, the whole business. He would begin his talk with a litany of all of the most famous engagements the

---

[6] *Fighting 69th-* The storied 69th New York Infantry Regiment, part of the New York Army National Guard, from New York City, has its roots in the Irish Brigade formed by Irish émigré revolutionaries. It has participated in four wars, beginning with the US Civil War, and 23 campaigns; it is said they were nicknamed 'The Fighting Irish' by Robert E. Lee himself. Source: 69th New York Infantry Regiment, en.wikipedia.org/wiki/69th_New_York_Infantry_Regiment.

Marines had been in, and he embellished it with how many men had died in each one. It amazed me that what he seemed to care about most was how glorious that was and, 'Here we lost 5,000 and here we lost 10,000,' and it was about how these men obtained glory for the Corps. I thought I wanted more humanity in a commander; I don't know what the military services are like today. There was not a lot of talk, free talk, among the men in general, as I recall, pro or con. Usually, talk was with one or two people that you would get to know better.

Landing at Makin

Men were taciturn about what they were going into. There was a reticence to show fear, or to let anybody else think that you did not understand what it was all about. I don't know if people are more loquacious today, or not. My sense was that these were people who, even among the draftees, realized they were there for a very serious job. And they were concerned, but most of their concerns were communicated to confidants, not out in the open.

I should qualify a lot of what I am now remarking with this: Once we had done Attu and Kiska, and had become this more or less special unit, taking others in, and we had been there, we knew what it was all about. We did not really associate that closely with the others. We were sort of separate and apart. You liked that, because it made you sort of special. Others looked to you like, 'They have been in combat.' I would say looking at my own unit, it had a great esprit de corps. We felt ourselves something apart because of the kind of work we did, and you develop that spirit. For instance, I can remember most of us sported beards. I used to get kidded about mine because of my age, but once we had been to Attu and seen combat, nobody told us to shave. We were the tough, grizzled veterans, and as long as we kept them trimmed, it was okay. It was

sort of like a badge. We were those grizzled guys that had seen combat. I guess we became more and more grizzled with every operation.

'I'll See You on the Beaches'

We [prepared by] packing our kits. The sergeant would come
down, see that everyone had what you needed, ammunition. We
would meet with the communications chief and get the codes. Our
preparation time was spent with specific housekeeping chores,
which, in a way, was good because it kept you from dwelling too
much on what you were facing. Always the commanding officer
would come down and give you a talk. 'Do your best... Keep your
head down.'

Then, over the loudspeaker, the orders to board the landing craft
would begin, and we would go down the cargo nets into the boats.
I met Father Joseph Meany, Chaplain of the 165th, who was aboard.
The night before, he held services for all the men who wanted it, all
three religions—Protestant, Catholic, and Jewish. I did not go to any
of the services but a friend of mine went to Mass. I remember we
had one fellow in our outfit who was a Quaker who really had a lot
of trouble with guilt, because he'd gone against his parents' wishes
to join us. Before every landing, he was sure he was going to be
punished for that. Father Meany sat and prayed with him sepa-
rately.

I still remember what he said before we went over the side of the
landing craft. I sort of stood back and listened and the last thing he
said was [*imitates Father's Irish brogue*], 'Now, let's go forth among
the heathen and do our duty. I'll see you all on the beach when it's
over. If I don't see you there, I'll see you in heaven. And for those of
you who don't make it to heaven, the devil took you. Now, let's get
to it!' He got wounded. I tried very hard not to think about stuff. I

tried to focus on the maps and the codes. If I started to think about other stuff, I would start to get worried.

The tension would mount. You would see other guys more nervous, that would affect you. I have to say, the military at that time was not that politically correct as it is today. If you were from any ethnic minority, you took a lot of ribbing, some of it good-natured, some of it not. Being Jewish, I took some good-natured ribbing, and again, some that was quite hurtful. I soon learned from my interactions with the rest of the company that there were non-Jewish members of that group that expected you, because you were Jewish, to be yellow and inept. I was determined to disprove that. A lot of my responses and the way I reacted, looking back now, were colored by that. I was determined to never be seen in a situation of acting frightened, or worried, or anything like that. Some of that was bravado, I am sure, but I felt very good as long as I stayed close to that sergeant of mine who was a tough guy. He said, 'You can stick with me.' And I did; the problem, of course, was that he really *was* tough and didn't care about going where it was dangerous. He was from Two Rivers, Wisconsin. His name was Elmer Kominsky, and he came out of the logging camps. And believe it or not, I talked to him about three months ago. He's now in a nursing facility, because of arthritic knees. I felt if I stuck with him, I would come out all right. I think he joined the Army probably in '39 or '40. He came in before Pearl Harbor. He would say, 'Think about the job. Think what you have to do, don't think about anything else, that will get you through.' Now, people who are into yoga say, 'Be in the moment'—that's what he [taught us].

*

[Gearing up to land], what you do is go in large circles, each boat goes to its assembly area, you just keep circling around and around. The destroyer goes ahead to the line of departure, drops a flare in the water or a marking buoy. Then they come alongside and say,

'First wave, form up!' Then [the boats in the wave] string out [*gestures with arms in a wide line*]. Then the bombardment goes out. The bombardment lifts, and the first wave hits the line and goes for the beach. As I recall at Makin, a line of Navy TBFs or something came in and strafed like crazy. It began to look like it would be 'duck soup.'

Then the Higgins boats ground up on the reef. You could hear them trying to pull off. Then the [coxswains] said, 'I'm sorry, guys, you have to get off here.' They dropped the front ends and off we went.

The Tides

[The water was] about waist high. It varied with the terrain underneath you. As it turned out, you know, it was a good operation. We didn't lose as many men as we might have, but the Navy screwed up mightily; you know they misjudged the tides both at Tarawa and Makin Island. And if you know anything about the Pacific, an atoll is formed by several little islands around the lagoon. And if you want to get in and out of that lagoon, you have to know the tides pretty well because if the tide goes down beyond a certain point, the lagoon becomes inaccessible. What happened at Makin and Tarawa was that they misjudged the tide by several hours; there was a phenomenon that year with tides that made it difficult for the Navy to plot the exact time of tides. The Higgins boats went in, and they all scraped [the bottom]. On the coral reefs, they didn't want to rip the bottoms out, so they dropped the ramps right there on the reef. Let us off, the water is about up to here [*gestures to waist*], and we have to go several hundred yards to shore.

'The Only Thing That Saved Me'

What had happened was that the bombing and the shelling [were not terribly effective]. They later learned that the Japanese had built tremendous reinforcements on these islands and the shelling didn't do a great deal to destroy them. We had to wade in, almost a hundred yards, we got to within fifty yards of shore, there were little jetties out there, and the Japanese had placed machine guns, and they had a field of crossfire, and they were just whipping it back and forth. I still remember I was carrying that SCR-284, which was wrapped in this rubberized stuff. It was all waterproof, and evidently in the shelling beforehand, a bomb of some kind, their shell, had made a crater in the water. I stepped into that thing and went down just as the machine guns opened up, and right after that picture was taken that you're looking at there, the guys who had been on either side of me were lying in the water face down when I came up. The only thing that saved me was that I stepped in that hole and pulled myself up on that floating radio and kicked myself ashore. [Stepping into that shell hole] was the only thing that saved me at Makin.

I recall there were still [Japanese] shells landing on the beach. I heard a lot of fire, but you could not tell what it was. Things were so hectic going in you were not sure what you wanted to do, [but] you see that beach, and you want to get there and lie down. That's the first thing you wanted to do! Not make a target, you know?

I just pushed like hell and headed for the beach. We made it, found my sergeant, he said, 'All right, you guys, follow me!' We just went. The guys from the infantry were there, of course; they just formed lines, skirmish lines, and we started to set up, running the radio, that was our job. They set up a command post immediately. We began to run communications. As quickly as the lieutenant got the lay of the beach, he had our guys run telephone wires to the different landing parties, make sure we were in touch with them, so we could send their requests back. We were the initial communications center for the beachhead.

The 165th in Action

[Of course, I got to watch the 165th in action]; they were all around us. I thought—and this is why I got so upset after I heard about the Saipan thing—that these people were businesslike, orderly, conscientious, followed their officers' and non-commissioned officers' directions.[7] They went about the business of taking that island. They did what they were directed to do. As I understand it, in the post-mortem period, Howlin' Mad Smith was very angry,

---

[7] *I got so upset after I heard about the Saipan thing-* The Marines on Saipan were joined by the Army's 27th Infantry Division, a New York National Guard unit federalized in October 1940, and it was the 27th which would bear the brunt of the biggest banzai attack of the war. Before the final attack, the Marine commander expressed his unhappiness in front of war correspondents with the progress of the Army soldiers and had the Army general relieved of his command. In fact, in the attack to follow, three members of the 105th Regiment would be awarded the Medal of Honor, posthumously. A 27th veteran in Vol. 1 remembered: *"The 27th Division got stuck in the mountains fighting. We had to fight cave to cave, hand to hand sometimes. And we had a General Smith, Ralph Smith, one hell of a good man. And he was relieved by this Marine general, 'Howlin' Mad' Smith. From what I understood back then, the reason he was relieved of his command was that the Marines said we could not keep up with them. Well, Jesus Christ, they had tank support down in the lowlands, which we didn't have! They confiscated half of the 27th's artillery... and we were supposed to keep up with them! The best we had was 60 and 81mm mortars, and half the time you could not use them because of the terrain. There were mountains, gulches, hillsides, caves dug into them. That's the way it was; it was really rough going up through the goddamn mountains! As much as you tried, you could not keep up with them. You go past a cave so small you never noticed the opening. The next thing you know, you're getting shot at from behind."*

because it ostensibly took two days longer than he wanted for the island to be taken. But they followed Army procedure, they didn't throw their troops in there to be shot down. They followed envelopment and recon, things of that sort, all good, solid tactics, and it all worked. I mean, they were not overdue, they just didn't do it as fast as he would have liked to have had it done. But they did it and they took their casualties.

"Soldiers of the US Army's 2nd Battalion, 165th Infantry, struggle to shore on Yellow Beach on Butaritari Island, Makin Atoll, November 20, 1943." National Archives and Records Administration, public domain.

Makin Mary

Several hours after we had landed, the battle was going on. Out of the bushes came two local people, a young woman and her young brother. She must have been somewhere around seventeen or eighteen, I guess he must have been about twelve or thirteen. He had a loincloth of some sort on; she had a grass skirt, period. I don't know who it was, but anyway, she decided to help us. She got her kid brother to run the generator when the guy got tired. We gave her some K-rations. They just hung around. They did not get in the way. They did not bother anything; they were just sort of there. They felt safe near the command post. We later found out that one of the first things that happened when the place was secured was an order came ashore along with several hundred Navy skivvy shirts, [looked] like T-shirts. I don't know who originated this order, if it was Howlin' Mad or anybody else, but henceforth, all native female population would wear T-shirts. Well, the females loved this idea, and they went ahead and wore them tied around their heads. [*Laughs*]. Somebody came ashore for the occupation of the military government unit, and requested a meeting with the chief, the elder of the island. I'm told that in that meeting, he was told that the population would not walk around bare.

The chief said, 'You have to understand, our people have done this for centuries, they don't see anything bad.'

'Well, you can't flaunt that in front of our people.'

At which point, the chief supposedly said, 'I can vouch for my people if you can vouch for yours.' [*Laughs*]

Anyway, we were there for four or five days. I thought it was a very smooth operation. There were no major gaffes anywhere; it was wrapped up, the island was secured, it was only afterwards that we learned that the Marine commander was upset about everything. He felt it took them too long; I thought it had been an efficiently run operation. None of the communications that I heard actively going on [at the time] were from anybody upset, or that something didn't go according to plan, or anything like that. It was just a battle [plan] that was followed and worked out. Interestingly enough, when it was over, the media reports were all about the Marines and the Gilberts and of Tarawa, and it was almost a throwaway report of Makin. And in some of the reports, it was almost as if the Army had not been there. The Marines had one hell of a PR outfit working for them, and they used it. I think the Army was there to do their job.

[The Raiders had attacked Makin before we got there, of course.] We had known about that; they told us all about it in training. By the way, there was an interesting difference between Colonels Carlson, Roosevelt, and Howlin' Mad Smith. Throughout our training with Carlson's and Roosevelt's Raiders, it was emphasized to us—I can still remember the talk we got from Jimmy Roosevelt, in which he emphasized how badly they felt about the few casualties they had had on Makin. Those were too many, he felt. They had fifteen or sixteen, I forget how many men were left on Makin, killed in the operation. But he kept emphasizing that if you do your job right, it will keep you alive. Our object is not to get you killed, it's to keep you alive so you can do it again. And he kept emphasizing that. It was nothing like you heard from Howlin' Mad Smith, who didn't give a damn, he wanted to get this thing done, 'I don't care what it takes.' And it was a callousness about the well-being of the people in his trust, really, in his charge, that he was prepared to sacrifice them. I am not saying that everyone doesn't think 'so be it, so be it,' but that shouldn't be the objective. The objective should be 'let's do this and keep as many alive as we can.' And that was the glaring difference that I remembered between what I'd seen at Pendleton in my training, and this general.

Kwajalein

The battle for Kwajalein and its airfield under construction began to unfold on January 31, 1944. Using the lessons learned in the Gilberts, Kwajalein in the Marshalls was subjected to the most concentrated shelling of the war, with 36,000 shells from naval guns and ground artillery, followed by B-24 aerial bombings.[6]

Kwajalein was a larger island [atoll] than Makin, it was sort of in the shape of a T. As I recall, the object was going to land one group down on one end, and one group down at the other end. They were going to work toward each other, cut the Japanese in half or something. It never goes according to plan somehow in these things because you really never know what the enemy is going to do.

I also recall that it was the first place I ever saw the use of flamethrowers because they were dug in. Really, they had these things dug right down into the sand with coconut logs and coral and stuff all over them and you just couldn't root them out. We went along. We weren't supposed to root them out. Of course, we were communications, but because the island was so small, there really was no room for a lot of artillery; they brought some tanks into one of the columns, armored trucks in with some heavy stuff. But, in reality, they used naval bombardment all the way up to the coast as we went, and our people were the spotters.

Now, there's a whole different scene [on these atolls]; you know, there wasn't a single tree in the Aleutians, but here, you know, it was underbrush through palm trees, all the rest of it covered. And the Japanese, who had been living there for a couple of years before we got there, were very adept at using that. They used all kinds of tricks, and we were told about a lot of the tricks that might be used. But you still don't know until you see them. So, you know, at night, particularly, they would use little phrases like, 'Hey, Joe!' 'Hey, Joe!' You know, to get you to answer and come out. We learned from our friends the Raiders not to fall for that.

We operated purely with taps and hand signals, but never talked at night. We were also told not to shoot because it gave away your position. So, at night, most of us had large trench knives on hand, just in case someone needed them. The nighttime was the worst because of infiltration, and they were very adept at that.

On Kwajalein I had an experience that taught me that Japanese soldiers are not much different from American soldiers. I have a chip right here in this tooth [*points to his mouth*]. On Kwajalein, our positions, we dug in with V trenches. In a V, you had a guy at the point, and a guy at each end. [*Uses fingers to make a V sign*] The guy at one end of that V was hit, and at night, the Japanese intruder came in through that end. And I was whispering and trying to see what was happening down at that end.

I said, 'You okay?'

[The intruder] said, 'Yeah, yeah,' something like that. But something was funny, so I started crawling toward that end, and someone was crawling [towards me], and suddenly we came face to face. Immediately you try to think about what you were taught about hand-to-hand combat. I assumed the position and grabbed his arm and came across like that [*turns his trunk*], never thinking that he had a foot free, which came up and caught me in the mouth. We both fell back, and he ran back like hell that way and I ran like hell [the other way]. So I figured, he was just as human as I was, glad to get the hell out of there. [*Laughs*]

Kwajalein was four or five days. It was interesting because later, when I read some of the reports by Marines observers and PR people, they always played down Army operations by comparison, and we doubted the figures that became the final figures. The Army people came up with that because they told us going in there were like 2,000 Japanese on Kwajalein, but I remember when we left that island, we walked about almost three-quarters of a mile or so down to where the boats were going to pick us up, and there was this makeshift road, and alongside that road, the bodies were stacked four and five high like cordwood, many of them burned beyond recognition from the flamethrowers, but it looked like three times as many as they said were on there. If that was 1,800 Japanese, it was more like 4,000 or so. In many cases, they underestimated the number. I mean, it wasn't a horrendous miscalculation, but there always seemed to be more than they thought there was. Also, the state of [Japanese] preparedness was usually either they were better prepared than we thought, or they just were stubborn as hell.

And as I recall, I think there may have been maybe a half dozen survivors from that operation. Most of them committed suicide, so you always knew when the banzai attacks began that they figured it was over and they were just coming at you. There was that banzai charge of sorts on Attu, but they were in worse shape than we were. And there weren't enough of them to really make it a horrendous affair.

It was the first time that the Japanese outer defensive ring had been penetrated. Of the nearly nine thousand defenders, nearly eight thousand were killed, unfortunately including Korean forced laborers. U.S. military records do not distinguish between Japanese military and Korean slaves killed in the battle.

The Rats of Tobruk

After Kwajalein, we took a rest. They told us we were going to take a rest. We went to New Guinea, and MacArthur's people were doing the island hops from New Guinea, the Solomons to New Guinea/Buna, all that way. What had happened was that after they had taken Hollandia and set up a large supply base there, which we landed on, they decided on the leapfrog approach not to try to take everything. And they tried what they called a 'process of containment.' So what they did was they launched a strike at the northern end of New Guinea, and they drove the Japanese back into the interior and they set up a perimeter like Hollandia. And what they would do would be to send patrols out on that perimeter from time to time, just to keep the Japanese back, to let them know we were there, and so on.

The famed Australian 7th Brigade, the Rats of Tobruk, were pulled out of Tobruk after it fell. They said they were sending them home, but they sent them [to Hollandia] to do R&R patrols, and they would take a group of us and send two of us with each squad that went out on patrol as communications. So we went out with the Australian 7th Brigade members, and I heard they were wonderful guys. Fearless.

The Aussies were very casual about it all. As a matter of fact, I remember we were attached for communications purposes, and with each patrol that would go out there'll be like a patrol of 15 or 16 Australians on this perimeter at Aitape, New Guinea, and there would be four of us radio people sent along. The Japanese really never showed themselves in strength. They did a lot of sniper stuff and hit-and-run things. It was the jungle. They would love to climb up into trees and tie themselves up there, and they'd wait for whoever came along and hit you with sniper fire. If they missed, that was it for them because these guys were very blasé about it. If somebody says, 'Sniper!' or all of a sudden you hear a rustle or something in the trees, [they would just] turn around with one of those little Sten guns, just spray everything in sight. You'd see the bodies drop out of the trees.

Excellent fighters. They didn't flap easily, you know? They got the job done. I can still remember going along in a patrol. You might have just had a hit from a sniper or two and they returned the fire, got rid of them, and somebody would say, [*imitates Australian accent*] 'Oh, it's four o'clock, time for tea!' They'd stop everything, set up these little alcohol lamps, take out their canteens, and sit around on their haunches and brew a pot of tea, and the whole war would stop for tea! Well, we didn't mind it. We got along fine with them. The one thing we didn't like about them was that they drank warm beer. They would carry bottles of it along and they thought the Americans were crazy to drink cold beer. I remember that distinctly. We would josh each other a lot. They were easygoing people, the Aussies. Not like the British at all. They'd tell us all about Tobruk and we'd tell them about our battles. We'd swap battle stories and we got along fine with them.

Mr. Elisha's story will continue.

CHAPTER FIVE

The Marine Mechanic I

When we think about World War II, it's easy to overlook the personnel who kept the armed forces moving, the people whose knowledge, skill, and precision under pressure could mean the difference between life and death. James Smith was a Marine tank mechanic. He sits in a comfortable chair, decked out in his red commemorative Marine windbreaker jacket. It sports a round patch on the left breast that reads, in red lettering on a white background, *Iwo Jima Survivor, 1945-1990*, circling an embroidered outline of the famous Joe Rosenthal flag-raising image. He is also a survivor of the 3rd Marine campaigns at Guadalcanal, Bougainville, and Guam.

"My first experience with any kind of service trouble with the tank was on Bougainville. When we made a landing there, we had the light tanks, and when I came ashore, one of my tanks made a left turn to go down the beach and it came to a dead stop, and I was behind him... What had happened was that when that tank went into the water, it got hit in the back end with a wave, and water got into that engine compartment. Now, the engine compartment has a radial engine with an updraft carburetor on it.

The saltwater got down in the bottom of that engine compartment, and the updraft carburetor sucked that water up into the engine and killed it.

While I was working on that, I heard something behind me, and I looked back and it was a Zero coming right down the beach, strafing as he came down.

I was in the Pacific for twenty-nine months, from Guadalcanal, Bougainville, Guam, and Iwo Jima. At my age, I still haven't gotten to the point where I can get my mind to [understand] that it really happened..."

He gave this interview in February of 2003.

James A. Smith, Jr.

I was born in Wallington, New Jersey, and I'm going to be 82 this coming April. I went to two years of [secondary] school in Passaic, New Jersey, at Saint Nicholas School; it's a parochial school and I graduated there in 1935. We moved up [to northern New York] from New Jersey; moving back and forth from the city to the North Country and to high school up here for two years, for economic reasons, well, that's another story. [We were] a family of six and things were really tough in those [Great Depression] days, because we had come from the city, living 'The Life of Reilly,' so to speak, and then to come up here with no electricity, no [running] water, nothing, absolutely nothing, and my father was an ailing veteran from World War I.

I had originally come up in 1932 and lived with my aunt, came up for the summer vacation. Then, when I had gotten back to Jersey from that summer vacation, I had grown so much and browned up so much that everybody wanted to know where I'd been. It was called 'God's Country' as it is at times now; several people today still call it God's Country. But to us, it was really hell on earth because we were experiencing pioneer conditions! We had absolutely nothing to fall back on.

Nobody was working, so I left high school and went to work on a mink ranch in the [lower Adirondacks], north of Porters Corners. There was a mink ranch started up there by a gentleman from New York City, a Russian Jewish fellow, a well-educated man. I went up there just to work during the summertime to earn a few dollars. Well, earning that extra money like that was like a gold mine to our family. So, against my parents' wishes, I decided to stay there, left school, and decided to work the summer out. As the summer finally wore down, I was wondering what they were going to do with me, and they offered me a job to stay there in the mink ranch and to work there as an extra hand. Over a period of probably two years I learned the mink ranching business, the breeding and the feeding and the pelting. Learning to grade the mink furs was quite an education in itself; I was able to do that.

The Japanese Gentlemen

While I was there, we had five Japanese gentlemen come in from Japan. This is about 1939. What had happened was, they were looking to start some mink ranches in Japan. They were going through the yards and we were explaining the details of what we were doing, how it was done, and all the different details of maintaining a mink ranch.

When they got all through, they wanted to speak to me and I had a little bit of a conference in a corner with them. They asked me if I would consider going to Japan to start a mink ranch for them! They would make a ranch, and they offered me a home and a salary. Here I am, a young fellow, and I said, 'I'm going to go home and talk to my mother and father about it,' and spoke to them, and my father was all for it. He wanted me to go, he said it would be a great chance of traveling, opportunities like that. He said, 'This is great!'

But my mother, she was against it, she was one hundred percent against it! She was really dead set against anybody that looked 'Oriental.' I'd have to say that, because I think I asked her several times, 'What is your reasoning, Ma?', and I think it was from [the stereotypes put out] from Hollywood. She brought up the fact that in the pictures that were being made in those days—I don't know if you remember the old Chinese or Japanese movies at that time, there were different people brought into the movies in those days and all—and all she could remember about them was the 'hatchet man!' They called them that; I don't know if you are familiar with that term or not. She carried that thought in her mind all those years, and that's the first thing she thought about [when I asked about] going to Japan! So I didn't go to Japan. I turned it down, and it's a good thing, because I would have been in Japan when the war broke out.

'Where's Pearl Harbor?'

I remember Pearl Harbor very distinctly. I was in Paramus, New Jersey; I used to go horseback riding in those days before the war, and I was horseback riding with my uncle, Leo Smith. It was bitterly cold, and my Uncle Leo was really having a hard time. So I had a '38 Chevrolet Business Coupe.

I said, 'Uncle Leo, I'm going to the car to start it up for you and get it warmed up,' so that it'll be warm, because he was really freezing. I had an old Motorola radio that used to hang from the dashboard that I put in myself, and because it was on when I turned the ignition on, the radio came on. As I was waiting for the engine to level off, the news broadcast came up on the air on the radio that Pearl Harbor had been attacked. That was my introduction to Pearl

Harbor. It was the same old question [everyone had], 'Where's Pearl Harbor?' [We] didn't know where it was.

I've often thought about [what if I had accepted the offer to go to work in Japan]. I think, [after Pearl Harbor] the first thing I did think of is the fact that I would have been a prisoner of war. Not of war, but in a prison, being an American and being in Japan. I often wondered what my fate would have been. It's something that has bugged me over the years. I wondered just what I would have done, but after a while, I immediately got to thinking about [getting into the service].

'I Want You!'

I never thought too much about the military at that time, but my father, he had been a sergeant in the army and had been overseas. I [started] thinking about that, because I thought [with the war], it might be possible that I would be in the army. But on my trips back and forth to New Jersey—I was working in New Jersey now, traveling from New Jersey up to Saratoga, New York—on our way up on the Old [Route] 9W, there were a couple of these [billboards] with Uncle Sam on it, and I can see that finger— 'I want you!'—following along, just like he was pointing at me! I know it was a great sign; the more I saw it, [the more it was] asking me to join the Marines. So that kind of stayed with me for quite a while until I was clutching right along, and would you believe it, I got stopped by a state trooper. He pulled me over and he said, 'Where are you going in such a hurry?'

I said, 'I'm on my way up north to Saratoga Springs,' and I said, 'I'm working down below and traveling north on the weekends.'

Then I said, 'I'm considering enlisting in the Marines.'

'Well, look,' he said. 'I don't know where you got the gas from...' but as it was, I had a friend in New Jersey who had a gas station, and gas was eight cents a gallon. I used to carry a five-gallon can in the back of the car. So I had enough gas for my return trip; [he let me off.]

I was a mechanic. I was a mechanic all my life and every weekend I was up, if the car wasn't functioning right, I pulled the head off. It was a Chevy, it was easy to work on. I'd pull it apart and work on it, grind the valves, then throw it back together again; I was always trying to make an engine run at its peak, and get the best miles out of the gas. I was very conscious of that in those days, even to the point where I had drilled a hole into the intake on the carburetor on the manifold and had a ball bearing in there that would, as the vacuum pulled that ball bearing, it would bring it in and [allow] an extra mixture of oxygen or air to that carburetor, and that increased my mileage quite a bit. That was back in 1939-1940, right in that era of time when I was driving that car, and that's what happened to me on the way home with the war hanging over everybody's heads.

Well, within six months I had enlisted in the Marine Corps; I went in August of '42. Those posters had a direct bearing on it, really. I never thought about the Marines; I knew about the Army with my father, of course, and I was always wanting to be a flyer. When I was a kid, I used to travel to what is known as Bendix Airport now, but it was Teterboro in those days. I used to walk down there on the weekends and look at all the planes and all that. Just before the war, I was going to the Academy of Aeronautics in Carlstadt, New Jersey. It was a naval school run by the Navy, and would you believe, a lesson cost 25 cents a night to go in, and I took that course to go into aviation, but before the war broke out, they closed the school down. There was a Navy commander who was the instructor there, and they knew that we were headed for war; they pulled him out of there and they closed the school down. That was the end of that, but ironically, my son, Jim the third, was born with that instinct for flying. He ended up going to the Academy of Aeronautics in Long Island. It was an academy run by, I think, three World War II pilots. It's still there, the Academy of Aeronautics. But that's where my aviation career ended right there.

I went into New York City to enlist because I was familiar with the area a little bit and I would leave New Jersey. I went down there, and the lines were around the block to get to the recruiting stations! So I said, 'Well, enough of this!' I jumped in the car and went back to Jersey. That Friday, I drove up to Glens Falls and it was an old school up on South Street. There was a Marine recruiter up there in the school.

I went into the school and looked for him. There was nobody there but I finally located him, a recruiting sergeant.

He said, 'What do you want?'

I said, 'I want to enlist.'

He said, 'You sure you want to enlist?'

I said, 'I made up my mind. Definitely, I want to be in the Marine Corps.' So he gave me a quick physical, checked me real quick, and then took me down. They made a date and they picked me up on Broadway by the post office. There was a bus that came down through, they were picking up guys from way up in [the lower Adirondacks], North Chestertown, Pottersville, and bringing them down, coming through and picking up everybody to take to [the state capital], to Albany; that's where the main recruiting officers were, and they gave us a general physical there. I think there were about 15 or 18 people that had requested to be enlisted in the Marines. We were sitting out in the hall and they were going in and they went in alphabetical order. Being as I was on the end of the line, [I noticed] a strange thing was happening.

As the fellas came out, some of them were pretty well down in the mouth and I couldn't understand, I was wondering what was wrong.

I said, 'Boy, this has got to be some kind of an exam.' What was happening was they were flunking, and they were being sent from the Marine Corps down to the Army and the Navy. They were there, their offices were posted down through the hallways, and these guys were going from one to the other to find the one that would accept them.

So finally there were just two of us out of the eighteen, whatever it was that went in for the exam. I was the last guy in, and I went through all kinds of calisthenics, whatever, you know. They would take your blood pressure and your heart rate, all that, examine your hearing. He kept asking me something.

I said, 'I can't hear what you're saying.'

I said, 'I can hear you, but I can't understand you.' They had the window open, in those days there were a lot of trains in the lot there. They're all steam engines, of course, and they're making a lot of noise. But I said, 'Well, give me another chance. Let me try.' He kept at it, so I listened to him. He was standing behind me, in between the window and me.

As he was talking, I heard him say, 'Can you hear me talking?'

I heard him now, and I said, 'Why don't you close that window?'

He said, 'Listen, if you're in combat, you want to hear what's going on behind, because there's going to be a lot of noise. That's what we're looking for. We want to make sure your hearing is up to snuff.'

So he said, 'Okay, get the hell out of here.' He said, 'You're elected!' So there were just two of us out of the eighteen. I think they gave us a week to get our business in order and our lives straightened out, whatever it was, to get ready to go down.

Parris Island

We went down to Albany and boarded the train, and the trip down to Parris Island and the conditions were really bad—we couldn't wash, there's no shaving or nothing, and the trains were steam engines. I'll tell you, the soot was thick and hopping onto our bodies, in our hair, and all that. You couldn't wash, couldn't shave, nothing like that. When we got close to Parris Island, I was trying to shave, and I hit this part of my ear right there [*gestures to left ear*] with the train rocking and I started to bleed. I'm telling you, I bled like a stuck hog. I couldn't stop the bleeding! They were using everything to try to stop the bleeding. Finally, after a while, it did finally dry up there. But there's blood all over; you'd think I'd been in combat already now.

But anyway, that's what happened there. Over the next eight weeks was really some rigorous training. It was really, really rough. I compare it now with, I've been to Parris Island twice since then—the Marine Corps flew us as a detachment [*gestures to Iwo Jima Survivor jacket patch*], flew us down there a few years ago. Let me tell you something, those kids—when you go through the Marine Corps now, you got to be really in tough shape, you must really want to be in the Marine Corps, because it's no place for anybody just going in for the glory of it or whatever. It's tougher than what we had because they're pushing us through, [due to the war]. The boot camp training itself was very tough. Learning to use your rifle was the main object of the whole thing. The toughest part about the boot camp training was that we were training with the .03 rifle. That's a Springfield. We had been snapping in with that for several weeks, and right about two-thirds through boot camp, they brought the Garand rifle in. Here we are almost through with boot camp training, and they hand us a brand-new rifle! Fortunately for us, there was a young fella in our platoon who worked in the

Garand factory and he knew the Garand rifle. We were lucky because we had a class right in our barracks, right?

Our barracks were nothing but a big, long shack made out of green lumber. There was no paint, anything like that, it was just a long shack that housed a platoon of Marines. The fella that was in there, he worked in the Garand factory and he really saved our butts. So when we came out of that morning, we were way ahead of everybody with our rifles, and we learned to fire them. It was tough to make the adjustment from the two different rifles, but I was a firing 'expert' all through.

The day before [firing for] record, I got hit [in the face]; the back of the Garand rifle has got a square butt there, and the .03 didn't have that. I was so used to the .03 that I finally got hit. I got hit right here. [Gestures to left eye] The drill instructor said, 'You're doing fine, just keep up what you're doing.' But then all of a sudden, I have that black eye when I needed the points to make 'expert.' I couldn't keep it, my eye kept twitching from the pain here.

Boy, he kicked me right in the head. He called me everything. He said, well, I don't want to tell you what he was calling me, but it cost me. But I mean, I could still use my rifle very effectively. Unfortunately, I ended up with the Thompson submachine gun, which I didn't have too much training with.

Learning the Engines

But when we were getting ready to leave boot camp, there was one fella I had become pretty close friends with. His name is Ray Charlebois from Glens Falls. In fact, Ray worked up in the post office up there for many years. We were pretty good buddies, and we were standing and dressed in our uniforms and packs and everything, rifles, in the pouring rain, just like you've seen in the movies

THE THINGS OUR FATHERS SAW [VOL. VIII] | 117

at one time or another. They're asking people what they thought they could do, whatever you thought you were good at.

He said to me, 'Go on, Jim, you said you're a mechanic. Why don't you?'

I said, 'I don't know. You read about these things where you'll [volunteer and] wind up with a wheelbarrow or something like that, all that kind of jazz.'

But I stepped forward; I was the only one in the platoon that stepped forward. I ended up in a tank battalion, a tank company, but the equipment we had then was like from the World War I days.

The 3rd Marine Division was activated in September 1942, training for combat to take the islands back from the Japanese. Smith's unit, the 3rd Marine Tank Battalion, would see heavy fighting on Bougainville, Guam, and later, Iwo Jima.

I ended up going to school in Camp Pendleton, that's where we ended up with our light tanks. We had to learn the whole electrical system of the tanks. It was an intensive, very quick course, because they were trying to get us moving out, because of the war and the way things weren't going that good, and they wanted to get into the Pacific to start taking the islands where they needed them the most. Actually, their main goal was to acquire an airstrip. That's what the story was for the islands, the airstrips. They wanted a place to get planes so they could use them to go forward and clear the way for as much as possible for us.

Some of the equipment was really bad. It wasn't anything that I would have liked to have gone to war with because nothing functioned right without being repaired, and it had to be repaired constantly. I noticed something in one of my tank battalion magazines, they were looking for anybody that had any experience with a

Guiberson diesel radial engine [for aircraft and tanks], which is a rare, rare bird. I have never heard of it since, but it was a diesel radial engine. It started with like a shotgun shell in the back—you put that into the chamber and the driver activates it with a toggle switch in the cockpit. That engine was a noisy thing, and it was loud, smoky, and we finally got rid of those. We ended up with some hand-me-downs from the army, some light tanks. They had the .37 millimeter [cannon] on them. They had the aircraft engine, it had a seven-cylinder Continental, and some had the Jacobson seven-cylinder radial engine.

Mud Marines

We did a lot of maneuvers. The tankers, we were classified as special troops. Our weapons were all automatic weapons. We all had .45 pistols and a Thompson submachine gun. [In convoys] on the way from San Diego until we first stopped off at New Caledonia, these ships were old banana boats, and we spent all of our time in the chow lines. From the minute you got up, you got in line for breakfast, and you got back in line again for lunch, whatever it was; you spent more time in lines, so that's why whenever I see lines, I get so disgusted and frustrated, it brings back all the things that were going on in those lines, and that's constantly what happened to us—a lot of our automatic weapons were stolen by the 'mud Marines' [while we were in these lines], the guys from the infantry. They were the ones that were in the frontlines, or whatever you want to determine as a frontline; in the jungles, there was no such thing as a 'frontline.' I mean, here we weren't in the trenches like in World War I. It was sporadic bunches of Marines here and there, trying to keep their lines together so that they weren't separated.

If they were separated, then they had to depend on radios. Most of the time it was just... you had to learn to take care of yourself.

You are going to take care of yourself [first]. We were trained to do that, because there were so many times where if you see somebody that's hit or wounded, whatever, you immediately want to stop and try to help them, it's a natural thing for a person [to want to help], and they told us not to do that. Don't stop to do anything like that. Somebody is trained to take care of somebody like that, and if you're not trained, you're not doing any good for that person, all you're doing is just causing [more] problems. If there is a hole in the line or wherever the firing is going on, you want to make sure that you're doing your job and not worrying about somebody. That may seem kind of tough to bear, even carry on your mind, on your conscience. But it had to be done that way. I remember a couple instances like that, especially on Guam, because I used to have to walk ashore with the mud Marines, I went ashore with our tanks. I was in 1st Platoon Maintenance, and I had six tanks to worry about.

The Early Landings

At Guadalcanal, we came in behind the 1st Division, the ones who made the initial landing there, for like a mopping-up operation. Now, ninety-nine percent of the time, people who were in the Marine Corps like me, we really didn't know what was going on. But actually what was happening was the same theme that will show up again later on in the Pacific campaigns, [again and again].

When we went down into Guadalcanal, when they made the statement that the island was 'secure,' that [implied that it] was the end of the fighting, but that was so wrong. It was unbelievable because there'd be, in some cases, several thousand Japanese loose on the island! They would form up in pockets or live in bivouac areas of their own. So with us coming up in behind [the 1st Division], it was a training area, [real] combat conditions, training people to learn how to fight a war in the jungle.

Jungle Rot

At Guadalcanal, a lot of us came down with a jungle rot on our feet. It came on with the rainy season—it rained for days on end, and we used to have to take our sea bags and dump them out and rotate our clothes so they wouldn't get mildew. Then there'd be jungle rot. It started to come out on our feet and there would be blisters; it's terrible, and I had them for a long time. After the war, I still was afflicted with it. I never went to the VA hospital for any help with it, but the only relief I could get from it in those days at Guadalcanal was, what I used to do is sterilize a razor blade and slice those blisters open and let the liquid out; it would relieve the itch, and then it would dry up. After a number of years, it finally disappeared from my system, whatever it was. Some of the fellas were really afflicted with it really bad to the point where they had to be taken right out. Their feet were in bad shape. the doctors used this [ointment] Merthiolate. It was a dark, purple-colored stuff like Mercurochrome. That's the only thing they put on it.

The other thing that some of the fellas were afflicted with was, I think they called it elephantiasis. It was from the mosquito and the infection ended up in the armpits and in the groin, in their testicles, and [those areas] would just swell up. They had to ship those Marines out. I remember they shipped them out to Oregon; a cold climate is the only place where they would ease this affliction. It would die down; what the medication was for it, I have no idea. But it was really a sad thing to see something like that happen from a mosquito bite.

US Marines in the mud at Bougainville. Marine in foreground center has been identified as Hans Wittmann, Company F, 2nd Battalion, 22nd Marines. US Marine Corps photo, public domain.

Bougainville

Operation Cartwheel, aimed at neutralizing the Japanese base at Rabaul, began in 1943. Rabaul was the principal Japanese forward operating base in the South Pacific at New Guinea, with tens of thousands of troops in reserve threatening the toeholds established at Guadalcanal and elsewhere. The Bougainville campaign, so named for the main island in that area, was part of this overall strategy.

Bougainville was really a tough situation, [because we landed and] you've got to maneuver with tanks. It was very difficult. On the Bougainville campaign, the thing that saved the whole campaign and really won the war there was the amphibious tractor. They call them the alligators, and they were indispensable. They were able to travel in the water. They carried a lot of ammunition, and they could travel in the jungle a lot better than the tanks could go. The tanks were a lot heavier than the amphibious tractor. The tanks, I worked on the tanks all the while. That was my job, to service the tanks, and the engines were the main thing that we had to be concerned about.

My first experience with any kind of service trouble with the tank was on Bougainville. When we made a landing there, we had the light tanks, and when I came ashore, one of my tanks made a left turn to go down the beach and it came to a dead stop, and I was behind him. I ran around to the front of the tank and I said, 'What's the matter?'

He said, 'It just stopped.'

So I said, 'Well, try it again.'

So we tried it; they had toggle switches for the starters. It would crank over okay, but it wouldn't start. Never even fired. So I went around the back, and when I got back to the back of the tank, the door is thick and they had bolts, they were inch-wide bolts. However, one of those bolts came out, I have no idea how there was a bolt missing. What had happened was that when that tank went into the water, it got hit in the back end with a wave and water got into that engine compartment. Now, the engine compartment has a radial engine with an updraft carburetor on it. The saltwater got down in the bottom of that engine compartment, and the updraft carburetor sucked that water up into the engine and killed it.

While I was working on that, I heard something behind me, and I looked back and it was a Zero coming right down the beach, strafing as he came down! I hauled my ass right out in front, I jumped in front of the tank, and I got down underneath the front of the tank and he went over. As he was banking, they got him—they hit him as he was banking, going down. He's going down the beach and strafing and they hit him, and I witnessed two of those kills. But

when we were in Bougainville, the campaign was pretty much under control. The Army was coming in to take over the positions
that we had taken. They took just about everybody that was available and that meant most of the division; we had to carry ammunition, barbed wire, and food, and put it in all the foxholes on the line
before the Army could take over.

The worst part about it was that we were doing this, and when
we got back, we're on the beach with all the confusion and things
are going on and these poor guys were making like [it was] an invasion landing; they had people on the shore with the camera taking pictures of them making the landing on Bougainville. We've
been there three or four weeks, and they were just coming in to take
over.

The Seabees

The Seabees were the greatest bunch of guys you would ever
want to be associated with. They did a lot to really hasten the war
because those guys were Johnny-on-the-spot. They were patching
up everything as fast as things were blown up. They were right behind, filling in the holes and cutting this and cutting that. They
were into everything and they had everything.

Pappy Boyington was there with us on Bougainville. I saw his
plane there, where they were bivouacked after the Seabees cleared
the jungle up and built an airstrip. It's uncanny what those guys did
with the equipment they had! They were right with us all the while.
I could go on and on with the different things. We were stealing
from them and they would steal from us.

Construction Battalion Navy Yard on Bougainville
with the Seabee Expression, 1943. U.S. Navy Seabee Museum

Keeping the Tanks in Order

We came back from Bougainville and got back to Guadalcanal, and we had hand-me-down Shermans. So what we really became was aircraft mechanics because here we have diesel now. They were General Motors 600 twin diesels and you know what they did? They sent in mechanics from Detroit to Guadalcanal, put up a couple of tents bigger than this room, and strung up two sets of diesel engines on racks.

They said to us, 'Take them apart.' So that's what we did. We tore the engines all down, detail stripped them. Then they told us to put it back together again, which we could do. But we couldn't start them; we didn't know the first thing about the injectors, and that's what they were using now. There was no electrical system, no ignition to worry about with the diesel. We had to learn how to adjust the injectors they had, what they call an injector rack.

Advertisement, World War II.

Each one of those racks had adjustments on of a locking nut with a tightening and adjusting screw on it. That was the heart of the diesel engine with us. You had to learn how to adjust those so that you got just the right type of spray into the engine, and also to control the governor. It had to be really fine-tuned, a very critical part of that diesel engine because if that governor went haywire, the diesel would run wild. It would go out of control, and it would blow itself up if you didn't shut it down. There was a big flap and if the driver senses something was wrong, he hit what we call the panic button at that solenoid flap to trip and shut off most of the oxygen to the engine. That's what a diesel thrives on, it's oxygen like any engine, and it will shut the engine down. That was our introduction to the diesel. It was just a matter of, as I said, adjusting those injectors because without those injectors running, there's a lot of loss of power.

In the Army, the Shermans, they had a Chrysler nine-cylinder radial engine, it's a big aircraft engine. Those things were easily blown up with a Molotov cocktail because we burned high-octane gas, which is what we burn in the light tanks.

But here now we were in diesel with these little twin engines, and it had clutches for both of those engines, and it had lockouts, a lockout like a choke. You pull that out and it disengaged that clutch from that engine, so if an engine got hit in combat, broadsided, and knocked out of commission, your temperature gauges would be telling the driver, over all the noise and everything, as soon as the temperature rose on the right or left engine. He would know immediately that there was something wrong with that engine, so he would pull the clutch lockout to see if it was running by his tachometer. If it wasn't running, he knew the engine was dead for whatever reason. But that other engine would pull that tank out of harm's way if it had to be taken out; it could get the crew out of there with that one engine. That was a beauty. It was a type of engine that could withstand most anything except for a broadside by an armor-piercing high-explosive round that would penetrate the hull and get to the engine. It was a good tank for what we used it for, and we used it more effectively in the later campaigns on Guam.

Guam

The [immediate] objective of all these landings [I was on] was to get supplies in on the beach, mostly ammunition, to get that in first. That's the first thing that's got to be done. Most of the time, with the tanks, we came in on the LCTs, or Landing Craft Tank. The LCIs were for the infantry, the Higgins boats, as they were called. Then there were the largest ships that were brought into the war a little later on, the big transport LSTs. They carried the tanks, trucks, all the heavy equipment. They had a huge opening on the front of the ship so that when they hit the beach they would drive up onto the beach.

On the LST, they had twin screws, and immediately, when they hit the beach, they reverse those to like an idling position. So, they kept the ship there, but it was also giving them a little pull off the beach, so that they wouldn't be stuck there. If it stayed there too long, the vacuum suction would hold it, and they would have a job getting it off. Now as they were unloading equipment, it lightens the ship, of course, it lightens the load. On Guam in particular, this caused a major problem, really. The water was a little deeper than other places, and when the LST would hit the beach, they would reverse the screws, but what was happening was it was pulling the sand from underneath the ship and creating big pockets in the ocean [floor], deep pockets.

When we were stepping off [our LCTs or LCIs], a lot of us would step off into those holes, and on Guam, it happened to me— I just went right out of sight. I had tools in my pack, and I had a rifle, because somebody had stolen my Thompson submachine gun, on that trip out from San Diego to New Caledonia. I had a rifle and I disappeared and went right down. When I hit the deck, the bottom of the ocean, I pushed myself back up again.

When I come up there was a [guy] who happened to be right there, and he put his hand out to me and pulled me out. He was there for just that reason; in fact there were a couple of guys, but I remember this one man who pulled me out.

"US Marines leap from their amphibious tractors for the sand dunes, Guam, July 20, 1944." US Marine Corps photo, public domain.

[On the way in], with all the confusion, there were a lot of dead Marines floating in the water. You were walking your way through, and the intense mortar fire was killing [us] on those beaches. The mortar fire was terrible.

I had a young fella with me who was new in the company. His name was Jasper Fane, and he had never been in combat. He was behind me, and when I turned around, I didn't see him. I stopped, I turned around, I was looking for him, and then I saw him step off the ramp and he disappeared. He went right out of sight. That fella was right there and then pulled him out. I waved to him, and I waited for him, and he caught up with me.

I said we had to look for a stream. That was our landmark, and we would go to the right of that stream, and that's where our tanks would have gone in. Well, we couldn't find any stream, the further we went down the beach.

I said, 'Jasper, the fellas are bunching up.' There was an officer standing on a 55-gallon drum and he had an old megaphone. He was hollering through that megaphone, 'Don't bunch up. Don't bunch up on the beach!' That's all he was hollering, 'Don't bunch up on the beach. Don't bunch up!' Some people start to disregard him, and they started to bunch up over to our left.

I said to Jasper, I said, 'Let's get out of here because there's a lot of mortar fire flying around and they're looking for targets. Let's move out of here!'

So we moved out up the beach, and they were dropping the 90 millimeters. One of them hit—it couldn't have been any more than fifty feet from me—so we hit the deck because I could hear it coming in, and I recognized the sound.

Jasper got hit. I don't know how he got hit; to this day I can't figure out how he got hit. He got hit in the leg, and I turned around and I said, 'Well, I'll try to get a corpsman.' I turned around, and to this day, I don't know what happened to him.

I went back up the beach, went back in the opposite direction. But just before that 90 millimeter hit, the Japs had spotted these guys bunched up and they laid a bunch of mortars in, and they got most of those guys. There were a lot of guys lying on the beach; some of the corpsmen were working there and the fire went through there and just tore everybody apart, right down that beach. It was—I don't even like to... in fact, at times, it just blacks out. I can't see those pictures anymore in my mind, of all those people that were being just blown apart after they had been lying there helplessly wounded.

So that's what happened there. There were a couple of Japanese officers too, lying there on the beach. I don't know why I remember all these things, or things like that. They were booby-trapped; really nobody was touching them. They lay right there; they were trying to psych us. It's—I don't know if you've ever been where there's been an accident, it's something that is really chaotic. There's so much going on that you wonder how anybody can get anything done because of the conditions, the things that are happening.

As we are standing there, those 90 millimeters are still coming. We got to the point where we were just standing around trying to get some direction, because here you are walking into a jungle. You don't know where you're going to be, if there's any place to meet, there's no direction whatsoever until you move in.

The Fever

On Guam, we used to set up ambush groups, two people in an ambush area, in different places in the jungle. I was in there with a Marine buddy of mine, Paul Ryan. He was a platoon sergeant; he became a gunnery sergeant after that. We had different things set up in the jungle where if anything rattled, we knew that somebody was out there that shouldn't be out there. It had to be about three or four o'clock in the morning, and all of a sudden, I heard him kind of groan a little bit.

I said, 'What's the matter, Paul?'

Boy, he said, 'I'm sick.'

The next thing I know he passed right out. Well, here I am. It's three or four o'clock in the morning, this guy's passed out, and I had no idea what was wrong with him. I finally got some word. There were another couple of guys a little further to the right. We had passwords we had to use at night, if you're going to do any moving, and they change it every day, every night, every morning, whatever, whenever. So I got word over and what was happening was that our relief was coming. It was a very timely thing, our relief coming in, and I said, 'Paul is unconscious.'

So they took him right out, dragged him right out, and left me there alone.

I said, 'Well, so here I am now, waiting, and no relief.' Finally, about two hours later, I started getting sick. I mean, I was really getting sick and I didn't know what was wrong with me, I had no idea what was wrong with me. I was feeling good and all of a sudden it hit me and I come down with it, the dengue fever, pretty close to two weeks that I was down with it. My teeth loosened up, hair fell out, your eyes you couldn't turn. If you want to look at anybody, you couldn't turn your eyes. You had to turn your whole body.

I was laid up for about two weeks just flat-out, didn't eat anything all day. All they fed us was aspirin, that's the only thing that they gave us at that time.

Zeroes

On the beach at Guam, it's about the third or fourth day and a Zero came and there was a dogfight going on with the Corsairs and the Zeros and we were watching that, crazy things happened. Two of the planes came down real low and they're all shooting at the first airplane and they wound up shooting at the Corsair Marine pilot and they hit him. Behind him was the Zero. This guy took a .50 caliber in his leg. He landed the Corsair on the beach and came out of there, and boy, let me tell you something, mister, he was calling out just about everything he could lay his tongue on. 'You call [yourselves] Marines?' But about that time, that Zero turned around, and he came back down the beach and was strafing.

As he was banking, there was a fella with a .50 caliber on this 6x6. He was pumping .50 caliber rounds into that thing just as perfect as you could. [A plume of black smoke appeared], just like you see in the movies, going right down the beach and crashing in the jungle. A colonel happened to be just watching all this. He took the guy's name and all that and he said, 'I'm going to put you in for a citation!' But I actually saw that, all those crazy things are happening, and you wonder how you survive.

Mr. Smith's story will continue.

Soldiers of the 27th Infantry Division review the bodies of dead Japanese soldiers following a banzai attack, July 1944. New York State Military Museum.

PART TWO

BANZAI

I'm telling you the way I remember it, no bullshit. I remember it was like I was reborn again. I remember music. I could see the sun. My whole life changed in front of me, and when I came to, there were guys all around me. They were still fighting! The Japs were down around where I was, but they were in a little ways away, like from here to my driveway. They were still fighting them off!"

—US ARMY INFANTRYMAN, SAIPAN

CHAPTER SIX

The Runner

One of seven children growing up in Troy, New York, Sam Dinova was working with his father as a bricklayer when he volunteered for the Army in the autumn of 1940. After his one-year stint, he returned home, only to be called back after December 7, 1941. He would go on to be an unfortunate participant, wounded in the most horrific banzai charge of World War II.

"Everybody was screaming and hollering. I don't know what the hell was going on, I can't explain it to you—kids hollering, women screaming, machine guns firing and rifles firing. I grabbed my carbine, ran back with the other guys, and somebody hollered, 'Let's stop and all form a line and fight them back!' We did that, but they overran us. Now, when they overran us, there were [just] too many of them. We had these two kids in my outfit, one kid, one soldier—I don't know his name, they cut his head off with a saber! The other kid got hit, too— [these guys] were machine gunners—the other machine gunner got his head cut off, too."

He sat for this interview at his home in Troy, New York, in January 2003.

Samuel R. Dinova

[I was born in 1922.] I went to the eighth grade, and I stopped; I didn't graduate because I just didn't want to go to school [anymore]. I was fifteen years old; I went out to Idaho, I went in the CCC camp. You've heard of CCC camps?[8] I was supposed to be seventeen, but I lied about my age. For six months, we chopped trees, built roads, fought forest fires.

[When Pearl Harbor happened], I was home. I had already been in the Army—I went in the Army October 15, 1940—I enlisted, [see,] I wasn't quite eighteen. Then, you had to be twenty-one to get drafted. My friends were going in the Army, and they were going to be twenty-one or they were twenty-one. So, they went up to the National Guard before it was federalized, then when I joined it, October 5, the government federalized it, and that's why I went in.

'We're Going for A Year's Vacation'

We left Troy from the Troy Armory; we walked all the way down to Federal Street, then boarded the train at the Troy Depot. We lined up, the whole 1st Battalion, and we were loaded on the train, and we were headed for Fort McClellan, Alabama.

When we first got there—our captain had said when we left the Troy Armory, 'Bring your golf sticks, your swimming [trunks], we're going for a year's vacation.' [*Laughs*] We wound up way the hell out of the camp, it was up in the hills and we had to put tents up. That's where we stayed; I was there for almost a year, then we went on maneuvers. Then, June of '41 we went to Tennessee maneuvers. We came home and I went on a furlough, and after we got back we were on the Louisiana-Arkansas maneuvers—that lasted

---

[8] *CCC camps*-Civilian Conservation Corps; New Deal work relief program employing young men on environmental projects during the Great Depression.

quite a while. I remember the big artillery, the trucks were pulling the guns, the 175s, the 105s; I remember the tanks being out there. I don't know if it was Patton's outfit or what, but they had tanks out there. At night, it was raining, so I slept near the truck and tank. We got up and we had to fight. We were the Blue Army, and we fought the Red Army—that's the guys with the bands on their arms. We fought in Louisiana down around near Shreveport and Monroe. They were the Texas 36th Division that we were fighting; as a matter of fact, one of the guys was kind of a wise guy. He shot with the goddamn blanks, and it hit one of the guys—you know the flame came out—so one of our guys hit him with the butt of the rifle, one of our guys hit him with the rifle. We stayed there and then some of the guys were captured, and they were sent to Lake Charles, Louisiana.

When we got back in the fall—it was the end of September '41—they called me in the office, and they told me that I was going home. My year was up. See, I was not National Guard; I was Army. There was United States Army, National Guard, and draftees. Well, I had only signed for one year. So, when I got out, after a few days home, I went looking for a job. I had put my time in the Army. I didn't think there was going to be any war or anything. I was looking for a job and my brother—he was only a young kid then—he picked up the mail. Well, when Pearl Harbor happened, I was looking for a job. I was coming out of the Lincoln Theater, and I heard the kids running around with the paper, extras, they were selling the extra—Pearl Harbor was hit. I knew I was going to go back in the service. Yes, I was a civilian. But when they hit Pearl Harbor, I said, 'Oh, what happened?'

A few days later I got a letter from Cluett Peabody to go to work.[9] Here I am, I didn't know I was supposed to get a letter from them to go to work, [but then], I got a letter from the War Department—they called me back; on January 14, I got the notice to report back to active duty. They gave me five days to be there by the 19th of January 1942. So now when I went in, I got the notice. We shipped out by rail out of Albany Depot down to Camp Upton, New York. We were assigned to this barracks. I met different guys there the week or two I was there, you know, I got talking to guys, they were from all over New York State. Then this guy—he was with a tank outfit, and he got called back in the service and he was always clowning around—he wouldn't let me in the men's room. I had to wash up because I had to go on KP.

I said, 'Come on, will you, I have to get going!'

He said, 'All right, come on in.' I went to look into the latrine, there was a guy, he committed suicide. What he did—he grabbed the wastepaper basket, and he got the rope from his barracks bag— the barracks bags used to have ropes on them; I don't know if you remember that. He threw it over the rafter, and he hooked it, and he kicked the barrel out and bang, he went down. He committed suicide.

I had to go on KP that day. I dipped out spuds, potatoes, about 2,800 guys [we had to feed]. They were from all over. While I was doing that, we had to clean up the mess hall and all that. I didn't get out of there until about nine or ten o'clock at night. The next day they had me on guard duty. The civilians were going to see their sons off, going back in the Army. They had a lot of civilians up in Camp Upton. I forget now if they gave me a club or not, you know,

9 Cluett Peabody & Company, Inc. of Troy, New York, was a manufacturer of shirts, detachable shirt cuffs, and collars. Troy had an early industrial history, and later, for its standing in the garment industry, became known as the 'Collar City.'

a billy club. I had to stop the people from going into the mess hall and things like that. I did that. At night I was on guard, and it was awful cold out there in January, so I used to go into—they had a little shack in there with coal furnaces, and Joe Louis the fighter was down there, too; he was stationed there when I was there. They called us out one morning; they told us to fall out. They called the sergeant to come out and he called you by your name and you went out onto the company street. And then they told us we were shipping out and we had to get ready, and we had to go down to the depot. I don't know how far the depot was from the camp.

Jungle Training

We went down to the camp and we shipped out. We went to California. We went down to Camp Haan, California, down near Riverside. We were there for a few days and they shipped us right to Fort Ord. We went over to Ford Ord, we stayed there and did training, going out in the field with the mortars; now we had regular mortars.

We went to California. We were out regular drilling every day like we did down in Alabama, you know, close-order drill, going out firing our guns and mortars and things like that, machine guns. [Then the 27th Infantry Division] shipped out to Hawaii, I think it was March 10, 1942.

On the barracks bag, they had a code word marked 'plump,' and we were supposed to be headed for the Philippine Islands. That's what I was told, I don't know how true that was. In the meantime, the Japs already took the Philippines, and we wound up going to Hawaii. We got off of that ship and we went on another ship called the USS Republic. It was a captured German ship in the First World War—the way I was told. I'm telling you everything that I know. So, from there on we went to the big island; we drove all around those islands, we did [more] training there. And then we went to Oahu where Pearl Harbor is; we were staying in tents.

We went on thirty-mile hikes, we did jungle training, amphibious training, and I know one time we went out up in the mountains and we had mules bringing us food. A couple of them went down—they fell off the cliff! We were on the edge, narrow passes there. And we stayed up there and we fired our mortars, and we started a forest fire with the mortars; we had to go down and put it out. I remember that. And then one day they took us over to Maui from Honolulu where we got on a ship; we had simulated landing. They had airplanes come by and throw down paper bags of flour, simulating that they were a bomb. They had these [landing craft]—they came down with a ramp on the side, landing craft infantry, LCIs—you came down and ran up, you know, they got as close as they could in the water, and we got off of them, falling in the sand and all that, with your rifle and all that shit there.

We took more jungle training. I'll never forget the day I burned my hand on the damn Browning Automatic, BAR. I don't know what made me grab the goddamn thing, and my hand got all blistered up. It was so white from the heat. The BAR, that was a good gun. We fired them, we fired a Tommy gun, we fired a pistol and the mortars and everything like that. And they took us out to a little village off of the shore to the ocean. They had like a lagoon. You had to swim with all your equipment on. A lot of guys were throwing it off—they were going down; you had to swim at least seventy-five yards with your equipment on, and as a matter of fact, I don't know how the hell I did it. I'll never forget the day a couple of guys went down, and they had these Navy divers go down after them, and they got them all right. Another guy went down, and he never came up; the Navy guy drowned down there. We did that and then they started trying us out with just the small haversack pack, a little bit at a time, with different equipment on. Then they had us go out to the ocean, out a little way, and they had like a wall, and they had the cargo nets and they had us go up and down on these cargo nets.

Shipping Out

After that training, we went back to the company and we used to go out to the field every day, training. As a matter of fact, I was in the hospital there for a couple of weeks. I had an operation on my leg. And we got the orders to pull out. We were shipping out—where, we didn't know. One of the guys told me, and I told him to get the lieutenant to get me out of there. I didn't want to stay up in the hospital; I wanted to go with my outfit.

We left Schofield Barracks on the side where nobody could see us, in these little freight trains; they used to carry sugar cane. We got in there, so many in a car, and they brought us all the way to the back of the island where nobody could see us. They brought us right into Pearl Harbor, where we got on the ship in Pearl Harbor. I think it was June 1, 1944.

We sailed out. I remember over the loudspeaker—June the 6th, the invasion of Europe started, Normandy. They announced that over the speaker.

Now when we were going out, I remember one night I was staying out on deck, sleeping on the deck, and I could see in the distance big flashes—must have been the Navy ships shooting at the shore because we were up near there. Then the next day, they got us, they assembled us on the deck of the ship, ready to go over the net. We started to go out, but they called us back. I was up on [the top of the cargo net] there and I could see the island, and the next thing I knew there was a flash. The [Japanese] had an ammunition dump and everything went up. Big balls of flame and all that stuff flying in the air. We pulled out of there.

In mid-June 1944, just over a week after the Normandy landings in France, 20,000 Marines of the 2nd and 4th Divisions landed and suffered heavy casualties. Reserves of Marine battalions and the Army's 27th Division followed a few days later. Guam, Saipan, and Tinian were seen by planners as essential stepping stones in the conquest of Japan, hastening defeat through economic deprivation of war materials and construction of long-range bomber airstrips. Awaiting them on Saipan were almost 40,000 Japanese troops controlling the high ground, every yard of the landing beaches cross-registered for devastating artillery fire. After nearly a week of Marine combat, it was time for the Army to bring in its reinforcements. The men of the 27th Division were tasked with the duty.

Saipan, <u>Stars and Stripes</u>, July 1944.

The Landing

They put us on [for the landing]; we went in on the 17th. See, we were supposed to be [reserve troops] for Guam—that's what they said, but we went in on the 17th of June, 1944. So, as we got in the Higgins boats, they made these circles, and they lined up going in. We got in so far; we couldn't go any further on account of the coral reef. They had these [amtanks], they went in the water—I don't know what the hell they called them—and we had to jump off on a beach. The Higgins boats couldn't go in or they'd rip the bottom up.

So, we got in there, and when I first got there, I saw a jeep with the blood plasma giving it to Marines who were on the beach, and then I saw three Marines—they were dead. One guy had a tank on him, a flame thrower, and he was shooting it at that cave where the Japs were coming out, and you could see some of the Japs on the ground. They were dead, scorched.

As we moved in that morning, we went up so far, all of a sudden we hit the ground, we got an air raid or something—you could hear the motor of the plane, and pieces of shrapnel were falling on the ground. They were shooting up at it, then we moved out. As we moved out, we moved into this area and the airport was there, Aslito Airfield.

So, we went in the airfield—I don't know who had it first, the Marines, or the Japs took it away from the Marines, but we got in there and I was digging a hole. The Japs used to put their planes in bunkers there so they wouldn't be spotted by the air. They weren't on the field; I didn't want to get near where the planes were; I didn't want to get near because I figured if the Japs came in, they could roll grenades. So, I dug in and the next thing I know, we were fighting. Well, anyway, while we were in there fighting up near the airport, the report came this guy got killed. A guy from Lansingburg [outside of Troy], Swede Johnson, they called him, he got killed. And then we pulled in, we dug our holes at night, and another kid [who would be killed later], Ciccarelli, I was near him when we hit this big cave. We were out there in front with our rifles, and we got them out of there. There were women and kids—old, old lady, old man, carrying the kids on their shoulders—and there were some Japs. They had G-strings on them, nothing on them, you know, to cover their privates. And they were sent behind the lines.

So I'm telling you what I did. That evening, we pulled up to this area, where the 165th, of the Fighting 69th, already had the foxholes dug, and we were supposed to take their holes that night. And this one guy that was in our outfit, he was a regular Army guy, he was a wise son of a bitch. He was from Arizona. He was made sergeant in our company, and he was picking on all the guys. So he happened to jump into the hole where all that shit was. Oh, was he mad as a banshee, smelled like hell! He was hollering and screaming like hell. [*Laughs*]

I say we went back in the holes right away because there was a Jap Zero dogfighting with one of our planes. You could hear the machine gun chatter; he came down and started strafing us. I leaped and [hit the ground], and I hit my chest on the frigging coral they had; I scratched my chest, I'll never forget that day. And [the pilot of the Japanese Zero], he lands down in the field there, and the guys opened up. We had guys there with .50 calibers down the field, and they opened up and they killed him. I didn't see this; this is what I was told. But I know they were fighting in the air; I could see the planes.

Coming in from the beach, when I got off the [amtank] to come in and land, I saw one of our airplanes. The tail was up in the air and the motor was in the ground, and a parachute was all loose and was on top of the tail of the airplane. And I was right there, me and a few other guys, and I was [poking] around near the cockpit. The plane was all scorched—I don't know if he got knocked down, shot down, or if he crashed or whatever happened. But it was in the ground, sticking in the air. So, I went to dig, I had that little pick mattock, and I was digging near his head, but I didn't see any head; it was just black ashes—I found just bone, skull, that's all I found there. I dug down a little bit and I pulled off his tag. His tag was near the skull and that was all black. The Navy has round tags; we got the flat one, they got the round one, and on that tag, it said, 'Paul Danna, United States Navy Reserve.' Well, then when I was digging farther down, you could see it was all charred, it was all ashes. His whole torso was all black and everything, so we started to scrape around that. We started digging a hole, and then we put what remains we could in there. Now what happened was, I got a stick; don't ask me where we got the stick and pieces of wood. We made a cross on it, we tied it with shoelace tight as we could, and we put the tag on there so the Graves Registration could pick it up.

Before we dug in that night, I went looking into [this concrete bunker]. I had my carbine outside, leaning against the thing, and the guys were scrounging around. And we found opium, rubbers, different things; guys were picking stuff up. They found rubbers. I found a nice silk handkerchief; I gave it to some guy about twenty-five years ago. Embroidered right on the handkerchief [was an image of] a Jap having intercourse with this geisha girl. It was a nice silk handkerchief.

In the meantime, we heard a big explosion. We went out, I grabbed my carbine—it was right on the end of the door there. One of our outfits, it was the 165th, dropped a mortar shell short; it hit in our area, and it killed a guy in my company—he was from Connecticut, Skiba—he was one of the replacement guys that came in from the Christmas Islands—and then there were two or three guys from B Company who got killed. There was a lot of confusion over that.

So now, that night, we dug in there. The next thing I heard while we were dug in—now, it's dark, it's pitch black—I heard a noise, a flutter, and something hit down right near my foxhole. I'll never forget that; I don't know what it was, I didn't look, I didn't get out of the foxhole, because you didn't know what they'd do; your own men might shoot you. It might have been a dud—whatever it was, I don't know. There was a roadway, and during the night, the Japs were trying to get out. They had these trucks, and our machine gunners opened up. You could hear them screaming— [our guys] opened up and they killed a bunch of them. The next morning you could see them all, leaning all over the trucks and everything, and then we pulled out of there.

We went up in this area where Mt. Tapochau was, where the banzai attack would come from, where they all came down. Now, we pulled up into that area, and we had these panel trucks with speakers on them telling the people to give up, we'd take care of them. There was a Jap general up there—he told his people that if they gave up, he would kill them. So, we pulled into that area; we dug in.

That day we were watching for snipers and out came women and kids, they had religious people on that island. They called them Chamorrans. These people were awful religious. We used to burn down the houses—they lived in shacks, the Japs took them over, you know. And one of the guys in my outfit was grabbing the gold teeth out of the [dead Japanese] with his bayonet. These [Chamorro] people were awful religious—they had the Blessed Mother in their shacks—they were like saints, and the Japs were raping the women and all that. They did everything. Well, we saw them coming out, and kids were bleeding, and we took them to the medics who were bandaging them up; some got hit with mortar shells, or whatever it was.

When I first came in, I did see a big, big wire fence. It must have been barbed wire, and they had had these Japs in there. Wiry little Jap soldiers, they were about my size, nice-built guys. They had them in there—we took them prisoners. The Japs had, in the mountain, a door cut out of the mountain. I don't know if it was square or what, but they used to open it up, pull a gun down, and shoot down into the ocean, shoot at the ships. And when we did find out, we knocked it out. At first, we didn't know where it was coming from, but they found out. I know that.

We're coming up this trail, and we're down near Tanapag Harbor, and this was before we got to the mountain, and there was a lagoon. I'll never forget—I saw a couple of soldiers, they had an old, old man. Why I say he was old, he had the goatee on him. He was a Jap from the navy—he might have been a naval officer or something, an admiral or whatever you call him, and they were on him with the gun, with the rifles.

We took a break down near this road and I'll never forget that day. Tokyo Rose was on; we were listening to her. In the meantime, we were waiting to move up to where the mountain was. We were in this area and Lieutenant Stark—he was from Ohio, he was a nice guy—he says, 'Sam, I'm going to make you a runner.'

I said, 'No, no, I don't want to be a runner,' because the guys who got out of the foxhole at night, they'd think you might be a Jap and they'd shoot you; they killed a couple of guys in the Signal Corps outfit who were attached to us. He was going to make me a runner and I didn't want to do it. But I was a runner anyway, this was when we moved out.

A jeep came down to the CP, where the officers were talking, you know they had their spot, and they were told to tell Lieutenant Ryan to stay put—in other words, not to move—but in the meantime, we were already starting to move out.

He says, 'Captain Callan, tell Lieutenant Ryan to stay put with the mortars.'

Now if he had done that, we would have been all right, but what happened was, [the captain] said, 'We're already moving out.'

So, up we went to the foot of the mountain and dug in. Up on the top of the hill I could see a big fire, just like they had a bonfire up there, and they were shooting down at us and you could hear the guns going off and they'd be peppering us every once in a while.

During the night, I was called out to the CP. There was Emmet Callan, our company commander there, Lieutenant Tuger, Lieutenant King, Earl O'Brien, and another officer, I don't know, there were four or five of them. I had to deliver a message, and then I came back to the company.

On July 7, after three weeks of fighting, the most horrific suicide charge of the Pacific War was about to get underway. Backs to the sea, rather than resort to surrender, the Japanese general ordered a full-scale frontal assault targeting a gap in the 27th Division's lines between the 1st and 2nd Battalions of the 105th Regiment. Over six thousand screaming Japanese soldiers, sailors, and even civilians broke through the lines; one officer likened it to a western movie cattle stampede that just would not end.

When I got back, about four o'clock in the morning—I was in my foxhole about four o'clock in the morning, four, four-thirty, in that area. Next thing you know, the sky lit up, it looked like today, you see how sunny it is out there—it was like daylight, it was like twelve o'clock in the afternoon at four-thirty in the morning, and you could see these women, kids, soldiers! They had bamboo poles with bayonets on them, shovels, picks, pitchforks—they had everything. These were civilians, with soldiers too. They came down on us; our machine gunners were out, and they started killing them— there were so many of them! I was at the foot of the hill. I couldn't get out of my foxhole because they were raking the dirt [with fire], and it was going in my hole. Then, me and these other two guys [got out]—where they went, I don't know.

Everybody was screaming and hollering. I don't know what the hell was going on, I can't explain it to you—kids hollering, women screaming, machine guns firing and rifles firing. I grabbed my carbine, ran back with the other guys, and somebody hollered, 'Let's stop and all form a line and fight them back!' We did that, but they overran us. Now, when they overran us, there were [just] too many of them. We had these two kids in my outfit, one kid, one soldier was from—I don't know his name, he lived in this little town outside of Rochester called Lyons, New York. They cut his head off with a saber! The other kid got hit, too— [these guys] were machine gunners—the other machine gunner got his head cut off, too. He was from Lexington, Kentucky; his name was Carneel.

When they did that, we had formed a line, and we started to fight them, but they still came at us; we had to push back. I ran down to the railroad track; it carried the sugar cane to the factories. Now, that night, it rained, I forgot it had rained. My carbine, the end of the thing had some mud in it. I threw a couple of shots, I just took a shot to clean it out. That was down near the railroad tracks, near the bunker I was looking up over. So, when I did that, they kept coming; I was shooting at them.

I ran down by the ocean. I don't know where the hell [I was]—I could see different guys running, and I saw one of the medical officers—he was with a guy from my company—he was on one side and he was running. Then I didn't see; everybody was for themselves. You couldn't help your brother if you had to; if your brother was there, you had to leave him. I saw the back of the officer's shirt and it was all blood, he got hit in the back, and then I ran down by the ocean, down the shoreline. They had a big silver-colored thing in the ground; it must have been a mine. I jumped over it and got behind a coconut tree, where I met two guys from Pennsylvania. So these two guys were with me, and we stayed behind this coconut tree, while the guys were running out in the ocean, swimming out in the ocean to get away from the Japs. The Japs were shooting all around; they circled around us—too many! There must have been at least five thousand of them. And we were only two battalions, 1st and 2nd Battalion. Then these guys got up, and they ran; I heard they got killed after. You know, [later] they're making the count for the guys that were killed, who got wounded. In the meantime, I'm behind this coconut tree. I got up over the coconut tree, and I crawled out towards the Japs.

They had big weeds—this big, tall grass. I met another guy there with my company. He was from Wichita, Kansas; his name was Ganz. I don't know what happened to him; when I crawled out, I lost him. I crawled back, I wiggled back to the same position I was in before.

Wounded

[The Japanese then] let [loose with] a barrage of mortar shells or artillery—whatever they threw at us—and then they hit the beach. I remember seeing the black dirt, sand, everything in the air. Next thing I know, I don't remember anything; I got hit in the leg. When I got hit in the leg, I got knocked out.

I'm telling you the way I remember it, no bullshit. I remember it was like I was reborn again. I remember music. I could see the sun. My whole life changed in front of me, and when I came to, there were guys all around me. They were still fighting! The Japs were down around where I was, but they were in a little ways away, like from here to my driveway. They were still fighting them off. I remember Lieutenant Stark—he was the medical officer—he put the sulfur drug on my leg, because my leg, when it was hit, you could see all of the flesh out of that hole where it had come out, all the guts from my leg, it was a mess. I lay there—I couldn't do anything. My leg wouldn't go, it was just dead. So, he put the sulfur drug on me and everything.

'They Had Baker Propped Up Against the Tree'

One guy runs by me—he's dead now, he used to live near me, too. When they had Baker propped up against the tree, he put a cigarette in Baker's mouth, lit it for him, and took off.[10] He went right by me, this Carlo, he's dead now. He came by me, and I gave him my rifle, [thinking], 'what the hell am I going to do with it,' not realizing, you know, I've got to use it myself. I gave him my rifle.

There were guys next to me, there were two brothers, and one of them—I don't know [what happened to the other that day]—but the one brother was killed. He got shot, he was next to me, he was shot in the head; this is after I was wounded. See, I lay on the ground, they kept coming, the soldiers—the American soldiers. They were fighting them off; they were right near me. This kid who got killed, his name was Bernhardt, he was from Petersburg. His

---

[10] *they had Baker propped up against the tree*- "Private Thomas Baker, also hailing from Troy, was a rifleman in Company A of the 105th. Baker had distinguished himself earlier in the campaign on Saipan by single-handedly destroying an enemy strongpoint that was holding up his company's advance. He exhausted his ammunition and used his rifle as a club. After he bashed his rifle apart on several Japanese attackers, Baker and a couple of his buddies pulled back. Baker was hit, and a fellow soldier began carrying him. When the soldier carrying him was hit, Baker insisted to be left behind. His buddies propped him up against a tree, lit a cigarette for him, and gave him a pistol loaded with eight rounds. After the battle, his buddies found him dead, with the empty pistol still in hand and eight dead Japanese bodies around him." Source: Decuers, Larry. *Banzai Attack: Saipan*. The National WWII Museum, July 7, 2020. www.nationalww2museum.org/war/articles/banzai-attack-saipan

other brother made it all right, and after the war, he went to California.

The lieutenant, the medical officer who put the sulfur drug [on my leg], he was there [with me at the time]. We stayed there until it got dark, around seven or eight o'clock, whatever time it was. I lay there and Nick Grinaldo—he dragged me and somebody else, he dragged me under a tree with all the wounded guys. I was next to Eddie Boudoin; he died here about almost a year ago, he had a plate in his head, shrapnel had hit him [that day] in the head. Then there were other guys, I don't know, I was out of it.

That night after I was under this tree, another soldier in my company got killed. He went out, he was all right until he went down to a little ravine to get water for the guys. When he went down, a mortar shell hit him there. He got killed. He was from Gary, Indiana—Mike Sabo. As a matter of fact, my brother [found his name]; he was in the Pacific, too. He was in the Navy and when he went to Hawaii after the war, he looked at the monument and he saw all the guys who were killed and wounded in the 27th, and I mentioned it to him about the guys in my outfit that got killed. He had the names, and he took a picture of the names on the stone, and he told me about it. My brother's dead now. He fell off of a roof. He was cleaning the roof of his house down in Florida. He's cleaning, and his wife says, 'Don't do it, the guys are coming to clean.' He was always a workaholic, always working, and his foot got caught in the rung of the ladder, tipped back and smashed his head on the driveway. He's the one who took a picture of this Mike Sabo, this guy from Gary, Indiana, who got killed getting the water.

What happened that night—it got to be around seven o'clock, eight o'clock. The [amtracs] were coming up to the edge of the ocean on the shoreline where the beach is. Guys were running out. The [landing craft] didn't have any guns on them, they carried personnel. Amtracs, they called them, and the guys were all jumping in, and they're getting on that, getting in the thing, and as they [were running for the amtrac], I grabbed this one guy—he and another guy in C Company—they grabbed me. I told them, 'Get me out of here!', because if the Japs could see me, they would have killed me, you know, when they ran by. So, they dragged me out and there was no room in the [amtrac]. So, they put me—they got a motor about half as big as this room—on the hood. The heat was bothering me, so a guy threw a field jacket on the hood of the thing, and I got on it. As we pulled out, the Japs were shooting at us.

The next thing I know, we go down this big, big open area, it looked like three football fields. I'm half out of it. A guy came up with the jeep, and they took me and another guy off [the amtrac], they shot me with morphine, put me on the jeep. They strapped us up on a jeep and they took us to this big open field.

Christ, like I told you, the next morning I was out of it. Everything was blurry. I was hurt, but I didn't know how bad I was. That night, they were operating right out of a big, big truck. Two-and-a-half-ton truck—they were operating right out of there with a light in there, emergency operations.

'He Swung the Sword'

I lay there all night long, and the next morning a guy came over to me, Sal Farina, he looked like Wallace Beery, he was a rugged-looking guy. I never told you about him, should I tell you about him? Well, when the Japs chased us down that morning—they pushed us—our tanks came up and they didn't have the hatch open, and he kept hitting his hand on the tank to tell them the Japs were all around us, and to get up and start shooting them with the machine guns. When he was doing that, a Jap came out of the bushes. The Jap came up—and I'm not making this up or anything, no bullshit—the Jap came up and swung the sword like that at him. [*Gestures with arms*]

Sal didn't know it, but he happened to see it from the corner of his eye, and he went down like that [*makes ducking motion with head*], and the sword went over his head. He told me that himself, he told me what happened when [the Jap] swung the sword at him—he missed him, and Sal let out a yell, 'AGHHH,' like that, like a big scream. And it's a good thing because that scared the Jap. One of the naval officers—he told me all this himself, and it's no bullshit, either—came up, and he shot the Jap.

The Replacement

Going back when I was on the ground there that morning, this soldier came by me, I think with a little chunk out of his arm, a bullet wound. He was with one of these new guys that came from the Christmas Islands; nobody knew him, though I knew him casually because we were shipping out and these guys were coming with us. Well, he was with us a couple of months. He was a machine gunner. Well, that morning when they broke through, he starts shooting at them with the machine gun, the water-cooled. Sal was his sergeant, the guy that the Jap tried to hit with the sword. He told him, 'Get out of here!', because they had killed a lot of them, but the gun froze up on [the kid], it warped from the heat. So, Sal got out of there. Before the kid could get out, he got killed. Those guys didn't know him. This kid I'm talking about, this soldier, he was with the 43rd National Guard Division from Connecticut—they broke it up, and they put so many in each of our regiments, that is how I got to know him. I didn't know him that well, but anyway, later, one of the nephews wrote to the 27th Division to say, 'I wish I knew somebody that knew my uncle.' The nephew was from New Haven, Connecticut—I imagine the kid's sister lived there—and that was his uncle.

Nobody up in the post knew him, they asked me, 'You know this guy?'

I said, 'I knew him a little bit.' Nobody knew him! They didn't know who he was! He was one of the new replacements. A mortar shell hit him and ripped his whole shoulder out. This kid here, he didn't get a chance to get out. He and Sal were firing the machine guns on the Japs, Sal got out, and by the time he got out the kid got killed. Now Sal—I saw him. I was on the ground in a big field hospital where they operate in the big trucks. Oh, it was a big field, guys were dying there, wounded. He says to me, 'Are you going to be all right?'

So, I didn't see him anymore. The next thing I knew, a couple of guys were picking me up; I thought they were Japs. They were Koreans, you know, they had Koreans on that island; the Japs had them do all the dirty work. So, anyway, they picked me up and they put me on a hospital ship, the *USS Samaritan*. I was on that hospital ship, and they were burying guys who died, throwing them off the ship after we left, and they took me to New Caledonia.

I lay in New Caledonia—I got there the later part of July. As a matter of fact, we were right by the island of Truk, where the Japs had that island. But they abandoned it, [we] didn't invade it. And when I got down, the Navy guy took me off, put me in the ambulance, and took me to the 29th General Hospital in New Caledonia. I forgot to tell you about—I was pulling guard duty. There was an open pass, this was just before the big banzai raid came. This guy lay next to me. He was from the 106th Infantry, and I was on guard. I was all dirty, needed a shave and everything—filthy.

I said, 'What's your name?'

He said, 'I'm from the 106th.' He said, 'My name is [so and so]. Where are you from?'

I said, 'Troy, New York.'

He said, 'I'm from Albany!'

I said, 'No kidding.'

'I'm in the 106th,' he said. 'I got a brother-in-law named Joe Merola from Troy; used to be the bread man, used to make the Italian bread.'

I said, 'Shit, I've known him all my life!' He was surprised. Then when I came out of the service, when I got discharged, I saw Joe Merola down in the neighborhood and I was telling him how I ran into his brother-in-law while we were fighting. I didn't know that guy from Adam.

And the next thing I knew I was on a hospital ship. They operated on me, and I got to New Caledonia, and I was convalescing. Then they put me on an airplane, and I went to Espiritu Santo. I was only a few miles from where the guys were stationed—my outfit, the guys that didn't get killed. Then they brought in all new replacements. I didn't know who they were. I was completely out now. I was in a different outfit, all new guys. Then they trained them and they went to Okinawa, then from Okinawa they came home. They went to Japan and they came home on the point system. I was over there thirty-two months.

[They sent me to] the hospital for a few days in Hamilton Field, California, and from there they shipped me to Lowry Field, Colorado, and then I was shipped to Washington. Two women picked me up, they were WACs. They had me down near Hagerstown, Maryland—that's outside of Washington. They put me in the ambulance, and I went down to Martinsburg, West Virginia. That's where I was in Newton D. Baker General Hospital. Then I went to Camp Atterbury, Indiana. They checked me over and they sent me home for three months. They said, 'Go on home for three months. You're still in the service, though.' They figured why [have me] convalesce in the hospital when I could do that at home. They said, 'Come back in September.' This was in the summer. I'd come back right after Labor Day. I went back.

They said to me, 'No, we can't let you out yet.' They sent me home again—three more months. And I got out December 22, about three days before Christmas 1945. But it was a long stay in the different hospitals and then I was hopping around. They were giving me treatment, whirlpool, they couldn't do anything. I have a big scar on my leg, a big hole there. [*Points to leg*]

Home

At first, I was so weak when I came home, I couldn't eat. I didn't want to be near anybody. I [normally] weighed one hundred twenty-eight, one hundred thirty pounds, but then when I was wounded, I went down to about ninety pounds. My aunt used to get two raw eggs—she said, 'I'll build him up,' and she mixed it with a shot of vermouth, and I drank it. It did build me up, though. See, I was small, but I was wiry.

My leg—this is the leg that got hit [*points to left leg*]—was big as that [*circles thumb and forefinger*], to the bone. All the flesh was up in here [*motions to thigh*]. That's an awful big scar; I'm lucky I didn't lose my leg, but I can hardly walk now. I got a bullet here that didn't go through [*motions to right lower leg*]; I have a scar there. Then when I was crawling after I got hit, I was hit [again] in the back. It's a good thing I got it in the back—I can show you, about the size of a nickel; the scar's there. As a matter of fact, when I went into St. Mary's Hospital quite a while ago, and they did an x-ray of my kidney, and they said, 'You have a foreign body in there.' They thought it was a tumor or something.

I said, 'No, oh no, I remember.' Yes, it was a foreign body, it was a piece of the metal!

[When I got home, I ran into fellow soldier] Joe Mariano. He told me when he came home—I asked him, I said, 'Joe, [what do you recall from that morning] when the Japs chased us?'

He said, 'I wasn't hit.' He was [fortunate]. They surrounded the medical department, they surrounded the headquarters, they completely surrounded, there were so many of them. It was hand-to-hand fighting.

He said, 'Sam, I don't want to tell you—where I live here, if you go up [the block] about a quarter of a mile, [and picture] dead Americans and Japs all on the ground, and a lot of the guys I saw the night before were there, dead.'

He said, 'I wouldn't touch anything because I don't know what was boobytrapped or what. They were all dead on top of one another!'

I hope I'm getting some of my stories accurate. But it is the truth.

Mr. Dinova was the recipient of the Bronze Star and the Purple Heart, among other decorations. He passed away on December 4, 2010, at the age of 88.

CHAPTER SEVEN

The Marine Gunner I

Albert Harris was born at home, the youngest of three siblings. When the war broke out, he enlisted in the Marine Corps, trained as a machine gunner, and saw action in the Marshalls and the Marianas, and at the battle of Iwo Jima. He was fast friends with his two other gun crew members, one of whom was subsequently killed the first day at Saipan, and the other near the end on Iwo Jima; he mourned them all his life.

In 1947, he and some fellow Marine buddies joined the Marine Reserves; it had a good baseball team, and they wanted to play together, however, when the Korean War broke out, he was recalled to active duty, training new recruits in his specialty, the .30 caliber air- and water-cooled machine guns. He served eight years as a Marine; after that, he never touched a gun again.

"There were some Japanese soldiers apparently up in the cave underneath where we were standing. A lot of other people were hidden in these caves all along. But they had gotten the people afraid of us, probably terrified of [us] coming. So, we went down there, we sent scouts down there [first]. A couple of them got killed by the snipers, so we pulled back to the cliff line and then had the Japanese speakers try to convince the people that

we weren't going to harm them. But I would imagine [they were] like, 'Who are they kidding?' There was nothing much we could do at that point. The killing just started. I saw whole families standing on a rock, right along the ocean, and explode a grenade, and then maybe a survivor would crawl off into that water. [But as an eighteen or nineteen-year-old in combat], I think by that time, I was a little deadened about anything shocking me. I thought much more about it in years after."

Albert J. Harris

I was born in Harris, New York, which is a small hamlet down between Monticello and Liberty. I lived there until I was through high school. I went to high school in Monticello and from then on, I moved to New York right after that in Brooklyn. I was in Brooklyn at the time the war started in '41.

My first thought [when I heard the news about Pearl Harbor was] I was wondering where the hell Pearl Harbor was, like everybody else. I don't remember any particular emotions really at the time. I didn't know much about the world; I wasn't following the world situation. I didn't know there had been a crisis for a couple of years. I was just existing in New York. So outside of trips down to the city to ballgames and things like that, yes, it was my first time really away from home.

During '42, I realized I better start looking for some spot. I was very vulnerable at 18 years old and single, so I shopped around. I didn't particularly want to go into the Navy, because I thought I might not enjoy life aboard ship; you're sort of confined there a good part of the time. The Army had no appeal. I don't know. It's just I was 18 years old, and I wasn't thinking things out too well at the time. I probably made a foolish move, but I just went and hit on and tried the Marines.

I enlisted and I was called up on December 7, 1942. They made a big thing of it at the time. There's a [recruiting station] on Lower Broadway, the room was full of people, and it made the front page of the *Daily News* and the *Post* and everything that day. Then we went into oblivion. [*Laughs*] We left to go down to Parris Island.

'Your Ass Belongs to the Marine Corps'

Parris Island was twelve weeks of hell. You just kept thinking that you were going to die and that seemed like a terrible prospect. But you're on the base about two minutes or less, and you already become molded in their image. They come down on you like just unbelievable. It was very hard.

They tell you not to worry about the people at home, [because] they forgot about you already. You better give your soul to the Lord because your ass belongs to the Marine Corps. They did everything they could to make your twelve weeks miserable. It had its moments, but I didn't think too much about it. I was too busy doing what they told me to; it was good training and discipline. It was massive training in discipline and that was the whole name of the game anyway. They just made you aware that you belonged to them. Then they started to build up pride and the fact that you were in an elite unit and that you better live up to the other people and stuff like that. But what they did, they did very well and did it fast. You got to know the basics of being a Marine. To tell you the truth, I didn't do that much socializing. I didn't have time to find out much about anybody. I didn't make any close friends.

Training to Be a Marine

Then they shipped me up to Camp Lejeune, which is in North Carolina. That's the east coast Marine training base. At that time, they were just forming the 4th Marine Division. I was one of the first people that came into the 4th Marines. We were there, just a nucleus of people, probably a month or two, that's all. Then they moved us across the country on a troop train to Camp Pendleton, California. At Camp Pendleton, they formalized the whole outfit. I became an assistant machine gunner in the 24th Marines, 4th Division, K Company.

Then I started to build relationships with the other people in the platoon. You never had much chance to socialize with the rest of the regiment. I wouldn't have known the rest of the regiment probably if I fell over them. But I did get to know people in the company. Our company was, of course, about two hundred, two hundred and fifty people. I knew them by sight and the people in my platoon were very close, of course.

Our sergeant was a post-[World War I] Marine, he was solidly of the old-school type. He wasn't a bad guy. He didn't work out too great in combat, but he wasn't bad, just ordinary. He knew what had to be done in the way of training. You see, the problem with the training at that time, they didn't have much to go by. By this time, it was obvious that they knew that the Marines were going to be strictly a Pacific force and they were fighting an enemy that was nothing like [we would face in] World War I. That's the only basis they had of how to train people, World War I, which was trench warfare. So, they trained us and spent a lot of time on things that were ridiculous, but they had to keep us busy. I remember I took a long time, two or three weeks [learning] semaphore [signaling]. In the islands out there if you raised a semaphore flag, you'd have been long dead before you got the second flag up there. It was useless stuff.

They trained very little live ammunition training—none. I never threw a live grenade. I was the assistant gunner on the .30-caliber machine gun, but the only thing I did was carry the ammunition, I never fired it on the range. They trained us on how to take apart the water-cooled, and how to carry it with the big tripod and everything. We never used it in combat. You couldn't use a water-cooled in the islands, carry a water-cooled machine gun. So, we used the air-cooled .30.

I'll tell you, all the training they did, it was kind of worthless because I think I would have learned how to dig a hole by myself or climb down the net of a ship. I could have figured that out without them telling me. But again, it goes back to their strong point and that was command and discipline. You've got to realize that you obey what you are told to do. There was no... you knew where you stood. They had to do something to pass the time. I see now a lot of times on the History Channel they show the Marine training, and it's so much more sophisticated now than it was then. But, it worked. We were young, probably most of the people were eighteen years old average; even the junior officers might have been twenty-four, twenty-five.

'Awed By the Destruction'

We were at Pendleton up until January 13, 1944. It was about a year. We shipped out from San Diego. We stopped at Pearl Harbor. At the time, it was still a mess. In fact, we stopped there for a couple of days to pick up the rest of the convoy. I remember they gave us a day off just to stretch our legs. They had planking going from our transport across the side of the *Oklahoma* and from *Oklahoma* to Ford Island where they had a little recreation for us. That was my first visit any place outside the United States was walking across the *Oklahoma*. It probably still had bodies in it at that time.

I was awed by the destruction. Of course, what they had released at the time to the general public didn't cover the situation. But anyway, we were only there for a few days. Then the whole convoy went out and we landed on the Marshall Islands.

The Marshalls

Following the heavy Marine losses at Tarawa in November 1943, military planners cautiously approved plans for an island-hopping campaign to break the outside Japanese ring of defense, beginning in the Marshall Islands, a grouping of nearly 100 small islands over 2,000 miles southwest of Hawaii, the largest of which is Kwajalein, over six miles long and two and a half miles wide. Within the atoll were two smaller objectives, Roi and Namur, in the north, and Kwajalein Island itself in the south. The 4th Marine Division would assault Roi-Namur, and the Army 7th Infantry Division would attack Kwajalein.[7] The Marine attack took place on February 1-2, 1944.

We attacked Roi-Namur, which was the first pre-war Japanese island. It was only two days, I think, to take this atoll. The atoll is very big, like a big pearl necklace made up of little islands. They moved the convoy in to the attack ships, which we were on. That morning early, they put us into the LCVPs—the tracked vehicles—and started to circle us around to get the waves together.[11] Then, when it was going to be the H-Hour on D-Day, they start straightening up the lines—I was in the first wave going in—they make these lines to get them just in the right order that they want. Then, so you go past the destroyer escorts, maybe we're a couple of thousand feet off the shore. As we went by them going into the shore, I remember looking up at them and having the sailors waving at us and thought Holy Christ, what have we gotten into here? [*Laughs*]

---

[11] *LCVPs—the tracked vehicles-* Mr. Harris may actually refer to a version of the LCTs—Landing vehicle, tracked, colloquially known as Alligators, and also known as amtracs, or in the armored versions, amtanks.

That was the first time I realized I should be someplace else. This is terrible. It looked like two-to-one [odds that] you won't come back.

Our particular ship landed in a pretty good spot—we didn't land right in front of the pillboxes, so it wasn't too bad. I jumped off. They're quite high, the [LCTs]—and I was so loaded up when I jumped off with gear, everything from gas masks to strips of ammunition. I was the 'instrument corporal,' theoretically. Nobody knew what that was, but I had all that crap. I had range finders and I had maps and I had binoculars like Rommel. [Loaded with all that stuff], when I went off the [landing craft], I went flat on my face in the surf. That was my first invasion.

'Lose It And It's Your Ass'

[My new classification], that was another thing going back to the old World War I philosophy. Everybody in the squad had a job, and that's all they knew, such as assistant gunner, or instrument corporal, and runners, all these World War I things that meant something. So, they told me I'd be the instrument corporal. That sounded good. I was only a PFC. I thought instrument corporal, I get a promotion. But, no, there was no promotion. Nobody did anything until we were about two weeks from sailing, leaving California, and suddenly all this fancy gear started to come in labeled for the 'instrument corporal!' I had this range finder that looked like a golf bag in a beautiful leather case. I had no idea even how to open the case! Why would we need a range finder on an atoll? I had another instrument which came in a smaller leather case, something to do with map making. I had a stopwatch. I had a pair of binoculars that big in a case again. I had a map case. And all my regular equipment, and my gas mask, too.

I said to the sergeant, 'What am I going to do with this?'

He said, 'I don't know, but you hold on to it! Lose it and it's your ass!'

I carried all this crap; I threw them away, first thing. Nobody asked me about it. That was the end of the 'instrument corporal.' I guess they felt they could win the war without instrument corporals. [*Laughs*]

The fighting at Roi and Namur was brutal. Massive explosions set by the Marines to destroy blockhouses killed nearly two dozen of their own. That night, a banzai charge decimated the Japanese; when the fighting was over, only eight-seven of the enemy were left alive, just two percent of the occupying force of 3,500. The Marines lost 190 men killed in action.

That [action] lasted two days. The Army 7th Division took Kwajalein itself, which is on the southern end of the atoll. It was very successful. Their losses [were high]; we only lost two hundred killed. In fact, we had a Medal of Honor winner—a guy named Sorenson who fell on a grenade and apparently saved the lives of some in our company.[12]

The 'Instrument Corporal'

Then they put us back aboard ship, and we went back to Maui which was to be our training ground. That was about [two] thousand miles back. So, the whole division was put into a tent camp which they had built on the side of the volcano. Have you ever been to Hawaii? They have a big volcano called Haleakala. They put this massive tent camp there, and that was our training grounds for

---

[12] Richard K. Sorenson [1924-2004] was one of only four surviving Marine MOH recipients [out of 27] who received the honor after shielding their comrades in arms from grenades with their own bodies.

about the next about four or five months. Then we went off again, to attack Saipan and Tinian. [With the lessons they learned in our first invasion], I think the only thing they had to learn was that they didn't need an 'instrument corporal'...[*Laughs*]

Now, one important thing that they did learn, not from that operation but from the one just before, was made by the 2nd Marine division. That was Tarawa. In Tarawa a lot of the landing boats got hung up on the coral, and people had to wade in. They were decimated.

This time, for our invasion, they had gotten a hold of all of these tracked vehicles which would go over the coral. So, everybody got in. That was a very important thing about them. But the position that the Japanese were in by this time was always defensive, and they were dug in. I never saw a live Japanese in my four battles. I never saw one live one.

Saipan

On our way to Saipan, they told us quite a bit about the contour of the island, of what we could expect; they had a mockup of the island on the ship. They told us whatever they knew about it, which was limited, but I would say that we had all we needed. The overall commander of that operation was [General] Holland Smith.[13]

---

[13] *Holland Smith*- Holland McTyeire "Howlin' Mad" Smith [1882 -1967] was a 'Marine's Marine,' the overall commander of the land-based Saipan operation. He harbored no love for the Army or the 27th Division's commander, General Ralph Smith [1893-1998], as discussed by veterans in Volume 1 of this series. Before the final attack, the Marine commander expressed his unhappiness with the pace of Army progress in front of war correspondents and had the Army general relieved of his command. This action, coupled with Marine General Smith's unrelenting criticism even after the war, badly exacerbated interservice relationships. Ralph Smith was exonerated by an Army inquiry shortly after his command was relieved. He lived to be 104,

I was with the reserve regiment. We came in about, I think, H-hour was about 11 o'clock—we landed at about five. We landed below Garapan, which was one of the large cities. Well, they weren't very large. By the time we landed, things were very quiet. Maybe it was a little later than that because it was starting to get dark. My platoon was in amongst a bunch of what looked like gas tanks or barrels. I remember I was looking at my squad leader, who was right in front of me. His shoe was practically right in my face, and things were very suspiciously quiet. All of a sudden, we heard that first shell coming in. That first shell, it exploded somewhere near me and I was looking at his shoe, and a piece of shrapnel took the heel of his shoe right off in front of me! Then, they just kept pouring them in on us.

'The Most Horrible Moment of My Life'

I remember somebody yelling to get out of there, because there's gas around there, but we didn't know where to get! Nobody's giving any orders or anything, but people started to move forward. This was the most horrible moment of my life. As you move forward, it looked like all of the World War II [movies] that you ever saw in your life were happening all around you, all of these explosions. I was in a daze. I went, I don't know how much further. We just kept moving forward.

Finally, we came to a ditch—a curved ditch—and somebody said, 'Get down in the ditch!' We plopped in there. All night long there was firing, and people were hit in the ditch. If you had wounded, you didn't know where to go. I didn't have the foggiest idea where the beach was or where to take anybody. You just felt if you were moving around, you were going to get killed. So, I remember that

---

and in all that time only once broached the subject of their tensions in an interview in the 1980s, but only to defend the actions of his men on Saipan.

went on all night. The whole thing—the whole episode from the time of the first shell, practically, is just like a dream. On Roi-Namur, we hadn't experienced anything like that. So, I was not really prepared for this.

The casualties were horrible. I remember that at just about dawn, I looked up from the trenches. It had quieted down a bit. I saw this Marine, sort of sitting up over the trench; I thought what's he doing up there? I looked up, and saw that he was decapitated.

By the next morning, it had quieted down. What had happened, the Navy—of course we had a lot of Navy all around us—was now able to see where the artillery was coming from up in the mountains, so they started to control them. We were able to start moving again. We had a couple more barrages but not as bad as [the beginning]. Saipan was very tough. It was physically demanding.

Our first night, we lost half of our people, either dead or wounded. The only thing we had left was what we carried. I didn't have a pack or anything. I just had my ammunition and a belt and my carbine and water. That was it. The organization was scattered. Nobody knew where anybody was because of the barrage. It took a while for that to get all organized again.

'The Place Was Full of Bodies'

They finally brought food in; the beach wasn't that far away, once they could stand up on it and do things. It was twenty-five days or so, of really a lot of things happening. It was the heat of the place. It's on the equator. It was in June and July, so it was hot. The place was full of bodies, [and the dead] bodies caused maggots, and the maggots caused flies. During the day, you couldn't even put any food up in your mouth or anything, because the flies would cover your spoon. You couldn't go to the bathroom, because they'd be after that. You'd have to wait until night to have a bowel movement.

You'd walk along, and the flies would get on every little scratch you had. You'd have five or six of them trying to get to the blood. You just had to walk along like this [*waves his hand in front of his face*]. That went on for most of the time.

The fear was worse at night, but the Japanese [there] didn't move around at night, and as it turned out, didn't fire much at night because they were afraid of the counter-fire. I know on our gun, we had to keep awake all night, so we did one hour off and one hour on, all night. It was bad. The thing about it too—the island was full of civilians. They got hurt too, badly.

Running Into the 27th Division

Once, in the middle of the island—we were going to the west coast through this trail—we [ran into the 27th Division]. They were coming in another direction, and somebody told me who they were—just two roads that passed there, in the day. They looked like they were older people than us. Old, they were probably twenty-two or twenty-three years old, but they seemed so much older than us. I guess they were just shifting positions between the two divisions. [But] communications, when you're just a soldier, you don't know much what's going on. All I knew about what was going in the battle was what I could see.

Soldiers of the 27th Infantry Division with Japanese souvenirs on Saipan.
New York State Military Museum.

An interesting thing happened there. About the fifth day on the island—as I mentioned there was a monstrous convoy that brought us there. There were battleships, transports, supply ships, repair ships. The whole harbor was full of ships. So, we were up on this high ground at this point about the fourth or fifth night. They were still there. When it got bright the next morning, we looked out and there was nothing in the harbor but a few little harbor boats! You thought, my God, are we doing that bad they just left us here? I knew we weren't doing very good, but...[*Chuckles*]

What had happened was that the Japanese fleet had been sighted and they had left for a big battle called the 'Turkey Shoot of the Marianas,' where they destroyed practically the air force of the

Japanese.[14] That was what they pulled out for. That Japanese convoy was heading for the Marianas to probably shell us.

Marpi Point

At the end of the battle, [I witnessed] the most eerie, bizarre thing that I ever saw in my life. Up at the end there was a place called Marpi Point. We were there for two or three days, just watching people commit suicide, civilians basically jumping into the water, blowing themselves up with grenades, having their own soldiers shoot them.

What had happened was the end of the island was covered with a shrubbery very tight, like a hedge. It was also coral, and it was pockmarked with these holes, so people could get in these holes all along there. Then there was a cliff just about a thousand feet from the edge, which had caves in the underside. There was a path going down into the flatland, before you got into the water.

There were some Japanese soldiers apparently up in the cave underneath where we were standing. A lot of other people were hidden in these caves all along. But they had gotten the people afraid of us, probably terrified of [us] coming. So, we went down there, we sent scouts down there [first]. A couple of them got killed by the snipers, so we pulled back to the cliff line and then had the Japanese

---

[14] *'Turkey Shoot of the Marianas'*- In the Battle of the Philippine Sea, June 19-20, 1944, the last major carrier battle of the war, American aviators destroyed nearly 400 Japanese planes to a loss of just 23, an action that became known as 'The Great Marianas Turkey Shoot'. Three Japanese carriers were also lost in their attempt to disrupt the landings in the Marianas and deal the punishing blow to US naval forces that had been the hope since Pearl Harbor. This, coupled with the losses sustained in the Battle of Leyte Gulf, put an end to Japanese carrier-based ambitions in the Pacific. One of the pilots later debriefed exclaimed, "Why, hell, it was just like an old-time turkey shoot down home!" Potter, E. B., *Admiral Arleigh Burke*, Naval Institute Press, 1990. 154.

speakers try to convince the people that we weren't going to harm them. But I would imagine [they were] like, 'Who are they kidding?' There was nothing much we could do at that point. The killing just started. I saw whole families standing on a rock, right along the ocean, and explode a grenade, and then maybe a survivor would crawl off into that water. [But as an eighteen or nineteen-year-old in combat], I think by that time, I was a little deadened about anything shocking me. I thought much more about it in years after.

The Little Girl

On about the third or fourth day after, I went down on a patrol to this big cave that was underneath; it was bigger than this room. It was carved out, and it was full of bodies—piles of Japanese bodies in the middle of it—a [huge] stack of them, with ten million flies! I remember because we carried a few [of them]. I remember, in fact, that I carried a little girl back, [still living], to the lines. She must have been about five or six. She had a shrapnel wound in her cheek, right through it, but she wasn't whimpering or anything. I remember I returned her to the civilians there, or to the Red Cross or whoever it was, but it was horrible. I remember, in the whole war, there couldn't have been a much more bizarre thing, and [all that] after Saipan was secured.

Tinian

We hung around there for a few days getting a couple of hot meals. Then we went back aboard ship, the same ship we came in on. It pulled up out in the ocean a little ways because Tinian, our next objective, was only three or four miles away. So, we went out just far enough to make another invasion and the next morning we came back and invaded Tinian.

It was very different because [the Japanese] expected us to land down on the part of the island where the beach was, at Tinian Town. We surprised them by landing on this very small beach on the upper end, a small, very rocky area. In fact, instead of landing us as a couple of people in a row, they landed us in company formation, one company right behind another. There was very little opposition. It put us in a good position. That night they had a banzai attack, but it didn't hit right in front of my line [like the one on Saipan]. The Japanese were decimated again by it; I remember when we finally moved out, walking through piles of bodies. They were lined up. They came up there from Tinian Town where they expected us to land. The troops came up during the night and just made that attack.

After that, there was just a scattering of resistance the rest of the way down, until you got to the end of the island. This was about seven days later. Then we were pretty well held up quite a while in a rocky area. We took a lot of casualties there. As I remember, tanks had to be finally brought up. Again, they're all firing, but you never knew where they were firing from. They were firing from cover.

[Still], we were in good shape; our losses [here] weren't that terrible. We had losses but we were in fairly good shape, [but] by this time, it just felt like 'God, we're going to be here forever!' There was never any thought about when you'd get back, or get home. You felt, 'well, this is my life, I guess, this is the way I'll spend my days.' The whole war looked at that point like if the Japanese were going to fight for every isle and every spot like this, there's no way [we are going home].

I remember we were on a patrol, sort of just a mop-up type thing, and there were five or six of us who went through this wooded area. We came into a clearing and there was a whole family of Japanese who had hung themselves. Apparently, they fastened a rope and then just sat down. There was a mother, father, and two kids hanging and bloated, strictly because they were, I guess, in fear of these invaders and they had probably been told [that bad things would happen]. Even with something like that, at this point, what could you do? You just looked at it blasé, and that was part of the day. It's the type of thing that now, fifty years later, you think about harder than you did at the time, but it doesn't bother me, I don't know, [though,] it puts a lot of things in perspective.

After Tinian, we went back, this is a very long trip back to Maui—it took almost a month and a half. We had prisoners; they had picked up some prisoners, so we had them in the hold. You never saw them. The only way you saw them was [if they died], once or twice a day they'd bury them at sea by sliding them down the plank.

'Nobody Knew Who the Guy Was'

I'll tell you as far as treatment of the Japanese prisoners and the dead, we never made any attempt to identify the bodies, who they were. All the Japanese that went into a shallow [grave] were covered over [with earth] by a bulldozer. They're all missing in action, all the Japanese dead [we buried], or else they were sealed in the caves they were in when they were blown up. I helped bury a lot of Japanese, but I never saw any attempt to identify anyone, even though I'm sure that they had identification on them. [I suppose that bothers me] now when I hear we are trying to get the North Vietnamese to give us all sorts of records on our dead and everything; I think we're being a little hypocritical here.

We went back to Maui to just get our replacements to fill in the ranks and did normal marching and training and stuff. A lot of time, the poor guys [brought in as replacements] were brought in right during a battle, and shoved in the line without knowing anybody.

That was very typical. That's the way a lot of them arrived. A lot of them came in and died and nobody knew who the guy was.

Mr. Harris's story will continue.

CHAPTER EIGHT

'Revenge For the Dead'

In 2011, I received a letter at my school address from a local citizen who was aware of my work with students and World War II veterans. In it, he enclosed a translated transcription of a Japanese soldier's diary on Saipan, which was apparently found after the battle, presumably recovered from his body following the final banzai charge previously described by veterans in this book and in Volume I, the largest banzai charge of the war. The World War II vet whose possession it wound up in "serviced the Enola Gay the morning of the bombing mission." Unfortunately, the original seems to have disappeared. The translated typewritten transcription is presented here for the first time and serves as a window into the thinking and character of this unknown Japanese soldier, apparently serving with a medical detachment; as the fighting grows more intense, it is clear he understands his fate.

The American Landings

11 June 1944

The second air raid since landings on Saipan Island. Same as before, bombing was carried out in large pattern bombing and receiving terrific bombardment right after noon and toward evening. The raid occurred while we NCOs were cooking, and we didn't have a chance to take cover in the air raid shelters. Although our AA put up a terrific barrage and our planes intercepted them, it seemed that the damage was considerable. Charan Kanca and Tinian areas were burning terrifically.

12 June 1944

Same as yesterday the enemy appeared. Spent the day in the air raid shelter and it seems that I have the dengue fever.

13 June 1944

Also today the enemy appeared and bombed. Each squad dug air raid shelters by order of the commander. In the afternoon, enemy fleets appeared offshore and commenced furious naval bombardment. Seems as if the bombardment was centered around Charan Kanca and Garapan.

The hospital was hit and burning. During the night our 2nd Company supplied material to the hospital. 1st Lt. Omur and 2nd Lt. Yamaguchi of the hospital units are in high spirits. We carried the patients and supplies to the air raid shelters.

14 June 1944

Toward the later part of the day, naval bombardment and bombing was prevalent. Today we transferred to the air raid shelter on the left side of the valley. In the evening we prepared to move medical supplies and tents, commencing moving at 12 o'clock, however, it was so far that it took us till dawn. On this day, enemy troops and supplies have landed and the time had come at last.

15 June 1944

During the evening the unit commander and a large part of the NCOs departed for the Saipan Shrine for the treatment of patients under terrific fire. Lt. Kunieda performed bravely and courageously treating the patients under naval barrage, and he should be considered an ideal model for the medical section. We administered medical aid to one of the patients and it was the first time that we had carried out medical treatment since our landing on Saipan Island. Under the terrific bombardment, an impressive ceremony for our country was carried out in Saipan Shrine. During the night, we transferred the patients to the 3rd Company on top of the hill. Upon returning, immediately departed for the rocks.

16 June 1944

Due to movements of the previous day, I was tired, so I rested in the air raid shelter.

17 June 1944

I and other NCOs plus five men were ordered by the commander to secure medical supplies. Today the enemy planes were in their glory, bombing and strafing at will.

19 June 1944

Today the order was given for the distribution of duty. I was placed in the pharmacists section, commanded by Lt. Yamaguchi.

20 June 1944

The enemy strafing is becoming heavier and because of naval gun fire I stayed in my shelter all day.

21 June 1944

Due to approach of strafing, bombing and artillery fire, we endured to dig shelters.

Moving the Patients

22 June 1944

Today the enemy attack was more furious, while carrying out duty below the cliffs, the artillery of the enemy found its mark and caused several casualties. During the evening we transferred the hospital unit to the top of the mountains.

23 June 1944

Today the enemy barrage is increasingly terrific. Through treatment of the patients cannot be accomplished. We obtained water and food for the patients, who did not appreciate it.

24 June 1944

Terrific assault by the enemy. They were overshooting the hospital, but one finally landed 10 meters from our dugout and regrettable though it is, we received a few casualties.

25 June 1944

Because of unfavorable conditions and near the vicinity, the unit received orders to move near the vicinity of Tata-Hoke, during the night, removed some patients to same. It is generally regrettable, but we had to abandon some supplies.

26 June 1944

Spent the night below the cliffs with the patients. Condition is becoming increasingly unfavorable and because of concentration of artillery fire, took cover among the trees. No casualties. During the evening, the unit received orders to move to Donney.

Some of the patients were committing suicide with hand grenades.

27 June 1944

Slept good last night because of the Saki we took last night. Upon being awakened by Capt. Watanabe, immediately departed for Donney. Proceeded to Donney under terrific fire by artillery. We received heavy casualties due to the concentration of fire by land units and tanks. Took cover on top of the mountain.

Preparing for Banzai

Was ordered by hospital commander to prepare for purpose of attacking the enemy with rifles, hand grenades, or bayonets on sticks. I was ordered by Lt. Yamaguchi to burn medical supplies. Because of furious fire by the enemy, one tank was destroyed and the enemy withdrew. It was decided that the severely wounded would be evacuated to Tata-Hoke by way of the mountain pass. On the way we were separated from Lt. Yamaguchi and lost our way and came out by the seacoast.

28 June 1944

We found the main strength of the company and were relieved to hear that Lt. Yamaguchi was safe. Suddenly we received a terrific bombardment as we were resting near the 'Y' junction. We immediately dropped to the ground and were covered by dirt and sand. I received a slight wound across the forehead. When the barrage subsided there were cries of pain and calls for help around the area. Took to the forest, assembled and waited. During the night received another barrage. Quenched our thirst with rainwater.

29 June 1944

'Sadness, Pity and Anger'

Dug foxholes due to scare of the previous night. Stayed in them till the afternoon and again received a terrific bombardment. When the firing was over everything was desolated. Took up our duty of treating patients again. During the night orders were received to proceed to Tata-Hoke, but the trip was hampered by a terrific rain squall. Under the flare lighted road we continued to Tata-Hoke. When we reached the Y junction, there was a feeling of sadness, pity, and anger, and we received a blessing to resolve and gain revenge for the dead.

30 June 1944

Toward the morning we reached the Tata-Hoke area. Immediately started on the construction of air raid shelters and received a rain of bombs from enemy planes. Stayed in the shelter all afternoon. Toward the evening did my duty as a medic. Ate rice for the first time since the 25th and regained my strength. Felt like stamping the ground and tears came to my eyes. On this day the hospital received concentrated fire and numerous casualties occurred. I received a slight wound on the thigh of my left leg.

1 July 1944

While working, everyone seemed to regain his strength and upon seeing this, I was greatly relieved. Stayed in the air raid shelter due to the concentrated artillery fire. During the let up, rice was cooked, which had a taste most undesirable. After eating, fixed dugout and attended to the medical supplies.

2 July 1944

At dawn, I visited the place where my friend lay dead with a bayonet wound through his head. Covered him with grass and leaves, after returning ate a breakfast of hard tack and pickled prunes. While eating, heard gun fire and orders were issued for security positions, however, no attack was received and so returned to the shelter. During the evening, took care of medical supplies and fixed up the shelter.

3 July 1944

At daybreak, the sound of enemy artillery and rifle fire reached throughout the valley. Immediately took up security position. The rifle reports seemed more terrific than yesterday, however, the situation cannot be comprehended. If the enemy approaches, the whole unit will repulse them and with every weapon at hand.

Toward the end of the day, took refuge in the dugout with Lt. Yamaguchi due to attack and fire from ground units. Later tried to transport rations under the command of Lt. Yamaguchi but failed due to enemy fire and actions. Today the casualties were the men in the pharmacists section.

'My Foxhole is My Grave'

4 July 1944

Different from yesterday; today is extremely quiet. Near noon the terrific artillery barrage and rifle reports came nearer, so immediately took the battle position. After the rifle fire subsided and nothing happened, at nine o'clock commenced moving toward the top of the mountain, but was greatly hampered by flares.

I was bothered by my wounded leg. Orders were given by the unit commander to fight in this bivouac area. Dug in with all my might. My foxhole is my grave. Heard that orders were issued by the commanding officer for all men to take part in the last assault.

5 July 1944

Lt. Matsumia came into our dugout saying, 'As long as I am going to die, I want to die with the pharmacist section.' He joined us, also [saying], 'If this is going to be our grave, let us make it clean,' so after reveille, we attended to cleaning up the area.

While waiting in the area in our hole after breakfast, the furious assault of the enemy began and the second company under the command of Lt. Matsumai formed into three squads and took up positions on top of the mountain.

Seeing that we were surrounded in the front and the rear, we were being approached by the enemy with the determination of annihilation. We fired at the enemy from the rear, but with the determination of killing and doing away with them. The enemy was advancing rapidly along the road.

We drank coffee and Saki while waiting for further orders. The order was issued for each company to carry out night attacks. Lt. Yamaguchi went to work with Col. Omura and the pharmacist section, bade the final farewell among themselves and awaited the commencement of the movement. Men committed pathetic suicide due to severe wounds. The Lt. and the pharmacist section bade farewell and was promised to meet at the Yakumi Shrine after death.[15] I, with Lt. Yamaguchi, was absorbed into the command section and was very happy. At last, under his command and Capt. Watanabe, the weaponless unit commenced night attack. As the units began movements, communications between the units could not be taken.

6 July 1944

Received an artillery barrage during the morning and took refuge among the rocks. As each round approached nearer and nearer, I closed my eyes and awaited it. Rifle reports and tanks seemed nearer and nearer, and everyone took cover within the forest and then the machine guns could be heard over our heads. I thought it was the end. We got ready to charge out with hand grenades, when ordered to take cover by the Capt. When I looked around the side of the rock I was hiding behind, I saw the hateful face of the enemy shining in the sunshine. With a terrific report the rock in front of my face exploded and the sergeant that had joined us last night was killed, also the corporal received wounds in his left leg. However, I could not treat the wounds, even though I wanted to. Everyone

---

[15]*Yakumi Shrine after death*- The author almost certainly refers to the Yasukuni Shrine, "a Shinto shrine in central Tokyo that commemorates Japan's war dead. The shrine was founded in 1869 with the purpose of enshrining those who have died in war for their country and sacrificed their lives to help build the foundation for a peaceful Japan. The spirits of about 2.5 million people, who died for Japan in the conflicts accompanying the Meiji Restoration, in the Satsuma Rebellion, the First Sino-Japanese War, the Russo-Japanese War, the First World War, the Manchurian Incident, the Second Sino-Japanese War and the Pacific War, are enshrined at Yasukuni Shrine in the form of written records, which note name, origin and date and place of death of everyone enshrined." Source: Yasukuni Shrine, JapanGuide.com. www.japan-guide.com/e/e2321.html.

hugged the ground and remained quiet, waiting for the opening in the enemy. As I stood up to get a rifle from one of the dead, a bullet hit between my legs and I thought that I was hit but glancing down, to my happiness, nothing was wrong.

A report was heard, and I looked around and Cpt. Ite, lying on his back with a rifle in his hand, had been killed. After fierce counter fire, the enemy was repulsed. I approached the body of Ite, who had a bullet hole through his left temple with his eyes partly open and his lips tightly clenched. I'll take Ite's revenge; so, taking Ite's rifle, which he had tightly in his hands even after death, I waited for the enemy to attack.

'Please Cut Skillfully'

Cpl. Yasuhire also had wounds in both of his legs. Pathetically he was saying, 'Please cut skillfully.' Matsumai with the sweat pouring down his head, took one stroke, two strokes, and on the third stroke he cut off the corporal's head.

The reports of the rifles outside subsided. Soon, however, reports commenced roaring in the frontal area. I pocketed the scroll written by Cpl. Onos' hand, and commenced moving to join the friendly troops by opening a bloody path. However, because of firm enemy security measures, this could not be carried out; this friendly force was the vehicle unit which we were supposed to meet at Mt. Tapochau. Soon a squall began, and everyone was drenched.

7 July 1944

While shivering from the wetness, orders were issued to move. Facing down [toward] the north, bowing reverently to the Imperial Palace, and bidding farewell to my parents, aunt, and wife, I solemnly pledged to do my utmost.

With Sgt. Hasegawa and Cpl. Watanit [we] departed for the rocks and came out of the forest. It is regrettable that we have separated from Lt. Yamaguchi because we promised that the place would be the same. Between the enemy bombardment we approached the cliffs where before we received the enemy barrage. We tried to reach the shore, but couldn't, on account of the rocks and cliffs.

The enemy is surrounding us in all directions. Helpless, we took cover in the forest. At the crack of dawn, enemy activity commenced on the road below the cliffs with vehicles, tanks, and walking soldiers.

'The End Has Come'

At last the end has come. We have separated from our unit staff and members of the 2nd company consisting of Sgt. Haswgawa, Cpl. Watanit, and Narusi and myself. And with the patients of the transport units, our group consisted of less than ten men.

Even though we have no weapons, we want to attack and with the determination of dying for the Emperor, both my parents, my wife and my aunt. I am grateful for I am 26 years old, thanks to the Emperor, that I have lived to this day. At the time that my life is fluttering stray like a flower petal to become part of the soil.

Since the enemy landing, to have fought against the enemy endeavoring with the utmost power in carrying out my duty and thus becoming a War God, I am very happy. It is only regrettable that we have not fought enough and that the American devil is stomping on Imperial Soil. I, with my sacrificed body, will become the white caps of the Pacific and will stay on this island until the friendly forces annihilate the hateful enemy and come to reclaim the soil of the Emperor.

Dear Kieko—Please live with courage. My sincere regards to Mother and Father.

Dear Brother—Take care of the family, wife and aunt. Take my revenge.

Dear Sumiko—Even though I am ending on this southern island, your brother is firmly convinced that you will continue in my place.

Dear Aunt and Uncle—thanks for your hospitality. I regret that I cannot repay you. Please take care of Sumiko.

8 July 1944

I am glad that I can die on the seventh anniversary of the Sino-Japanese incident.[16] I firmly believe that the enemy will be annihilated and will pay for the certain victory of the Imperial Land.

[END OF DIARY]

---

[16] *seventh anniversary of the Sino-Japanese incident*-Japanese expansionist aggression triggered the full-blown war with China known as the Second Sino-Japanese War [1937–1945]. The 'Marco-Polo Bridge Incident' of July 7, 1937 marked the start, culminating in many Japanese atrocities committed in the following months and years.

General Douglas MacArthur wades ashore during initial landings at Leyte, Philippine Islands. Army Signal Corp Photo, National Archives. Public Domain.

PART THREE

'I HAVE RETURNED'

"People of the Philippines: I have returned. By the grace of Almighty God our forces stand again on Philippine soil—soil consecrated in the blood of our two peoples. We have come dedicated and committed to the task of destroying every vestige of enemy control over your daily lives, and of restoring upon a foundation of indestructible strength, the liberties of your people."

—GEN. DOUGLAS MACARTHUR, LANDING IN LEYTE, OCT. 20, 1944

CHAPTER NINE

The Invasion Radioman II

The decision to invade the Philippines was discussed in Hawaii in July 1944 by the top brass and President Roosevelt. Admiral Nimitz initially favored blockading the Philippines and invading Formosa; MacArthur pressed for his 'return to the Philippines as promised,' with landings at Leyte. The Seventh Fleet would be tasked with naval and logistical support. The attack would go forward in October, with a preliminary assault at Peleliu. On September 15, 1944, the 1st Marine Division and Army troops began the attack on Peleliu after three days of heavy bombardment by Navy gunships. Peleliu hosted a major Japanese airfield that, in the planning stages, was deemed a major threat to any U.S. advance on the Philippines. The island was heavily defended, and casualties were very heavy. The 1st Marine Division lost 1,252 killed and over 5,700 wounded or missing. The 81st Infantry Division, sent in to relieve the Marines, lost over 540 dead and 2,700 wounded or missing in action. The battle remains controversial since it was never used as a staging area for the invasion of the Philippines or any other subsequent operations, though it did draw some Japanese troops away from the Philippines. Nearly 10,700 Japanese were killed on the tiny island.[8]

Paul Elisha had completed four first-wave invasions. After R&R, the men of the 75th Joint Assault Signal Company prepared for the return to the Philippines.

Paul Elisha

Normally, [our initial assaults] like Attu, Kiska, Makin, Kwajalein, were all fairly short operations. The first one at Attu was a month-long operation, but nobody knew it was going to take that long, so we were stuck in it until the end. Normally, in a larger operation like with the Philippines, we would stay until the battle was, let's say, twenty miles inland, and they would pull us out once all of the support and logistical people came ashore. They would pull us out and we would get ready to go on the next one.

Aitape was in June, we did that for a little over a month. Then we went back, I think to Manus, where we got ready for Leyte. They'd send you into a place where there was a PX or a service club. You did lots of drills, lots of calisthenics training. Always training, you'd go out on amphibious training exercises. That's what the R&R was all about. They didn't want us to get rusty.

Leyte

For Leyte, we were again attached to the 7th Division, I think it was, and we were in the first wave at Leyte Gulf. Getting ashore was not nearly as bad as making it at Kwajalein. First of all, the Japanese had more room to maneuver. When you hit a small coral atoll, they were there to throw you off immediately. So it was a tough landing. Leyte, as I recall, going in was not as bad as we thought it was going to be. Once we got ashore, we caught mortar fire and some machine-gun fire. There were some counterattacks. As I recall, the immediate objective when we landed on Leyte was the town of Tacloban, where there was an airstrip. The objective was to get to Tacloban so they could capture that airstrip and bring in the air support. I think in about two days, we were close to Tacloban. Once we got 18 or 20 miles in so they could land artillery, you were just about beyond the range of battleships' [guns and communication], so that was it and they pulled us back.

Abandoned

The Americans had landed successfully over 200,000 men. The Japanese Navy set into motion a complex 'oceanic banzai charge' to destroy the landing fleet and isolate the Americans now on land.? The Japanese Navy was converging from three different directions to take the gamble at destroying the invasion fleet. From October 23-26, 1944, complex maneuvering over thousands of miles and several sub-engagements wound up in the nearly complete destruction of the Japanese fleet. The Battle of Leyte Gulf was the largest naval battle of World War II.

The thing that complicated Leyte was that when they did pull us back to the beach, just after the landings at Leyte, the Battle of the Philippine Sea took place.[17] I don't know if you remember that or not. That was a major naval battle of the Pacific War. When they found out that the Japanese task force was bearing down, and actually they didn't know about it until the last minute because it came through the Straits between Leyte and Luzon rather than seaward.

---

[17] *The Battle of the Philippine Sea-* It was indeed a major battle, sometimes referred to by air veterans of the battle as the Great Marianas Turkey Shoot, totally destroying Japan's capacity to conduct carrier operations. However, this occurred on June 19-20, 1944, before Mr. Elisha's arrival. He is certainly referring instead to the great Battle of Leyte Gulf, the dates and details of which coincide exactly with his time on Leyte. In his defense, this battle is sometimes referred to as the SECOND Battle of the Philippine Sea.

So the Navy didn't want to get caught bottled up in there. So every ship was yanked out of there, even the LSTs around the beaches. What happened was they were told to dump everything they had. The beach suddenly became this massive chaotic place with piles of ammunition and all kinds of supplies and everything. The Navy just took off!

At the conclusion of the three-day Battle of Leyte Gulf, a sinister new development began to harry the weary American crews. Out of the skies came suicide planes, armed with bombs, often closing on a target in pairs, intent on crashing into ships. The kamikazes, or 'divine wind,' took their inspiration from the typhoons that had saved Japan from Mongol invasions centuries before.

Kamikazes

You may recall, if you've read any of the histories of the Philippine invasion, that shortly after just two days, I think, after we landed there, the Japanese sent a fleet up through the Straits there to hit the invasion force. So they pulled out. Well, you realized you were on your own now. As a matter of fact, for a while, it was an alert because they thought that if the land force got word of it, they would counterattack. What did happen, however, was we were subject to some pretty intensive kamikaze attacks by air. We were on the ground; the Japanese from Manila and other places sent air strikes in with kamikaze pilots.

What [the Navy] did was, they dumped everything on the beach. So they pulled the LSTs, everybody else out, and they went out to meet them, and so we were fairly certain the aircraft carriers were gone. We had just a couple of destroyers cruising offshore. And so, the Japanese pretty much had the air over the island to themselves, and they sent kamikazes in. Now, in Okinawa, they were really bad.

But our first experience was on Leyte when they came in on the beaches.

We'd been told that there were such things and to expect them, but until they happen, you don't know what they're like. As a matter of fact, the day that we were pulled off of Leyte, we were up toward a small village called Manaoag, as I recall, which was inland about a mile and a half, and we had a little encampment there and then they told us we were leaving to get ready for the Luzon invasion. They were pulling us back and they had some LSTs up on the beach and we were to go back and go aboard. Just as we got to the beach, the siren went off for an attack, and in came the Japanese planes. I remember there were several of us—eight of us, I think—and two or three of us dove under a big truck that was pulled up on the side of the road when we came down to the beach. We dove under this truck. The other four or five raced like hell and ran up the ramp of the LST. As luck would have it, one of the kamikazes came down and dove right into the fantail of that LST. It blew the back end right off and two of our guys were killed in that. We were just lucky that we dove under the truck.

They just pulled everything out of the belly of this LST and dumped it on the beach and pulled out. So, here was this huge dump of ammunition and we were just across the road. We'd set up our radio and stuff at the command post. And all of a sudden, we heard the siren and the code red for a raid, and they came in and one of them just dove right down into that fat pile and all hell went up [*throws both arms in the air*]. We went up in the air, radio, everything else. And I had this arm that was broken, [*clamps right hand on left forearm*], this arm had just what they called a 'greenstick fracture,' [*moves opposite hand to right arm*], but I could move it and you couldn't do anything. I remember another guy and I laid behind a stack of #10 rations. It was about four cartons this way and about that high [*gestures with arms*], and we just lay behind it for hours and the bullets were just going, you know, you didn't dare stand up. And then, finally, I remember a warrant officer came along with two other men and he said, 'There's a cart loaded with 155 mm shells over there and we got to get it the hell out of here because when that blows, you know everything is going to go.' So the four of us with the warrant officer went and we just pushed this cart. I remember there had been a group of Black troops who were transporting people, unloading at the time, and one of them came and helped us move that thing. I've always wondered what became of him, because without him, we'd never have done it. And I'm sure nobody ever wrote him up in a book, but we got it moved.

'You Don't Want to Get Stuck Here'

Then, we just threw ourselves back down behind those #10 rations and waited for the firing of bullets to stop. I ended up in a field hospital, with both arms in splints, and one of my buddies, about four or five days later, came in and said, 'God, you don't want to get stuck here.'

He said, 'We're getting ready to go down to Luzon. You better hurry back!' I can't explain this, but there is a feeling, if you stay with your own group, you're better off than if you're a free agent out there somewhere. God knows what'll happen to you. It's like the devil you know is better than the devil you don't. So I went AWOL from the hospital. It was broken, it was healing. It was wrapped, and then they splinted it. [I didn't have much of a problem with] my CO; I had the feeling he was trying to kill me anyway. But I remember the night before we went down to get on the ship to go to Luzon, I was sitting on a cot, and we had by then set up tents. The battle for Leyte was practically over and we were down near the beach when he came in and he threw this thing at me, which turned out to be a Purple Heart medal, and he said something like, 'I don't know why I am giving you this.'

He said, 'Don't think that arm is going to get you out of anything.' He said, 'That'll teach you to go AWOL.'

The Luzon Campaign

The Luzon campaign was not an easy campaign either, I recall, largely because the plan of attack was changed. Originally, when the maps we were given, we were landing in Lingayen Gulf. If you look at the map of the Philippines, there are two sets of hills and mountainous terrain down the sides of the island. Then there's a valley in between. The original plan is to hit the beach at Lingayen Gulf and run right down that valley to Manila. Cut the island in half. Also because there were both civilian and military prisoners in Manila being held in prisons and stuff, they wanted to liberate those people. MacArthur wanted to capture Manila intact if he could. For some reason, toward the end, before we landed, we got other maps and instead of going down the valley, we went down the coastal areas and some of that was literally hill to hill to hill.

I can remember outside of Baguio, which is called the summer capital of Luzon because it's up in the hills, I can remember there was one large mountain. We were there for communications, and for fire support. We must have gone on to that mountain at least three or four times and got thrown off three or four times before they actually secured it. Heavy casualties, really; there was a rumor going around. One of the rumors was that many of the wealthy landowners who own plantations in the valley were close personal friends of MacArthur's. He was trying to do as much as he could for their plantations not to be torn up. If that's so, we paid a hell of a price for that territory. I always felt there were a lot of unnecessary casualties in Luzon.

"An abandoned Japanese baby is adopted by front line medical unit of the 27th Div. The baby was found with a scalp wound, in the arms of its dead mother, by a tank crew during the fighting below Mt. Tapochau." Saipan, July 1944. New York State Military Museum.

The Baby

It's impossible for you to see death and that kind of human degradation and not be affected by it. I can remember in Leyte, we had left the village of Manaoag and we were advancing toward Tacloban. We set up communications and across the road, all of a sudden there was a commotion. Of course, coming from the village of Tacloban, trying to reach the American lines were civilians, once the Filipinos heard the Americans had landed. They began streaming toward the beaches to greet us. They were waiting to be liberated and I remember my sergeant said, 'What the hell is going on over there? See what that's all about, Elisha.' So I ran across the road, I had my carbine just in case. One thing you have to be very careful of in places like the Philippines where there were a lot of civilians was that the Japanese didn't try to get in among them. The commotion was about a ditch where a shell had landed on the side of the road, and there was a woman lying in the ditch and she was giving birth! So there were some units going by toward the front, and they had medics with them. I yelled for a medic, and one of the medics came over and he helped this woman give birth.

I remember I was standing there, and I shouldered my carbine, and I'm keeping people away. I said, 'Keep away. Keep away. Stand back.'

Then, all of a sudden, I hear this, 'Whaa.'

And then the medic turns around, he says, 'Here, take this.'

He had it wrapped in something, I don't know, a khaki towel or something, and he handed this baby to me while he finished up with her. I'm standing there in the middle of this. You see guys on stretchers waiting to be taken back, and you could hear the gunfire and everything else, and here you're standing with a newborn baby in your arms. You know that affected me tremendously. But all of these things, you know, I think what affects you most is that you see life and death in such basic terms. Cheek by jowl, [close to-gether, side by side] as it were, and that is bound to affect you.

'I Have Returned'

I personally witnessed what turned out to be one of the biggest publicity events of the war. There was a historic newsreel of Mac-Arthur's landings at Luzon and Leyte, keeping his promise, 'I shall return.' I think [the view of MacArthur is] overblown because he had a tremendous PR staff.

Several of us had just come back; they had finally taken the town of Tacloban, where the airstrip was. That was the first priority, and that's when we were supposed to be pulled out, because they had to land planes there so they could bomb the rest of the Philippines and Okinawa. They finally took that airstrip and Tacloban, and we were relieved.

They said, 'Go back to get some hot meals and showers,' and we were standing on the beach, watching a bulldozer push this sand out into the surf. And there was a little knot of men, and Kaminsky, our sergeant, asked, 'What's going on here? What are they doing there?'

They said, 'Well, they are pushing the sand out, so the general won't get his feet too wet when he comes ashore.'

We could see this boat waiting offshore, and then it came up and they dropped the door. And these guys came off with Thompson machine guns at the ready, you know, and then MacArthur behind them. And just before this happened, there were a whole bunch of photographers and press people and PIOs— 'Public Information Officers.' And this major came down and shooed everybody off to one side.

He said, 'The general does not like this profile, go to that side!', you know, they set the whole thing up. And then, he's coming ashore, everybody with the guns at the ready, and then he stops on the beach there. There is the body of a dead Japanese, and he kicks it over and he says, 'That's the way we like to see them.' And we just... you know, I could just see 'Willie and Joe,' and what they would have said.[18] [*Chuckles*]

After Luzon, we prepared for Okinawa.
Mr. Elisha's story will continue.

---

[18] '*Willie and Joe*'-American cartoonist Bill Mauldin's scruffy GI infantry characters, who offered their down-to-earth take on the stark realities of war in humorous fashion in *Stars and Stripes* and elsewhere from 1940 to 1948.

The Marine Mechanic II

Iwo Jima, or 'Sulfur Island,' was eight square miles of sand, ash, and rock lying 660 miles southeast of Tokyo. It could serve as a refueling stop for the B-29s and B-24s that were now flying almost daily out of the fields in the Marianas to bomb the Japanese mainland.

In late November 1944, aerial bombardment of Iwo Jima with high explosives began and continued for a record 74 straight days. The 21,000 Japanese defenders survived this with scores of underground fortresses connected by sixteen miles of tunnels stocked with food, water, and ammunition. The surface was covered with concrete pillboxes and blockhouses housing some 800 gun positions.

On February 19, 1945, the attack began as the landing ships brought the Marines towards the beaches of blackened volcanic sand. A total of 27 Medals of Honor were awarded for individual acts of heroism under fire at Iwo Jima. The island was deemed secure on March 25—25 days longer than planners had counted on. Nearly 7,000 Americans and 19,000 Japanese died at Iwo Jima.

It was the Marines' costliest battle ever.

James Smith

Iwo Jima

We were on the way up to Iwo Jima, see, we were a floating reserve; the 3rd Division weren't supposed to land there. As we were approaching the island, there were three LSTs on starboard and port sides as we were going up through, just kind of floating along nice and easy. No big rush to get anywhere. Then, we were attacked by the kamikazes; on the port and the starboard sides, they got hit.

It was in the early morning. We were at chow, breakfast. They had worked out a scheduled system for people eating because they didn't want everybody eating at the same time. So as it happened, it was foggy, and this kamikaze hit [one of the ships] on the right and another Zero came over. He couldn't have been fifty feet over our heads—I could see the pilot, he came right over, and he missed our ship, misjudged by fifty feet. If he had come down, I wouldn't be here today. But he went right over the bow, right into the drink; whether he was hit by us, I don't know, because he was so close that you couldn't even get a weapon on him.

Yeah. Well, we were hit by the kamikazes the day before the flag raising, and they had lost, I think, half a dozen doctors on the starboard LST. We were offshore and they were getting ready to send in different sections of the division and to help out because things were going bad to worse. Everybody was champing at the bit, and here we are out here, and we want to go in and do something. It was so bad, everything was starting to get rough, and the beach was cluttered from the mortar fire—if you were there, you could just envision a thousand people on the beach with the equipment, trying to get out of that sand, out of that volcanic ash. We were offshore, as I said, and watching. Then somebody said, 'There goes the flag!'

But that was the first flag. The second flag, I didn't see, but the first flag I did. It was so rough that they brought the guys back and they got back on board the ship again. It was so bad, they couldn't get in. It was really bad. It was unbelievable, what was happening there, because from what I've read in my history books, a lot of these people came right out of boot camp off to Iwo Jima. Now, I can't imagine what was going through those guys' heads. Here we are, we've been in the Pacific for over two years now, and had come through three campaigns, and here we are up here now [just] floating and not able to do anything. I had found out later that they were actually trying to keep our division [intact] for the invasion of Japan. I don't know whether it was true or not, but that's the scuttlebutt that was going around.

"Trapped by Iwo's treacherous black-ash sands."
Mount Suribachi in background.
National Archives. Public domain.

Now, the whole division didn't go in, but at the same time, we went in whenever different sections were needed, whatever they needed. The Sherman tanks had a .75 on them. As far as the all-around use of the tanks, Bougainville, [with the jungle], was the worst. It got better as you traveled up the island of Guam. It was a lot better and they were very effective; some of the tanks were equipped with flamethrowers, and on Guam, they used them quite a bit. We didn't have too many flamethrowers in our company. We were B Company, and A and C may have had some other newer tanks that were equipped with the flamethrowers to use up there on the different caves. We used them quite a bit up on Iwo, too. On Guam, we used a lot of bulldozers. We had a bulldozer, what we call a retriever tank, with a big bulldozer blade on it.

We finally brought in all of our tanks, and we had sixteen tanks in the three battalions of tanks—A, B, and C Battalions. We lost all of our tanks. The Japanese used 500-pound aerial bombs that were buried all through where the tanks might travel. We lost a lot of them that way. I think we had one tank left, and what we were doing at the time was salvaging parts from other tanks that were knocked out.

Tank Retrieval Under Fire

We were assigned to pull out some tanks for parts. Schwintek, Bob Reevey, and myself took a tank retriever to go up on the second airstrip to pull one of the tanks out. It had hit a landmine, and one of our fellas was still in one of the tanks. We couldn't get him out because he was in such a dazed and shocked condition that nobody could get near him, because he had his .45 out. He was the assistant driver, and he was sitting there, and he thought that everyone who came near him was Japanese. They tried to talk to him, and finally they did get him out after he passed out. He's still alive today in Massachusetts.

There was another tank beyond us that we were trying to get to. We had hooked up the cables and we were going to tow the tank out, and as I straightened up, I looked at the airstrip, and here came a bunch of mortars. They spotted us, and they started to lob the mortars at us. I quickly unhooked, pulled the pins on the cables, and hollered out to Ray Bebob, the retriever driver, and we jumped up on the tank, and they chased us right across that step. To this day, I don't know how we made it; I really don't know how we did. The Lord was on our side out there because as we were clutching along, they were just dropping [shells] behind us. They were on our sides and behind us, but they just didn't get zeroed in on us the right way; we were ducking from all directions and I can remember Schwintek saying, 'What are you ducking for, Smithy?' I just looked at him.

We just laughed at one another, and we got back okay. So this fella Schwintek I'm talking about, was awarded the Silver Star. He was formerly an MP on the beach at Guam and things were going pretty good except on our left there was a place called Sunita Bluff where the 3rd Regiment, I think, was having a bad time. They were losing people by the score there because it was a place where they had to go up, and the Japs were rolling grenades down. They tore the company all apart and the corpsmen were trying to pick up survivors, putting them in the trucks they had right there.

Now, these guys are working under fire all the time. This isn't like, 'Okay, fellas, wait a minute, [stop shooting], we got to pick up this guy,' it wasn't that way. They were under fire all the while, and unfortunately when the driver got hit, he was killed. This fella Schwintek was an MP. He jumped into that reconnaissance truck and drove the truck out of harm's way, and got the guys out of there.

Later on during another campaign, we were supposed to make another campaign landing, Kavieng was the name of the island. We got all loaded up for that and came back to Guam. So to keep the morale up, what they did was they put on the parades and paraded all the tanks, cleaned up and refurbished. Then they had a formation fall out, and then they start calling people out of the ranks and they awarded him the Silver Star for what he did, evacuating that reconnaissance truck with all those injured, wounded guys onboard.

Hit on Iwo

I did get hit on Iwo therewith, I think it was the Japs were using anti-aircraft guns on us too. If they could depress them enough, they would shoot across and they hit our machine shop.

One of the mechanics, Dan Tupper, was a second platoon maintenance man. Colonel Withers was in charge of our tank battalion at that time.

We had a machine shop. I was working on a tank up on a second airstrip and they got hit, and I got blown against the tank I was working on and got cut over my eye. But I just went down and picked up my tools, and went back to work again. Our corpsman, his name was Mendez, he said, 'You're bleeding.'

I was, 'Well, that's all right. I hit the tank. I don't know what it's from but just forget about it.'

'Well, let me take care of it.'

I was lying there in this hole with him, and he was cleaning my face off and the Japs had, I think they called it a spigot. It was a huge mortar. You could hear it; when they launched that it sounded like an old rusty gate opening. I knew that one of them was coming. But they didn't have much direction with it, because over half of them would end up in the ocean, would end up on the other side in the water. I was then on my back and one of those went over and of course, everybody scatters and heads for the hole. They don't know where it's going to land and I was lying there and I said, '6-8-9-4-2.'

He said, 'What the hell's the matter with you?'

I said, 'I just read the number on that mortar.'

I was on the island from February 22 to March 16. I was there pretty close to a month.

Going Home

We went [back to Guam] in an LST that had been hit by a kamikaze but was still usable. We made about seven knots, just enough to steer it from Iwo back to Guam; where my bunk was there was a hole in the side of the boat, and probably you could put a tank through it.

The thing that I remember most about before the invasion of Iwo was that we had the old *Saratoga* aircraft carrier with us. She was on our starboard side, and I used to be interested in aviation. I was always up very early up on topside—in fact, I slept topside quite a bit; I just lay there and watched those guys take off in the morning when they were taking off and flying in and going in close air support and it was quite a feeling.

Many months, in fact, after we had got back from Iwo, we knew we were going home, and we had our sea bags packed for about a week and they told us that there was some scuttlebutt around that one of us mechanics was going to stay behind to break in some new mechanics. Nobody knew anything about who it was going to be. So when the company fell out that following morning, they're calling off the names to pack sea bags, and then we're going, but they didn't call out my name. I was stunned; I was staying. I said, 'Oh my God, it's me!' I went right out, in fact, I ran, down to this tent where this really new second lieutenant was. I went down and I charged into that tent like a bull, and I said, 'Lieutenant, let me see that sheet!'

So I must have had an awful look on my face, because he handed me the sheet without even asking why I wanted it. I looked at it, I went down the page, and there was my name! We had been told that I'd made sergeant and it was still listed as corporal. I said, 'There's my name, Corporal James A. Smith, Jr!' He looked at me and I said, 'That's my name and you didn't call it up.' I turned around and shoved off, went back up the hill.

The guys said, 'What happened?'

I said, 'He just went over my name.' There was a Jesse R. Smith in A Company, there was a Dolph N. Smith in there somewhere. [Someone] said, 'Well, we're all [going to be] made sergeants now.'

I said, 'Listen, I'm going home. I don't care what they're making me.'

Jim Riley, our warrant officer in charge of the men, came back and said, 'I got some bad news for you guys.'

'Where are we going now?' The first thing we're thinking is, we're stuck here again.

He said, 'There's only one sergeant rating [available]. It's come through for you [three] guys, but I don't know what to do. So I don't know who it's going to be, guys. So let's cut cards.'

So we cut cards—I just cut the cards and looked back and this fella by the name of Packy, a good friend of mine, had the high card. So he makes sergeant; we didn't care. At that time we just wanted to go home—enough is enough. So we got on board; they put us on a brand-new aircraft carrier called the *Kwajalein*. We got on board that ship.

Boy, when we left our camp to go onboard, it was like driving down into New York City, that island had changed so much. It didn't look at all as if we had come in and made the landing there, you couldn't recognize it. It was like a city had been born! There were roads, the Seabees had built a core highway down through there, a three-lane highway down through the town off the beach. It was like seventh heaven, we couldn't believe it, didn't know where we were, didn't know where to go. It's a good thing we're on this truck that took us to the aircraft carrier; it was like a dream.

We got out to sea, and to wash our clothes, we used to tie all of our clothes on a rope to wash them in the ocean. We got really clean, really salty. So that's where the term came from, salty Marines. We were standing there on that fantail and washing the clothes and this fella comes walking up behind us. He was standing there and we had a lot of ropes, a lot of clothes we were dragging in. Out of all the ropes on the end of that fantail, whose rope does he pick on? Mine. He pulls my clothes up, and he drops the rope. I said, 'Hey, mate, what the hell do you think you're doing?' He just looks at me.

I said, 'Whoa, wait a minute. You're going to lose my clothes. What's the matter with you?' He just looked right straight through me—he just had that blank stare and looked right straight through me. I knew something was wrong with him and he just stared at me.

He turned around and he walked away. When he turned, I saw that he had some holes in his head. He was an officer, but he wasn't wearing his bars, whatever his rank was, and he just walked away. Well, we found out that we had some people who had lost it and they were onboard ship with this [condition], walking around and they didn't even know who they were. That's how bad some of them were. I don't know where he was from.

I was onboard the carrier on the way to Hawaii when [President Roosevelt] passed away. It was in April, my birthday was April 5, and I was onboard ship when we got that word. It was kind of a shock when you hear something like that; it's really disturbing to think that somebody like that didn't live to see the end of the war, the results of what we had done. That's a part that kind of stayed with me, thinking about when he was leading a country in war and all, and to pass away before he saw the end results of it.

'It Saved a Lot of American Lives'

I often think about [the dropping of the atomic bombs on Hiroshima and Nagasaki]. That's kind of a tough one. I think of the stories that we had heard later. There was a rundown on what the Japanese were doing to prepare for our invasion of Japan. In this book I read, in some of the pictures and some of the stories, they had 5,000 kamikaze planes on the ground waiting for us. They had planned to line the beaches with the women and the children. I think about that part, it keeps coming back to me [in thinking] about when that bomb was dropped.

I hate to say it, but I was glad to hear that [the bombs] had slowed them down, in trying to stop them to get our message through. That it's useless [to continue to fight on]. Why should they go on fighting and not give up? I have so many mixed emotions about that, it's hard to pin. I don't like to say I'm glad it was dropped, because I know how many people have suffered because of it, and are still suffering because of it. But it saved a lot of American lives. I wondered how many millions of our people would have been slaughtered on the beaches; we would have lost an awful lot of people. It truly saved a lot of people's lives, because I know there would have been a terrible amount of slaughter on the beaches with their people there and our people too. I mean, it would be tough for our guys to go ashore and face women and children.

The Japanese soldiers were good. The thing that they had on their side is, they just didn't care about living. I mean, they were just fanatics, it was unbelievable, the slaughter, what they did. [Climbing up and] banging on tanks—it's hard to describe why a person would do that, he has to be out of his mind. But most of the time they were full of sake. They did a lot of drinking and I think that's what drove a lot of them, they were so psyched that they got so wound up. I mean, they would just charge into a tank that was shooting, lead flying, and they would walk right into it. You and I, we wouldn't do anything like that. You would try to protect yourself, you want to survive, you want to do your job and survive, but they just didn't care.

It was unbelievable what they did. Some of the atrocities that they did on our Marines [was so bad that] you wouldn't want to hear about it. I still have a bad feeling about them. I can't shake it off. I really can't. [But another thing is] that whatever they accomplished something at times, they seem to me to be winning, and all of a sudden, their winning would stop, that sometimes they just didn't follow through. They would stop.

I know that some of them [were scheduled to meet us]; we were scheduled to go back to Guam for the 50th Anniversary Landing, the liberation of Guam. Unfortunate as it was, my mother at that time was very ill and she ended up in the hospital three or four times. So we had to cancel our trip to Guam, but some of the fellas went, they took a lot of pictures. In one incident, they had some little boys [there whom they befriended]. Well, they got back to Guam, and lo and behold, some of those people are still living and they came forth. They took pictures with them, and they had it posted in a newspaper on Guam, and they sent me pictures of these people who were kids, now 60-65-year-old people.

*

I've stayed in contact with all those guys that are living. I think there are about 35 people, maybe it's right in that figure somewhere who would be left in the original company. I write cards. I handwrite a message to every one of them every Christmastime. If [someone] answers back, I write the widows, there are a lot of widows. I write to them, and they keep in touch. A little story behind that fella, Schwintek. For over 50 years I'm writing him letters, at Christmastime, short letters, but I never heard a word from him. This past December, I finally received a card from him, and it was written by his granddaughter. She wrote on the card that it was good to hear from me and that [he was] so glad that I've kept writing. So I wrote another letter back to him. I haven't heard from him. I don't know what's happened. I don't know whether I have to wait another fifty years; it's a long time ago.

The Truck Accident

I'll tell you about one incident that crops up from time to time, and just about three years ago, it was finally resolved for this one Marine on Guam.

We were on the beach probably about a week or more, and our tanks formed up on a line, and they were shooting at different targets, whatever. They relieved some of these fellas to bring them back so they can have some warm chow. I was working on a tank. I was underneath one of the tanks dropping what we call an inspection plate; I was going to change the starter. Don't ask me how I remember these things.

Suddenly heard some terrible screaming. The hair stood on the back of my head, I thought it was a banzai, I thought some Japanese had broken through and were coming through the bivouac area. I crawled out from underneath the tank and stood up, and I can still hear the screaming. I looked off to my left and there was a sort of a hill, the road went up and turned. What had happened, this 6x6 truck, they had a bunch of guys on the back of it. They were loaded with the fellas that were from the tanks, and they were taking them back up the hill. As they got halfway up the hill, the fella who was driving the truck, it stalled on him. Of course, with those engines, they had a vacuum brake system on them. If the engine stalled, there was no vacuum for the brakes, but there's always a reserve so that you could stop the truck. But the truck driver got excited or something, he turned the wheel and turned it into the bank. When he did that, it rolled over. It had about probably a dozen guys in the back of that truck. That's what the screaming was. The truck tipped over [and trapped the guys underneath], and one of our tanker men is [dead]; unfortunately one of the stakes went right through him, pinned him right to the ground. Now, these fellas are underneath the truck, and we came running up, and to this day I don't know how we did it—we just picked that truck up. We picked that truck up and turned it, to let those guys out. My friend Tom Murphy was underneath. He said the only thing that saved his life was that there were a lot of packs in that truck and he said, 'It cushioned the blow for us.' But there were at least twelve guys underneath that truck and one of the fellas was killed and the other fellas were pretty well mangled up. His name was Miller. He was killed, and for the rest, there was some real bad results of that accident.

'He Hugged Me, And He Started to Cry'

One of the fellas who was a truck mechanic, Frank B., for years he and I both played guitar and we used to entertain the troops back then, but he would never show up at the division reunions. Over the years he'd write, but then he didn't write at all. Finally, I called him up when we were at Savannah at a reunion; he lived close to that area. I had a phone number and called and I talked to him. He said, 'Yeah. I'll come to the next one. I'll come to the next reunion.' He was always promising. So finally the next reunion was in Philadelphia and he said he was coming. He kept saying he was coming. When we got to the hotel, the rooms were all filled up. We had quite a bit of a problem with that, but I kept checking at the desk.

I talked to the woman at the desk, and she said, 'He's here. He's in the hotel.' We're trying to find him. I called his room and a fella answered, I found it was his grandson who was there [with him].

I talked to him, and I said, 'Where's your grandfather?' I told him who I was.

'Well', he said, 'he's downstairs somewhere, Jim.' I don't know how he knew my name but evidently Frank had been talking about us. He said, 'He's downstairs somewhere.'

So I hung up the phone, and I walked into the hospitality room. As I walked to the hospitality room, I saw two or three of our guys, and here comes Frank walking. We just grabbed each other. Now, this is a long time.

I said, 'Frank, how the hell are you? Why did you wait so long?' Now we kept talking back and forth and he kind of looked around.

I said, 'What's the matter, Frank?'

He said, 'Hey, can I talk to you alone?'

I said, 'Yeah, what's wrong?' So we sat down on a bench.

I said, 'What's the matter, Frank?'

He looked around and I said, 'For God's sakes, what's wrong? You look like there's a ghost behind you or something.'

He said, 'You remember that accident with that truck?'

I said, 'How can I forget that? So what's that got to do with you?'

He said, 'I was a truck maintenance man.'

I said, 'Yeah, so what?'

He said, 'I heard somebody said that those brakes failed on that truck. That was one of my trucks.'

Now [I realized that] this fella carries this guilt. All those years he thought that that truck flipped over because it was his fault. He carried that guilt all those years.

He said, 'I overheard somebody saying it was on one of Frank's trucks that the brakes failed.'

I said, 'Frank, those brakes didn't fail on that truck. The fella just stalled the engine. There was nothing wrong with the brakes on that truck. He rolled it into the bank and the truck flipped over. The brakes did not fail.'

Well, he took a hold of me, and he hugged me and he hugged me, and he started to cry.

I said, 'For God's sakes, Frank, all those years you were holding it.'

He said, 'It just about killed me to think that it was my fault.'

I said, 'But it wasn't your fault, Frank. Those brakes did not fail.'

'Boy', he said, 'you don't know how glad I am that I came to this reunion to find out. I'd have taken that to the grave with me!' That's another side story, about Frank.

'So Many Stories'

I'm active in the Marine Corps League. I've been involved in that for many years, was commandant over a number of years back. I'm serving as a chaplain now; whenever one of our members passes, we have a little ceremony for them. There aren't too many of us left; I'm the oldest one of the detachment. We are active in this respect, [but] we don't have anybody to work with anymore; there's only four or five of us that attend our meetings. I think we had three Vietnam veteran Marines. Tragically, two of them committed suicide.

I don't know if I mentioned before, I'm a musician. So I'm involved musically too; I had a band for over 50 years. Some of these people are musicians too, some of the wives, these widows, are playing and singing like I am. I could go on and on; I've got more stories than you can shake a stick at. Some of the fellas are completely blank. There's so many stories that I get goosebumps just thinking about all the things that happened, and [the fact] that I can still remember them. In my own mind, I wonder sometimes at the fact that I can remember all the things that happened.

[I have learned a lot about what we were really doing since those days]. I don't think I'll be any kind of a strategist or whatever, but from my experience being in the campaigns, and then doing a lot of the reading, and most of all, watching The History Channel, I can [better understand] what we were doing there, and it's crazy [to think about it].

My wife said to me, 'Why do you watch?'

I said, 'There are so many things that happened that we were completely unaware of. There are so many things [to tie together], if you only just stop and think about [them].'

I was in the Pacific for twenty-nine months, from Guadalcanal, Bougainville, Guam, and Iwo Jima. At my age, I still haven't gotten to the point where I can get my mind to [understand] that it really happened, that I was [part of it all], that I was able to survive all those campaigns and not [really] get a scratch.

James A. Smith, Jr. passed away on April 8, 2015, having just celebrated his 94th birthday.

CHAPTER ELEVEN

The BAR Man

A lifelong resident of western New York, educator and author John Kolecki was a Marine Corps BAR man who was wounded twice during the Battle of Iwo Jima. He was awarded the Purple Heart and Bronze Star for his actions.

"We had to look for a cover, and I spotted sort of a made-up Japanese foxhole with some rocks arranged. I didn't want to jump in because sometimes these places were booby-trapped, you know, but I had to take a chance, so I jumped in there and to the side of me, as I jumped in, there was a dead Japanese soldier. Apparently, somebody shot him right through the head. Now, there was enough room for me to kind of crawl up to him, which I dared to do, because I had no choice, and he had a little picture of a girl that he had placed among the rocks; it must have been the wife or the sweetheart of this dead Japanese soldier. And so, I had a dead companion for the night with a picture of his girlfriend or wife, I don't know. I spent the night with a dead Japanese soldier. Yeah, that was something sad."

He gave this interview in 2006 when he was 85 years old.

John H. Kolecki

I was born in North Tonawanda, New York, on August 14, 1920. I was a graduate of North Tonawanda High School and I was in my junior year at Canisius College when I volunteered to join the Marine Corps.

[When Pearl Harbor happened], I believe I was at my girlfriend's home. It was a Sunday afternoon; either I was there for brunch or lunch, I'm not sure. Oh, I was very much surprised. I didn't think that anything like that could happen in our times. Although, I was intrigued with the negotiations going on in Washington because, at that time, there were two Japanese ministers that went to Washington to negotiate some kind of an agreement dealing with lifting the embargo on scrap iron and on oil. And somehow that the Japanese economy was very adversely affected by our [punitive economic] actions in the Far East.

Soon, I was jealous of all the other guys that were going into the service, and I was still a student, and I was left alone. And that kind of put me in some bad straits. I didn't feel good. So, there was a speaker that arrived at Canisius College and there was some assembly, and I was impressed with the Marine Corps speaker, so I decided to join the Marine Corps. I believe it was in 1942 but I wasn't called to active duty until about maybe four or five months later.

'I Had A Premonition'

I went to San Diego for my boot camp. It was rather strenuous, but I didn't mind the rigorous demands that were imposed on me. Actually, the first two weeks were the hardest. Then the third, fourth, fifth week, we spent three weeks on the firing range where the pressure was somewhat off the recruits. The totality of basic training was seven weeks. We had a choice of whichever services we want to go, either into artillery or infantry, whatever. And I joined the paratroops, I wanted to go to the paratroop school. [See], I was a pilot; I actually had a private's license. I could have joined the Air Force, but for some reason I had a premonition that I would die in an airplane, but I wouldn't die on the battlefield. So, I abandoned my hopes of being a pilot to become a paratrooper, and I joined the paratroops at Camp Gillespie in California. And strange thing happened that in the course of my training, the paratroop program was abandoned. So, consequently, here I was ready to get my wings, so to speak, and the program was canceled, [along with] the 4th Paratroop Battalion, which I was in; the 4th Paratroop Battalion was [to be formed as] the nucleus of the 5th Marine Corps Division.

I never got to [make a jump]; I got as far as folding the parachute. I did a lot of running, believe me. The calisthenics and the exercises and the running that we had to do were quite extensive, quite demanding. But I accepted the challenge, then the paratroops school was disbanded. I went to Camp Pendleton where they were forming the 5th Marine Corps Division.

From there, we went to Hawaii, the main island, and there was Camp Tarawa where we did extensive training. Even at one time, we had maneuvers under round fire, real fire. And from Camp Tarawa, we then went aboard ship and took us just over a month before we hit Iwo Jima. We stopped at several places. We stopped at Kwajalein, Saipan, and Tinian. And then finally, we assaulted the island.

'You Won't Have a Scar'

We were in the first wave at Iwo Jima. And I remembered just before I hit the beach, somebody offered me a chewing gum, of all things. Why not? I took the chewing gum and we landed on shore, and I hopped over the side. I was a BAR man, by the way, Browning Automatic Rifle. I hit the beach and was running very hard. It was sort of an ash, deep black and gray sand; [getting] traction was very difficult. I made it up to a slope and I placed my BAR and I hurried to my friend, Pak. 'Pak, bring me the ammo.' Just as I turned, Pak gave me the ammo; a bullet grazed my eye and the top of my nose. Had I been looking forward, I probably would have lost both of my eyes and the bridge of my nose. Fortunately, I turned to my right [just at that instant], and that kind of saved my life.

But a stupid thing happened. A corpsman immediately gave me a shot of morphine and bandaged both eyes so that I couldn't see. Somehow, I crawled into a deep shell hole, you could even put a little cottage in there. It must have been from a 16-inch naval gun, I assume. After a while, I said, 'I got to take a look and see what's going on.' I was feeling some slight pain because the morphine immediately took action. I lifted my right eye and I looked at the crest of the shell hole and there's a huge floating Japanese mine there! How did it get there? I don't know.

I tried to crawl out of the shell hole, but I couldn't. So, some other Marine came by, saw me, they start yelling, 'You get out of here before that thing explodes!' And he gave me a hand. He took his sling off his rifle and handed it to me [to grab onto]; he got me out and then I was escorted to the beach, and I ended up on the hospital ship.

I was on the hospital ship about a week or more. Well, being aboard ship, they treated my eye and nose with some kind of compresses, so I questioned the nurse.

'Why don't you apply sulfur powder?' That's what we were using at that time on any wound. Sulfur powder was the thing.

She says, 'No, we have to put these on,' like Vaseline compresses. She says, 'We want the wound to heal from the inside out. This way, you won't have a scar.'

So, I went along with it, 'Okay.' Well, about the third or fourth day, I was ambulatory aboard ship. In fact, the chaplain came to me and says, 'John, I see you walking around. Would you serve as an honor guard? We're going to have a burial at sea.'

I said, 'Of course, Father. Sure.'

So, this was a very sad situation. Here they put this dead Marine into a plastic bag with some weights, which I assume were at the feet, and they headed out with him on something like a stretcher. They put the colors, the flag over the corpse. The taps were played. And then the chaplain read a verse from the Bible he said, and then, gingerly, we kind of lowered the stretcher. The deceased was dumped into the blue Pacific. It was very sad. The whole thing was over in about five, eight minutes. And I sometimes think about being the honor guard at that very, very sad funeral. When I go to funerals today, it's a half-day event. Flowers and the coffin, and all that lamenting and services of some sort, and here was a boy that died, and the parents didn't even know what it was all about, what happened. Yeah, very sad.

Well, anyway, to make a long story a little longer, I bumped into a friend of mine from my platoon aboard ship. Tucker was his name, and he told me he got wounded through the calf of his leg. He showed me his beautiful wound. So, we had lunch together. We conversed about things going on, and then about the sixth or seventh day, the announcer came out and said, 'Now here this. Here this. Any Marine desiring to return to shore with the doctor's permission may do so.' So, he looked at me and I looked at him and we were briefed that the whole operation would be over in seven days, and there might be three additional days mopping up the fanatics.

I said, 'Okay, you want to go, Tucker?'

'All right, let's go.'

So, he went to the doctor. The doctor gave us the okay. We went back ashore. And I had the hardest time finding my outfit, but I finally did. An artillery observer told us, 'The 27th Regiment and Company B is in this direction.' We finally got there.

'The Horrors of War'

As I was trying to get in touch with my platoon, I really saw behind the lines the horrors of the war, of the combat. That's where I saw many of our GIs being stacked like logs, under a lean-to before they were buried. There were all kinds of dead Japanese soldiers in trenches where they committed hara-kiri; their modus of operation was that they would take a grenade, put it under their chin, pull the pin, and blow their heads off. I saw many dead Japanese defenders with their arms blown off and their heads blown off or they would take a rifle and take their sandal, whatever—they mostly seemed to be wearing sandals—and they would put the toe into the trigger mechanism. Put the rifle under the chin and blow their heads off, rather than surrendering, which would be, well, most humiliating and dishonorable. And there were scores of these dead Japanese defenders, and I understand that only about four hundred surrendered after the battle out of 22,000 defending Japanese soldiers. The rest were killed, and they were buried in mass graves anywhere. Yeah, very sad.

'A Dead Companion for the Night'

I had an operatic experience, too, [on Iwo Jima]. Night was closing in, and we were moving up on the front lines and somehow the Japanese spotted us and started peppering us with mortar shells. So, naturally, we had to look for a cover, and I spotted sort of a made-up Japanese foxhole with some rocks arranged. I didn't want to jump in because sometimes these places were booby-trapped, you know, but I had to take a chance, so I jumped in there and to the side of me, as I jumped in, there was a dead Japanese soldier. He was clean-shaven. He had a clean uniform. He just had a trickle of blood on the side of his head. Apparently, somebody shot him right through the head. Now, there was enough room for me to kind of crawl up to him, which I dared to do, because I had no choice, and he had a little picture of a girl that he had placed among the rocks; it must have been the wife or the sweetheart of this dead Japanese soldier. And so, I had a dead companion for the night with a picture of his girlfriend or wife, I don't know. I spent the night with a dead Japanese soldier. I was kind of safe, and I felt safe, too. Yeah, that was something sad.

We had replacements that sometimes lasted a day or two. In my platoon, five lieutenants were either shot or wounded. Lieutenant Stan Holtz, who was our original platoon leader, had been killed on D-Day. I became a squad leader; the corporal of our squad became the platoon leader. So, the replacements that followed, they lasted a day or two, and it seemed that they were primary targets of Japanese snipers. Some of these platoon leaders, I never got acquainted with them, I don't even remember their names.

The Japanese were very crafty soldiers. Their camouflage was something unique, something they could be proud of, really. To spot a live Japanese soldier was not easy because they were camou-flaged and they had all kinds of foxholes, caves that they jumped out, fired a few rounds, and they would hide. I liked the BAR very much but, you know, in combat, I don't think I fired more than five rounds. The only Jap that I saw, Japanese soldier, I saw him in a trench, and I saw his helmet and he threw a grenade at me. And it wasn't a shrapnel grenade, it was a concussion grenade, and it bounced around, it exploded, but nothing happened. I tried to shoot at him, but he was so fast. I fired after he had gone already.

The Explosion in the Cave

Now, there was an incident towards the end before I got wounded the second time. Our platoons surrounded a cave, and a Japanese officer came out with the white truce flag, and he starts mumbling something, and eventually, we caught on, he wanted a translator. So, some half an hour or something later, an American translator started to communicate with this Japanese officer. And what we were told was that there were sixteen men in this cave, and they're going to come to a decision what they're going to do. So, this Japanese officer says, 'I'll be back at eleven o'clock in the evening, and we'll see whether we're going to surrender or not.' Well, there was a bushido code that every Japanese soldier's supposed to tell American soldiers before he dies.

So, we figured, 'Well, maybe they'll surrender. Maybe they won't. Maybe they'll come out and make a banzai charge against us rather than surrendering.' Because they were fanatical fighters. The Japanese did not honor themselves in surrendering to the Americans. Well, anyway. So, I was stationed above the cave and the rest of the platoon were outside the immediate area of the cave because if they come out and banzai charge, we got to have room to fire and that's so we don't fire at each other; that could be done very easily. Well, eleven o'clock came and nothing happened. And we began to whisper, 'What are they going to do?'

So, we sit tight. It must be about maybe after 11:00 and there was a volcanic explosion. I guess what they did was they stalled for time to get any kind of explosives together, figuring they're going to commit hara-kiri and they'll take us along with them.

It was a humongous explosion, really; the mouth of the cave was like a huge shotgun, the blast came out with dust and fire. I just curled up and nothing happened to me, but there were some guys who just were so shell-shocked they could not speak, the ones that were close to the mouth of the cave. I remember this Olmsted; he was a corporal. The guys had to carry him [*shakes arms vigorously*], his nerves were gone—I could see a person suffering from shell-shock. The blast was so terrific, so frightening that you think you're going to die, or you might even feel that you are dead. I've seen it with my own eyes.

Another night, there was a case where some Japanese soldiers were left behind our lines. And then, in the middle of the night, might have been one or two o'clock in the morning, one tried to run back to his line. I didn't even fire because I didn't see him. Of course, when he ran from behind our lines, hoping to reach his lines, he took a chance because they would sporadically shoot these flares, parachute flares. I didn't see him, but the Marine next to me, he says, 'I got a shot at him.' And the next morning, he said, 'They got this fella who tried to run for it.' The strange part was, we had a dog on the front line, and the dog never sniffed him out. He some-how got through but never made it back to his lines.

Friendly Fire

I had some very unusual experiences under friendly fire. We made several assaults on the ridges, and before we made an assault, they would soften up the ground with mortar shells or artillery. [The second time that I was wounded], I happened to be in a fox-hole, and one of the shells, I think, landed too close. I was curled up, and the shrapnel hit me above the wrist and in my leg, my thigh. Another time we moved up on the ridge, and someone goofed back at the lines, and they thought we were Japanese, and we got peppered with American artillery and that was horrendous, it was un-believable what artillery could do.

After the dust cleared, it was unbelievable. The havoc that that artillery barrage can create. We lost seven men; we lost our executive officer. It was a very, very unfortunate, sad situation that our boys opened up on us. It was some kind of a snafu, but it didn't last long. It probably lasted a minute, but when you're under fire like that, you think it will never let up. It was a terrible experience. After the barrage lifted, and the assault was made, I got up and the corpsman just escorted me back behind the lines and, fortunately, he waved down a jeep and he took me to the field hospital. And at the field hospital, the doctor looked me over, put me aboard the plane, and I ended up in the Guam hospital. And I was there for a week, and later, I was flown to Hawaii, Honolulu. I stayed there and about four days afterwards, I rejoined my unit on the main island at Camp Tarawa.

'Drowning in His Own Blood'

I was wounded twice, so I was entitled to a furlough, so I went home for ten days, and then came back [to Camp Pendleton], and they didn't know what to do with me because I had been recommended for officer's training and the war was coming to a close. So, they put me in charge of a recreational hall, ping pong and pool table, at Camp Pendleton. So, I was on duty eight hours and two days off. I didn't have enough money to enjoy the weekends off, so I would go to LA. There was a Catholic Church, cost me a dime or twenty-five cents, I don't recall, for a bed, a towel, and clean sheets to spend the night. So, naturally, I went to LA as often as I could, and the way I got there was mostly hitchhiking. Sometimes I took the train, but the train was packed, standing room only, unbelievable how congested public transportation was from Pendleton to LA. So, I preferred hitchhiking. At least I had a little elbow room, you know. And usually, the truckers were pretty good, and even civilians sometimes picked up Marines and took them to LA.

I might have been at the recreation room [when I heard about the death of President Roosevelt]. I thought more about the guys, [frankly], the friends that I lost in combat than I did about the president [when he died], really. I had some very close personal friends and I saw one of them get shot in the neck and I saw him die. I couldn't do anything about it. The corpsman came, started applying a bandage to prevent the bleeding. He tore it off. He's shaking. I think he actually died probably drowning in his own blood. He died a terrible death. So, my thoughts were more on what happened at the battle. Of course, I knew the president died; the word was out already. The war's practically over. The Germans and Italians were surrendering. I was thinking more of going home than anything else.

I do remember I had a reaction [to the dropping of the atomic bombs]. Now, I recalled my high school chemistry teacher. We discussed atomic energy, and he gave us a very cursory explanation of the atomic bomb.

He says, 'Once they perfect this separating the atom, only an ounce could blow up a city block.' And there was quite a discussion. And so I associated that lecture, that one ounce of split atoms blowing up a city block, with that bomb, blowing up a city. I had a very vague idea what the atomic bomb was, and I tried to imagine what the city would look like after the atomic bomb.

Going Home

At the time the war ended, I was already on my way hitchhiking to Pendleton, back to camp, when the announcement came. Oh, that was a good time. Great celebrations, yeah. It was a great relief. And I had enough points, you know. They had a point system and I think I was six points shy of being discharged from the service. So, something happened that later, they even lowered the points, and I was discharged in November of 1945; I came home a little after Thanksgiving. And so, when that happened, I went on a visit to Canisius where I was matriculating just before I went in the service and the dean spotted me. I remember Father Sullivan said, 'Oh, John. Good to see you.' I never knew he knew my name.

'I see you're back in school.'

I said, 'No, I just came in to see if I could bump into some of my old cronies.'

'You mean, you haven't registered?'

'No, I was late two weeks.'

'You come in Monday. You're registered.'

I said, 'Well, there are some courses that I need to take that are not available.'

'Don't worry about it. You just come on Monday. You're registered. You're starting school on Monday!'

So, I'm back. The following year, in March, I got my sheepskin. Because I was twice wounded, I was [covered] under Public Law 16, entitled to forty-eight actual months of education. Canisius is only eight or nine months a year. So, I had all those forty-eight months to chew up. So, I went back to Canisius, got my B.S. Then I went to Niagara, got my master's degree and Master of Arts.

Then I got a grant to study. You know, when they launched the Sputnik, there was a cry for more Russian language, so I went to an adult education course also and I took Russian. I had a little bit of Russian, so I applied for this federal grant, and they accepted me. The federal government sent me to Northwestern University for the summer. And then the following year, the second part of the program, they sent me to Indiana University to study Russian language and culture, and the second part of the Indiana program was five weeks in the Soviet Union. So, I was an exchange student in the Soviet Union in 1963. That's when that Vietnam War really got [underway].

Well, anyway, I spent five weeks in the Soviet Union and the program entailed visiting several universities, museums, art galleries, conversing with Russian students. The Russian students wanted to speak English and we wanted to speak Russian, because they wanted to sharpen their English, and we wanted to sharpen our Russian. I was fortunate to be one of the sixty-four students that were chosen under this program to go to the Soviet Union. I came back. Now there was a New York State grant to study Russian. So I applied, and I got that state grant, and it was offered at Canisius College. So I went there, continued with my Russian language. And it was in the summer of '66, I was an exchange student for the second time to the Soviet Union.

I spent the entire summer. It was sixty-some days. I had a good time, but some of the students had a hard time acclimating themselves, and [for them], some of the food that was served was not palatable. I'm of Slavic descent, so I'm used to sour cream, and I'm used to buttermilk and sauerkraut, pig's feet, and all of that. You know, for breakfast, they would serve, not orange juice, they would serve kefir, which is like sour milk, as a breakfast drink. For me, I drank sour milk, buttermilk, and it didn't bother me. Some of the students complained about the food, but we were treated very, very well by the Communist hosts. And we went to various art galleries, and we visited several cities. We didn't stay long. We spent some time in Kyiv, in Leningrad, in Sochi.

We went as far east as Baku on the Caspian Sea. I still recall we were going by bus, and we were outside the city limits, and you could smell naphtha. You could smell the oil. And when we got closer to the city, there was a forest of oil derricks, all wooden ones; they were not steel. Wooden derricks. You know, they need it to pump the oil from the ground. Yeah. And the architecture was sort of a mixture of European and Asiatic; you could tell by even the fences that they had. They were unusual and the buildings were different. It was a very enlightening experience for me under these programs that I participated in.

I went back to school to Niagara. Got my M.A., and then I still had so many months left. So I went back to Canisius, got another master's degree in education. I ended up being a schoolteacher at the North Tonawanda and in the Sweet Home school systems, and I also taught in the evening division at the Niagara County Community College, Russian language, Western Civ 101. I didn't know too much about western civilization or whatever, but I knew enough for me to get by.

'People Who Detest War'

I'm a life member of the American Legion, and I'm a life member of the Disabled Veterans. Sometimes Hollywood portrays an unfair picture of what battle is like, with the exception of the truest image of combat, I think, which was the movie called *Saving Private Ryan*. To me, it was pretty close, very close, true to life in combat, yeah. For example, in our company there were three platoons, one hundred forty-four Marines. When I returned to Camp Tarawa after I was wounded, the second time, just nineteen of us made roll call out of the original one hundred forty-four, [so] I can empathize with [the conscientious objector]. I can empathize with people who detest war, because I wouldn't want my son to go through the same thing that I went through.

John H. Kolecki passed away on December 31, 2008, at the age of 88.

CHAPTER TWELVE

The Marine Gunner II

Albert J. Harris

Iwo Jima

We left for Iwo Jima probably about November. The convoy took quite a while forming. Once we were aboard ship, we knew where we were going. By that time, we had a pretty good guess anyway because they had been bombing Iwo for about two months. A lot of talk was that we were going to Truk, if you've heard that name, but that was a big base that we eventually bypassed.

It took a long while to get up there. [In my first sighting, it] was pretty awesomely bad! It wasn't very picturesque. We landed again as a reserve regiment. We came in, again, about six o'clock at night; we were sort of hanging around all day waiting to get on boats—the landing boats.

When we went in, the Japanese commander had built such an intelligent defense. The upper part of the island was honeycombed with caves—completely a network of unbelievable caves. The lower part, the lower one-third was the landing area, and Mt. Suribachi was at the end. He let almost two divisions of Marines get on the island with only a modest amount of resistance. Then he just massacred the guys on the beach for four days; he stopped the front lines from going any further through his line-of-caves network. For four days, people were on the beach. The beach was only about the size of one hole on a golf course! You had all these bodies and anything you threw there is going to hit something. [*Pauses*]

Oh yeah, Iwo. I never saw a tree on Iwo. The part where all the caves were looked like a massive rock pit that had been hit by an atom bomb. No organization to it. Bodies. Small boulders. Big boulders. Cliffs.

The beach was like, on both sides there, black sand, sort of [more] like—I don't know if you could call it sand, it was more of a black gravel. When you stepped in it, it made a very big [footprint] like an elephant.

'Somebody Made A Big Mistake'

I came ashore at the time I had been transferred to the battalion intelligence section. I was what they called the 'intelligence scout.' Theoretically, I was supposed to find material of intelligence value. It didn't work out. I ended up being a 'gofer' for the colonel in charge of the battalion whose name was Vandergrift. He was the son of the Commandant of the Marine Corps. He was a wild man. I think he was trying to live up to the name. He was a lieutenant colonel. Anyway, I had two guys in my little group when I came ashore. The shore, you couldn't believe it because they had hit a lot of boats coming in, so the shore was just amazingly [crowded] with every sort of debris, and junk, and bodies, and everything.

I came ashore about when it was just getting dark again. I fell on the ground just as soon as I got out of the water, orientating myself; there was a guy lying there right next to me, with his rifle out and everything—I looked at him and he had been shot at some point during the day, right through the helmet [*points to his forehead*]—he was looking perfectly normal, no blood. I didn't see anything [to indicate he had been killed], but he was dead.

Now, we didn't see any of our guys that were supposed to be with us, or any in our company. So, we ran ashore about two hundred feet or so, three hundred. I told the guys, dig in a little spot. I dug a hole next to [the dead guy]. Other people start to dig in all around us, [and soon], the whole place was full of guys digging in. That's where we were for three days because the front-line troops had been held up on the other side of the airport. Somebody made a big mistake by putting that many people on shore. But the Japanese who were firing from the upper artillery and mortars, they couldn't miss. Any time they fired a mortar, it could hit some of us.

I remember once during the night—this was in the midst of a barrage—his thing came flying in on me, I felt it and I felt a face. I thought, oh my God, if this is the face, I've had it, but it was part of a gas mask that resembled a face. That's what I felt.

'That Was My Last Visit to A Cave'

After three days, I didn't know where the company was; I wasn't going to walk round looking for them. They weren't looking for me, that's for sure. I finally did locate them, where I was supposed to be. Then I went a number of times up to the lines with the colonel and the other times I went with my group just trying to find things that were of intelligence value, but actually it turned out we were just souvenir hunting, [really]. We went down a number of caves, foolishly. One time, we went down, just the three of us in this cave, it was covered with branches and everything, so it was camouflaged, but it had steps down into it, carved out of the stone. Stone wasn't easy to carve. So, I went down maybe ten steps, and there was a dead Japanese in the middle of the steps, so I walked over him. I have a flashlight and I have a .45 that I borrowed. I went down the cave, then right ahead of me it went about thirty feet and then curved. It was full of boxes and stuff. Then off to the right and left there were other caves. So, I am looking at all the caves and everything, I raise the flashlight and I am sure that I saw a face looking around the corner at me. So, I shot at it and the whole [place] lit up! I started backing up out of the cave, like a western, up backwards all the way, up past the dead body. That was my last visit in a cave. Holy Jesus! Then I heard later on that people got in real trouble in these caves, just foolishness.

'I Hope It's Our Guys!'

I could see that flag raising, but it really didn't make much of a difference to us at the time. It wasn't any strategic value; I think now when I heard more about the flag raising and read about it, I think I must have seen the original where they just put up a flag and the boats made all the noise. We didn't know what was going on. Suddenly, we looked back; it was about a mile back from the front line. We looked back and saw the people on top of Suribachi. I thought, 'I hope it's our guys!' That's all I thought about, and apparently a couple hours later, they did the famous Rosenthal shot. It was symbolic.

I didn't know that was a famous photograph until months later. I think I was two to three years back home before I realized what an impact the thing really had. It was a sensation. It was a perfect thing. People considered that the end of the battle and everything, but it wasn't the end of the battle. It had nothing to do with the end of the battle, but it was symbolism that counted.

'You Didn't Get a Cake'

I was on Iwo about a month. I celebrated my 21st birthday on Iwo—a very mild celebration. You didn't get a cake. [*Laughs*] No, no. They kept me alive. It was funny. The way it turned out, I think this is true for a lot of people there, I could have gone ashore on Iwo or any of the others carrying a six pack of beer and a ukulele and it would have done just as good. I spent the war being a 'shootee,' not a 'shooter.' [Unlike] in the war movies, there were no firefights going on where you're shooting [after aiming]; I never saw anybody aim. You just had to aim at caves, or you had to send the flamethrowers in. You had to protect the flamethrowers while they went in; you didn't see the [enemy on Iwo].

Then they took us back and the same routine again back to Maui, and I know we were supposed to go into the invasion of Japan, probably early the next year. I got a little break; they sent two people who had been in the division awhile over to temporary duty working in Pearl Harbor. I worked there for a couple of months and that's where I was when the war actually ended.

I was on guard duty in this prisoner of war camp in Pearl Harbor on Ford Island [when the war ended]. Not much reaction. We were no place that anybody celebrated. The people who were celebrating that you see in a newsreel were people that had never been any place; they wouldn't be sitting around in Times Square if they had been in a war.

[Now], at the time, I was very happy that [the bomb] had happened, because I could just visualize what an invasion of Japan would be, and comparing it [to my experience], they would have fought for every little village on the whole [Japanese] islands. I have had a lot of thoughts on it later; I realize it was a decision and you can't quarrel with [it, but] I sort of wondered why they ever dropped the second—the Nagasaki one. That never made any sense to me at all.

After about a couple of weeks, they brought us back to the camp again with the regular unit. They brought us back on an escort carrier to San Diego. We were then brought back up to Camp Pendleton. We were there a few days, and then broke up. So, when we broke up after all this time together, there was nothing. Nobody said 'goodbye'; I never said goodbye to any of the people I was with. I was by myself. I didn't know anybody when I was going through the discharge.

After three days, I caught a train up to New York; the only one meeting me at Penn Station was some bum. I got the early train, and that was it. That was the end of my war. Two months [later], I went to work for the New York Telephone Company. I was with them for twenty-five years, then I went to AT&T and retired from AT&T.

'I Never Saw a Hero'

The war years, they shaped my whole life. I think I was able to accept things better, I could put things and people in perspective much better. Items that might upset other people, I could roll with them, for better or for worse. I didn't have the drive maybe of a lot of other people. Whatever my life became, it was shaped by those years completely. It's a satisfaction, I guess, knowing that you can put up with things and were able to accept it and you didn't do anything to be ashamed of.

In my experience, here I was in four battles, some of the most vicious of the whole war, and I never saw a hero. I never saw one hero! I saw people trying to stay alive, doing their job, doing what they were told. I never saw anybody above and beyond the line of duty. I read about all of these wonderful things everybody was doing and thought, 'What's happening to me?' [*Laughs*] I mean, even the Persian Gulf, which lasted two days, and maybe a hundred battle casualties, yet they came up with all these medals. Even the Oklahoma City bomber got a medal—Bronze Star. It must have been a different caliber of people, or they are a lot more talented [in] writing up their citations. But that's beside the point.

'My Ten Minutes of Fame'

I never really talked too much about it. I didn't have a very active social life before, and I didn't really have a lot of friends. Most of my friends were also in the service in other services. [Those guys] shared a lot of that type of thing.

Back in 1950, I went [to a reunion] in New York. I haven't been to any of the others. It would still help to go, but I don't travel much and it's fewer people that I would know. Of course, they're dropping off, but it was an experience. I don't like to be an old soldier. I don't think I ever had any psychiatric-type problems associated with being in a war; I like to talk about it when somebody wants to hear it.

I really didn't develop many profound thoughts when I was in there. It was just life; it was the way the ball had bounced in my life. For the first time, I was with more people; I came from a small town and I never had a lot of people to associate with, and suddenly I am living with these people for long periods of time, and I've got to say it was kind of enjoyable.

I saw things that are history now. On that little, teeny island, I had my ten minutes of fame, with no fame. [*Laughs*]

Albert Harris passed at the age of 89 on October 4, 2013.

B-29 Superfortress bombers near Mount Fuji, Japan, 25 July 1945.
National Archives. Public domain.

CHAPTER THIRTEEN

The B-29 Radioman

Strategic bombing raids to Japan began in earnest from the newly liberated Mariana Islands as the fighting ended in the early summer of 1944. By summer 1945, wave after wave of the sleek new B-29 Superfortresses began to arrive in the skies over Japan. A quantum leap in aviation technology, the B-29 was much longer, wider, and faster than previous heavy bombers, and capable of carrying a much larger bomb load over vast expanses of ocean.

The coupling of the B-29 with the development and deployment of incendiary 'firesticks,' six-pound cylinders filled with napalm, or gelatinized gasoline, was a very serious development that brought death and destruction on a scale never before seen in warfare. Veteran Sam Kamerman described his impressions as a young man on this new, top-secret weapon of destruction, giving insights into some of the earliest fire-bombing missions over Japan.

"About a hundred and fifty miles from Kobe—anywhere between a hundred and fifty, two hundred miles—one of the crewmen in the nose over the intercom says, 'What's that spot out there?'

I had to manipulate around to get up front, but I got up front, and at approximately twelve-thirty, one o'clock there is this little orange dot. You can't tell distance at night, but there's this little orange dot. Nobody knew.

I said, 'What the heck is that?' It's all black, then there's this little orange dot. It could be a plane, it could be a light, it could be anything. As we keep going to the target, this little orange dot starts getting larger. I'm back in my seat and somebody hollers out, 'Kobe is burning!' Approximately a hundred and fifty miles away you can see a fire; you can't believe it...

When we get to the target, the bomb bay doors open; everything's burning. We're over the target. At this point, there comes up a smell that was awful. It was [burning] debris, and also bodies."

This interview took place in 2005, sixty years after the missions, when he was approaching 82 years of age.

Sam L. Kamerman

I was born on March 16, 1923, in the Lower East Side, New York City. I had two years of high school. That was it.

[I heard about Pearl Harbor when] I was in the park playing basketball with a bunch of fellas. I was eighteen years old, I guess. This is a Sunday, around one o'clock or so. In comes Harry, into the park. All of these young kids are playing basketball. He hollers, 'The Japanese just bombed Pearl Harbor!' You know what all of us did? We all asked each other, 'Where is Pearl Harbor?'

I enlisted because all the fellas around me, my age, were being drafted. I didn't want to go into the Army or be in the dirt kind of thing, so I enlisted into the Army Air Corps, in New York City. I went to Miami Beach for basic training. Two things I remember, I got KP twice down there and I did pots and pans. These pots were like three feet high; for seventeen hours I'm digging into the pots.

Somebody didn't like me. I caught this twice in the month's time that I was there.

Flight Training

From there, I went to Madison, Wisconsin, Truax Field, radio school for a couple of months, and then I went to the Sioux Falls, South Dakota, radio school for about five months. Upon graduation, an officer came into the classes.

He said, 'We need flying operators.'

I was not interested.

He said, 'You get an extra stripe.'

I still was not interested.

He said, 'Well, you get fifty percent [more] flying pay.'

I still wasn't interested.

He said, 'Well, there's no KP,' and that did it. [*Raises hand*] Don't laugh. This is the truth. KP, I got out of it; that was it.

I went down to Philadelphia, a special school, radio school. Learn a little of EIR, voltage and capacitance, resistance, that kind of stuff. We also learned Morse code. Being a flying radio operator, you had to know your Morse code. From there I went back to Madison, Wisconsin. From there, I was sent to Salina, Kansas. This was the 20th Air Force, the 58th Bomb Wing. When I got there, I went on one or two practice flights in a B-17. The first time I was uncomfortable, because I was looking out the window all the time and just enjoying the sights.

I got my flight gear. The flight gear was very, very impressive stuff. You get a summer flying suit. You get a winter flying suit. You get a .45 caliber gun. You get a watch. You get goggles. You get a parachute; it just keeps coming and coming.

So, now I'm part of the 58th Bomb Wing. I'm attached to them. They send me down to Great Bend, Kansas. I'm there for about two months. From there, they send me to a place called Marietta, Georgia. I'm there for like another couple of months, this is all part of the 58th Bomb Wing. From there, I went to Walker Army Air Force Base in Kansas.

After I was there about six, eight weeks, this officer says to me, 'You don't have to volunteer, but we need flying radio operators to go overseas.' At this point, I've been in the service like seventeen months or so, a year and a half.

I said to the officers, 'Let me get a furlough [first] so I can go home. I'll come back.'

He said, 'We can't do that.'

In one of the best moves I ever made, I said no.

'I don't want to go.'

A couple of weeks later, this 58th Bomb Wing—which was the first B-29 outfit, by the way, the very first combat outfit—they went to the China-Burma-India area. They flew out without me.

Two weeks later after they leave, I'm sent to Pratt, Kansas. This is a new bomb wing, the 73rd Bomb Wing, and I am now part of a combat crew. Well, the B-29s at this point, for testing, were very unreliable. Most of our B-17 combat training had to do with B-17s. This is from about April to around August. This is about a five-month thing. I was in with a very nice crew. By the way, in this crew, which is eleven crewmen, we had four New Yorkers in my particular crew.

We flew in all kinds of weather. It was lightning. It was thunder. What are you doing out in this weather? We flew one combat training mission that was approximately seventeen hours in the air. We left Kansas, we flew to the Caribbean, then flew east over Cuba. From there, we flew north over the Atlantic to Massachusetts, then we flew approximately to Michigan, and then back to our base; it was a long, long time. This was one of the few times I flew with an oxygen mask, because the B-29 was the first bomber in World War

II that had a pressurized cabin. It was quite an experience being up at 25,000 feet with the oxygen mask, and tapping away at a speed of like, five, six words per minute. You can't type fast in an airplane, not that I was any good or special at it. You don't recognize the shaking but when you want to do something, [the airplane] lets you know its shaking. I was commended on this particular flight for being in touch with the Army Airways Communication System.

Our commanding general, by the way, was a New Yorker, Rosie O'Donnell, you ever hear of him?[19] He ended up a real big deal. Now, we finished our training and we're all going home on furloughs from Kansas, to New York, for me. A B-17 on a training mission was going from Pratt, Kansas, to Mitchell Field, New York City. We flew into Mitchell Field, it took us about five hours or whatever, instead of the forty-eight hours. Coming back, me being a kid, and knowing I am going overseas, I wanted to stay home a little longer so I took extra time; on the last day, I went back to Mitchell Field hoping to catch some kind of a ride. Sure enough, I got lucky, so as not to be AWOL—there was a B-17 going to Kansas. This plane is dropping me off in Kansas, but not my base. I got up on a highway and thank the Lord, the people there were wonderful. You get out there and they'd pick you right up, 'Where you going, soldier?' I got back to my base about eleven o'clock at night, an hour before I'm AWOL.

Now we're getting ready. We finish our combat training. In the 73rd Bomb Wing, there's the 497th Bomb Group, the 498th, the 499th, and the 500th Bomb Group. There are ten crews in each squadron, three squadrons to a group. We've got one hundred twenty combat crewmen in a big hangar place in Harrington,

---

[19] *Rosie O'Donnell*-General Emmett E. 'Rosie' O'Donnell Jr. [1906-1971] led the first B-29 attack against Tokyo, and served as Commander in Chief, Pacific Air Forces from 1959 to 1963.

Kansas. All these crews are going there to pick up a new B-29 Superfortress.

A Pioneer Crew

For the Pacific, I consider myself [part of] a pioneer crew. It's a [phrase] I made up because we were the first ones. Each crew will eventually get a new B-29 Superfortress. We get ours. We get in. We take off. In about an hour and a half, we blow an engine! I get in contact with the home base. I let them know we are making an emergency landing in a place called Kingman, Arizona. The funny part about this is that, at this time, this plane is top secret! When I went home, I never mentioned that I was flying in a B-29. They didn't know about a B-29 anyway, and I never mentioned that I'm involved with that.

We made the emergency landing in Kingman, Arizona. When we get to the stand where the plane ends up, we have about thirty, forty MPs around the plane. Nobody's allowed to get near the plane, because it's top secret. When I walked down, I felt like I was somebody who came in from outer space. This is the feeling. Of course, they're all looking at us. We had different types of jackets at the time, they made us look pretty exclusive, so [that contributed] to the feeling.

Two days later we have a new engine. We go to California. From California, we go to Hawaii. From Hawaii, we went to a place called Kwajalein, which is a little atoll, all they got is an airfield, anything else you can forget about. From there we went to Saipan, and the beginning of where we are going to be involved, somewhere in late October 1944.

The B-29 was much larger than the B-17. It went further, it flew higher, it flew faster, and in reference to bombs, we had two bomb bays that were tremendous. The B-17 had a small, little bomb bay.

I was the radio operator, but I didn't know too much about what was happening. I had to read up [on it later] to find out. They didn't give me enough medals. [*Laughs*] With all I went through, I said, 'All right, that's their game.'

Let me see, where was I? We got in some training missions. We bombed Truk Island, it was Japanese-held at the time. Now in November, approximately November 23, 24, 1944, we go on the first ground-based bombing mission of Tokyo. Two and a half years before [our mission], Doolittle bombed Japan. Now we are going on the first one [since then]. We didn't do a good job at the beginning, but we let them know they were in a war.

'We Got Clobbered'

We went over, there was flak; there's always flak, and as a rule, there's always fighters. Not only were we the first ones, but our particular group was also A Group; we were like the first ones to go over targets. We got clobbered. We got clobbered.

The next day, the day after this, in this country it was plastered all over the papers. I have it here. [*Pretends to read headline*] 'B-29 Superfortress bombs Tokyo!' This was great for the public, you know. You read this, and you say, hey, we're going after them, that kind of stuff.

We had eleven in our crew, and [almost] all of us were from up north, but the pilot was from North Carolina; I can't think of the name [of the plane] offhand. It never got a splash, like today you'd see these books and they have beautiful [nose art] paintings and all, and loads of different good names.

On January 27, we had another mission. We were the first group, the 497th, to go over. In this mission, we had seventeen planes, and most of our missions at the beginning were to try to knock out the airplane plant in Tokyo. On this particular mission—

and this is the week after Curtis E. LeMay took over our outfit—
You've heard of him, Curtis LeMay?[20] When LeMay came into our
outfit, he made changes. All of us cursed this guy all to hell. We
cursed him all to hell. We were bombing at 25,000 feet; he brought
us down to 16,000. These are daylight raids. Then, he brought us
down in night raids to approximately 6,000 feet. Everybody was
cursing this guy. I even said what's this guy up to, [but] this is the
best thing that ever happened to us. He had the answers for us. He
came up with the incendiary bombing; this was a big thing. We
were one of the small percent. My crew was one of the small per-
centages, approximately ten percent, of the crews that flew on these
five missions, because they were tough missions on the plane, it was
tough for the engines to handle.

---

[20] *Curtis LeMay-* (1906-1990) Andrew Doty, a B-29 tail gunner featured in
Volume I of the series, recalled: '*General Curtis LeMay, head of the 20th Air
Force, concluded that individual B-29s, flying in at 5,000 to 8,000 feet at
night, would be far more accurate than if they bombed from 25,000 to
30,000 feet. They could burn out large areas of the Japanese cities, 'de-
house' the population, and destroy the many cottage industries that supported the war effort.*
*Another major advantage was that the bombers would not have to make the
long, demanding climb to high altitudes that strained the engines and drank
up fuel. Nor would they have to assemble in formation and jockey about on
the way to the target. Consequently, they could carry twice the bomb load.
Engine maintenance would be reduced, which would result in more bombers
over the target.*
*LeMay's decision had dismayed the B-29 crews. The low-level raids obviously
were much closer to ground anti-aircraft and searchlight batteries and left
less room for crewmen to bail out if their plane was shot down. Many B-29s
were seen to catch fire, explode, and plunge to earth. The incendiary raids
against major cities were not welcomed by the airmen.*'

Over The Target

Over the target, the Japanese fighters shot down two planes. [Don't forget, that's] an average of eleven men per plane. A third plane sort of lingered on the side somewhere, we never saw this one again. The fourth plane [lost] ditched a couple hundred miles off Japan. They never saw them again. That was four planes. The fifth plane made an emergency landing on Saipan. The crew was all shot up. So, out of seventeen planes on this mission that my crew was on, we lost like thirty percent. I figured it out—two more missions like that, and we're not around. That's all it took. That was the fear.

The fighter opposition was fierce, we have it in a book. Five hundred and fifty fighter attacks just on our seventeen planes; we got away with that. I didn't know it at the time, but we got away with that.

The Incendiary Blitz

I'm going to jump to March 1945. The middle of March was what they called the incendiary blitz—March 9, 11, 13, 16, 19. We hit Tokyo, Nagoya, Osaka, Kobe, and back to Nagoya. This first one over Tokyo, March 9, is considered one of the most horrific bombing missions of any war. We burnt out like sixteen square miles on that one. Fifteen point eight, sixteen square miles, what's the difference, two-tenths of a square mile? Eighty thousand plus died. A hundred thousand injured. A million homeless. Ridiculous kind of numbers, but this is what actually took place.

I'm the radioman on my ship. We're getting close, about a hundred and fifty miles from Tokyo. At this time, I'm not doing my job properly, because I'm listening to music. Wah-wah, you know that music, I'm the only one listening because I'm the radioman on the radio frequency. I'm listening to it, and all of a sudden it cuts out. I look at my equipment. I try to figure out what happened. There's nothing wrong with my equipment. I figured it out. I got on the intercom and said, 'Radio to crew. Tokyo Radio just went off the air.'

They knew we were coming. We were a plane by itself at this time. They knew it. We're coming over to take photos, that was one of the missions, a photo mission. They just went off the air. There's a procedure. A plane comes close, they go off the air.

As I said, we were an A group. Many times, we were the first, or the early ones, to go over. When you go over Tokyo early, you drop your bombs, your incendiaries, and you leave. You may not even see anything burning, because you're the early one. We did this with Tokyo, Nagoya, and Osaka.

'Kobe is Burning!'

Going to Kobe, we were one of the latter planes. About a hundred and fifty miles from Kobe—anywhere between a hundred and fifty, two hundred miles—one of the crewmen in the nose over the intercom says, 'What's that spot out there?'

I had to manipulate around to get up front, but I got up front, and at approximately twelve-thirty, one o'clock there is this little orange dot. You can't tell distance at night, but there's this little orange dot. Nobody knew.

I said, 'What the heck is that?' It's all black, then there's this little orange dot. It could be a plane, it could be a light, it could be anything. As we keep going to the target, this little orange dot starts getting larger. I'm back in my seat and somebody hollers out, 'Kobe is burning!' This is a hundred and fifty miles out! You can't believe it! Approximately a hundred and fifty miles away you can see a fire; you can't believe it.

Now we are in the latter part of the mission. There's been, I don't know, three hundred planes that dropped their firebombs on this area. When we get to the target, the bomb bay doors open; everything's burning. We're over the target. At this point, there comes up a smell that was awful. It was [burning] debris, and also bodies. We're at six thousand feet approximately; we're very low. Now at this point—and this is all in books, but here I'm not quoting books; this is what happened to me—we get the turbulence from this big fire. It comes up into the plane, and this plane gets shook up. This is a big plane and my top gunner, he hurt his head because it shook so much where he was sitting. When it shook so much, my question was, where did we get hit? We're supposed to get hit because of this [lower-level mission], but we didn't get hit. Turbulence coming up—you've flown, you've heard about turbulence, but you don't know what turbulence is! This thing is out of [control]...

[Now], they give cockamamie stories about one of the planes was turned over [by the turbulence]. I don't believe that. One of the things in reference to telling these stories is there is a tendency to fabricate. I don't fabricate. I know what I've been through—what I saw, I should say.

We were on these missions, one after another. You're not sleeping. They give you a [pill] that you take before you get to the target, Benadrex, I think it was—I remember one time my eyes were like this! [*Chuckles, holds hands apart wide*] Everything looked so beautiful. We're right near the target. And when you come back, they're giving you a shot of whiskey, so you can relax. You've got [it] coming up. You've got [it] coming down. You're not getting the proper sleep, whatever it took. Curtis E. LeMay, who was our boss then, at the end of the five missions, he said, 'My boys are a little tired.' What an understatement. For a young guy, I said, 'Why am I feeling like this? Why am I feeling so lousy?' This kind of thing can take its toll. A round trip [from Saipan to Japan and back] was thirteen hours.

We got flak, we got fighters, it was all there. I can tell you one time, we're over the target, and I hear a 'ping' and my navigator is right pretty close, and I look at him and say, 'What happened?'

You can't talk. The noise is tremendous. You can't communicate. I said, 'What happened?'

He said, 'I don't know.' When we got back to the base I immediately jumped out; there was a nice big hole there right by the bomb bay, very close to us. The holes were there in many planes. The flak was up there. Like they say in the movie, you look out the window and you can walk on the stuff. As long as you can see it, you're all right. It's when you don't see it, it comes up, bam, it could hit you, it could hurt you, but it wasn't like it was in Germany. In Germany, the Eighth Air Force, I'm glad I was never involved with that. They got [plastered].

At the beginning [I wore a flak vest], yes, but it was so cumbersome. The first time or the second time you wear it. You throw it right down there where you're at and leave it there. [You think], all right, if they are going to kill me, let them kill me.

We flew for five months without fighter protection because the fighters couldn't go from Saipan to Japan and back; we had to wait until they captured Iwo Jima. Once they captured Iwo Jima, there were many B-29s that made emergency landings there. The Marines and the Army who sacrificed their lives on Iwo Jima, it was for a good 'B-29 cause.' The B-29 people, it saved a lot of us.

I was on a crew [where actually] very little happened. I didn't even catch a cold. I was sitting at a desk; I could have sat at that desk the whole war with all that going on, and not look out. I remember looking out, one time. Somebody said there's a plane way out there, at two o'clock. I got up into the Plexiglass where the navigator shoots his stars. I looked at about two o'clock and there's this plane just staying ahead of us.

I heard somebody holler, 'He's turning!' That's when I took a look, and there's this plane coming right at us. I'm watching and, again, you don't hear anything. I see on the wings there's this orange stuff coming out; it's a matter of split-seconds. I realized, with this orange stuff, he was shooting at us!

There was another incident that's very hard for somebody to believe. I had to read about the same incident to know [more about it]. It's a nighttime mission, and we're over Japan, and we're heading towards a target at five, six thousand feet. I'm up in this Plexiglass, and I'm looking around—it's all dark out there. But I notice at about ten-thirty, a plane—it had to be fairly close to us and going in the same direction. The first thing you say to yourself, B-29. But I took a better look. This was a two-engine plane.

I said, 'Well, we don't have any. What is this all about?' This plane was staying ahead of us for about five minutes, that I observed. Then I went back to my desk. Then I read about what it was all about, I didn't know at the time. This plane was sending [information] back to the base in Japan about our altitude, our speed, all the information, but I had to read about it. I didn't understand this particular thing [at the time]. Somebody would say, come on, it's your imagination. I know I saw this thing for about five minutes.

We dealt with 'kamikazes,' as they say. The Japanese had a squadron of what they called 'rammers,' who were not [technically] kamikaze people. They came in and tried to hit the tail a certain way to hurt the plane. They, in turn, would parachute out. I read a book on that; this is what they did. They rammed the plane, whereas the kamikaze went in just to blow up.

Now another thing. In April '45, the kamikazes were clobbering the Navy in the area there. They flew out of the southern tip island, the southernmost island of Kyushu. They hurt the Navy a lot at this time, so we went in, we bombed their air bases in Kyushu. Three days later, they'd have the holes filled in. You couldn't do too much about it, but one of the funny stories I tell is that my crew bombed 'USA.' On one of our missions over Kyushu, the name of the [Japanese] air base was 'U-S-A.' We bombed the USA; I consider it amusing. [*Chuckles*]

The number [of missions completed] for our outfit to go home was thirty-five missions. We were one of the small percent that flew only thirty missions. When they told me, 'This is your last mission,' I knew I hadn't flown thirty-five and, as a kid, I'm not opening my mouth. If they're telling me I'm going home, I'm going, I'm not going to question them. [But] after looking at it, we were involved with rough stuff.

I can tell you I met my radar man about ten, fifteen years later. He was at some Army air base. I sit here, he sits there, and we were talking about 'the good old days.' After we finished, I left him, and I said to myself, 'Was he in the same war I was in?' He had a different story altogether; this is what you have to deal with. Maybe you were right, maybe he was right. You know where I learned that? I learned that from somebody who said to me the dog can only see from this angle [*gestures low*] and we see from this angle [*gestures high*]. [It all depends on] where your perspective is. This is what happened.

Saving the Crew

One time—this is like January 3, 1945—my pilot's friend ditched his plane between Iwo Jima and Saipan. He went on a mission, came back, couldn't make it, and into the drink he went. They had an idea, the radioman or whatever, of the [last] position. The next morning, my pilot comes in and he says, 'Sam, get your chute.' 'Get your chute' means you are going on a flight. He says to me, 'Get the chute and get in the plane.' This is a plane where two new engines have just been put in.

There's about six or seven of us in the plane. He needed a plane to try to find his friend, but if the people upstairs knew about it, they'd hang him for it; these things aren't 'dumbo' kind of things.

We got in the plane. I'm always in the front. This particular time—we have a tunnel in a B-29 Superfortress. It's a crawl-through tunnel—when you crawl through, it's just about like this [*motions narrowly with hands*]. You can't see anything on your right. You can't go back. If you have a case of claustrophobia, it'll kill you. I'm halfway through; I'm moving. I'm moving. Very funny. I went through this thing twice. I went to the side gunner's spot, [looking out]. There was another side gunner there, and all the officers were up front.

What was my pilot doing? [It's] hundreds of square miles and he's just circling and circling, doing smaller circles for an hour, hour and a half. I'm in there, I'm looking out; I can only tell you, don't be in a life raft in the middle of the ocean—it's worse than a needle in a haystack, and with an airplane, you're moving quick, two hundred miles an hour. What's below, you just don't see.

Very luckily, somebody said, 'Down below!' From where I was, I looked down, and in a split-second, I saw a life raft. I thought there were six or seven people in it, crewmen. That was it. We circled around; I never saw them again. He called in a destroyer or sub in the area, and because of my pilot, they saved about six or seven crewmen. There's more of a story to it, but they were saved. I was very proud of my pilot.

Close Calls

One mission we went out very close to Japan. We flew about nine hours, and we aborted a mission, which means that we flew and flew and when we got close to the island, we had a malfunction of the engine. If you're having trouble with an engine, you don't want to go over the target in a bombing formation, because when you fall back, they're going at you. You can forget about it. They just look for somebody to have a little problem, then they leave everything else, and they go for this one. So, we aborted. We dropped the bombs in the ocean, and we came back.

Another time, we're coming back from a target. Now, we have some bombs hung up, the bombardier couldn't release them. These are big bomb bays; it's twelve, fifteen feet from the front of the bomb bay to the rear of the bomb bay. These bombs happened to be stuck way in the rear in an awkward spot. Our bombardier comes and opens the bomb bay door. This bomb bay door [gestures with hands] is open, we're flying over the ocean. All you've got down there is water, water, and more water. He's climbing out, and if he slips, he's gone. Any kind of fall, that's the end of him. He's going along the side of the fuselage. There's a little ledge of about nine inches, and he's moving along this little edge. He's moving toward the back of the bomb bay to get to the bombs. It's hard to believe. At this point, my stomach couldn't take it. I had to stop looking. He released the bomb, came back, because if you're going to land, these things are subject to going off. They're still armed and they have to be released. I don't know too much about armament. He did a great thing there.

I was back in the States by the time the atomic bombs were dropped. I finished my last mission the end of May. It was all top secret. They were on Tinian, we were on Saipan. My crew, my outfit, made it easy for these guys, because we took all of the clobbering. I'm not putting them down, but we took all of the clobbering, and they came along. By the time they got there, who's attacking them? They're not being attacked. How far is Tinian from Saipan? There's a little inlet; it's about three to five miles. I saw Tinian when

I went down to the beach to soak on the beach. One time, I looked at Tinian and I see a plane taking off. I'm watching. This is like three miles away. I see another plane taking off and I say, 'Oh, they're going on a mission.' Another plane, and I'm watching for a while. This one plane takes off and instead of going up it goes down, down, down. There's a big splash. I don't hear it. I'm too far away. That's all there is to it. That was all there is to it. When the engines don't give you enough power, you're not going up, so you're going to go down. This is one of the things that happened.

We didn't live in barracks, we lived in Quonset huts on Saipan. In my Quonset hut we lost one crew that went on a mission and never came back. Then we lost a second crew. They come, and they go.

When we finished our combat missions, we were put into tents from our Quonset hut. They're keeping us away from the combat flyers, we've finished our missions. Now at this point I'm figuring we go back in a couple of days. They kept us there for like a month. I myself said I don't understand why they kept us there. We're finished. Put us somewhere where we can start heading back. They didn't do anything about it. Later on, I read a story of a crew that finished just about the same time, or maybe a little ahead of us, they got into a B-29 and were flying back to the States. They flew from Saipan to Kwajalein; from Kwajalein, they were supposed to go to Hawaii. This crew that just finished missions over Tokyo, over Japan, they crashed in the ocean! Now, from this I deduced that the wing doesn't want to lose any more men. So, this is one of the reasons I feel that they kept us there. When they finally make a move, I'm the first one they pick in the crew, and they put me in a B-29 to go back to the States. The officers and all the enlisted men, they all stayed; I don't know how long they stayed. After reading this story, I thought I was a guinea pig. I was the only one.

'I Kissed The Ground'

I hit California the 5th of July, 1945. I got off this plane, and, like they do in the movies, I kissed the ground. After that, I never flew in the service again.

I went to work in November of '45. I didn't use the GI Bill, and let me say to all of you people, use the GI Bill. That's one of my negative moves. When I got out of the service, I did a little night school work.

I would say the whole crew lost contact with each other until they started with the reunions; the first reunion that I went to was like ten years ago. Our bombardier was there, one of the gunners, my radar man, and myself. We were the only ones at that time. Since then, our radar man passed away. Our bombardier became a lieutenant colonel, eventually. When he goes out of the house, he gets in the car, he doesn't walk much. The other one seems to be in a senior type of home, something like that. He says he's happy there. I spoke to both of them around the holiday time. I move around but not easy. I'm hoping to go to Florida maybe. Maybe one of these cruise ships, but I'm single, they don't want singles. It's a negative thing to be single. To go with another fellow, oh my goodness, that's so tough, they got their own way of doing things, they're self-centered, my goodness. A couple of months ago, I went away with another fellow my age who I got along with quite well. By the time we got back, I didn't want to speak to him at all. I'm saying to myself, 'I know it's not me.' I'm only too glad to bend with somebody, it's not me. [Laughs]

Aftermath of March 9–10, 1945 Tokyo raid. Ishikawa Kouyou.

Over sixty Japanese cities had been incinerated by the B-29s. Howling firestorms devoured civilians and workers in sheets of flames, burning hundreds of thousands to death.

When asked after the war about the morality of his orders to the crews of the B-29s, General LeMay responded, 'We knew we were going to kill a lot of women and children when we burned [Tokyo]... Killing Japanese didn't bother me much at the time. It was getting the war over with that bothered me.'

'We had to kill in order to end the war,' one pilot remembered. 'We heard about the thousands of people we killed, the Japanese wives, the children, and the elderly. That was war. But I know every B-29 air crewman for the next two or three years would wake up at night and start shaking. Yes, [the raids] were successful, but horribly so.'[10]

Sam L. Kamerman passed away on October 16, 2014, at the age of 91.

PART FOUR

OKINAWA AND BEYOND

"We tried to coax them to give themselves up. Some of them killed themselves with hand grenades and others went to a cliff at the end of the island and just jumped down on the rocks and were killed. Mothers with little children in their arms did that. So they were really committed people.

We were lucky. By rights, if you look at the odds, we had had eight combat landings, and a number of us were literally in the first wave of every landing. We would talk about it. The last couple I remember we were saying, 'You know, if we come out of this one, it's a miracle,' because we were pushing the odds."

—US Army Radioman, On His Final Landing At Okinawa

CHAPTER FOURTEEN

Hacksaw Ridge

Situated less than 350 miles from mainland Japan, sixty miles long and nearly 900 square miles, the island of Okinawa hosted perhaps 120,000 defenders on paper, but once taken, American planners reckoned it would be big enough to support 800 heavy bombers to rain hell on the enemy for the planned Operation Downfall invasion of Japan, scheduled for November 1945. As the winter of 1945 gave way to spring, it was clear to the Japanese that the island had to be held at all costs. Taking it was not going to be simple or easy. The logistics for the largest combined amphibious operation in the Pacific War took months, and over half a million Americans were to be committed to the battle in the newly created Tenth Army, a hybrid force that included the Army's 7th, 27th, 77th, and 96th Infantry Divisions and the Marines' 1st, 2nd, and 6th Divisions supported with nearly 20,000 naval personnel on land. From the sea, troops were ferried and supported by the nearly 300 ship armada of the US Fifth Fleet, which included the firepower of 18 battleships, 39 aircraft carriers, and 3,000 aircraft, and almost 250 British Commonwealth planes.[11]

Early morning on Easter Sunday, 1945, the invasion of Okinawa began. The first of four initial divisions of Marines and soldiers to hit the beaches that Easter morning were somewhat perplexed, however, to find little or no opposition. Others noted the irony of the date: besides being Easter Sunday, it was April 1—April Fools' Day. The defenders were waiting. Japanese troops had by now fixed on defense-in-depth tactics and chose to consolidate defensive positions in a rough and precipitous area in southern Okinawa, known as the Shuri Defense Line, with its treacherous escarpment riddled with the defenders' tunnels and caves.

Henry Huneken was committed to the battle with the reinforcing 77th Division. He became acquainted with a young man from Lynchburg, Virginia, who wanted to serve his country but as a devout Seventh-day Adventist, refused to carry a gun and was trained as a medic. Desmond Doss became the first conscientious objector to war to be awarded the Medal of Honor.

"The Japanese were using that as an artillery observation outpost, and they had the natives dig a network of caves and tunnels, three stories deep, in that thing. And that's why we could not cross it. Every time fellas got to the top, [the Japanese] had machine gun crossfire up there, and they just mowed them down.

I came ashore early in the morning and I saw six litters lying there, with the ponchos covering them, [glistening from the] moisture from during the night. They were just beginning to steam up from the sunshine, and I thought to myself, 'Oh, for heaven's sake, what am I doing here?'"

Henry C. Huneken

My name is Henry Huneken. I am eighty-two and a half years old. I was born 2-2-22 near Bremen, Germany. And I came to the United States, my parents brought me here when I was almost five years old, in 1926.

My educational background is the public school system of New York City; I didn't quite finish high school. In 1939, I went on a trip to Europe to visit my grandparents, and while in Europe, I saw that there was a lot of activity, militarily, and I thought it would be best that I get out. So I left and I came back.

I enlisted in October of 1942 in the United States Coast Guard. And I was in the Coast Guard Station in New York City and what we did was called port security; we boarded every ship that came into the harbor and acted as security. The port security system was brought into being because of the *Normandie* fire; on the ship *Normandie*, the French liner, they were doing what they call 'burning' with acetylene torches and the sparks ignited and the ship caught fire, and when the New York City Fire Department tried to put it out, they poured so much water on it that it capsized, right in the dockside.[21] And that was the reason why they enacted this port security system.

Now in the port security system, I was stationed in three different places. I was on Ellis Island for a while guarding the hospital nurses there; I walked to the seawall with a rifle that wasn't even loaded. And I was also stationed in Stapleton, Staten Island, at age 18, and that was where we had our detail boarding all the ships.

Now, I had requested that I be advanced in rank to a quartermaster, and one day I got notice to come over to the 3rd Naval District. And I went with the hopes that I would be promoted at that point. Instead, they handed me a discharge. It was an ordinary discharge, and it was for the 'convenience of the government,' and the reason for that was at the time, the Coast Guard was overcrowded, so for

---

[21] *Normandie* fire-The luxury French ocean liner was docked in New York when the Vichy government, loyal to Germany, came into power following the fall of France in June 1940. The Navy seized the liner to convert it into a troop ship; in the process of converting it, it caught fire.

whatever reason they could find, they were discharging personnel and I was one of them that was chosen.

I asked the officer at the Coast Guard what I should do, and he said, 'Well you'll have to go back to your draft board.'

'Greetings from Uncle Sam'

I said, okay, so I went back to my draft board and about two months later, I got a notice from Uncle Sam. It said, 'Report for physical, Grand Central Palace' on Madison Avenue, I think it was.

I went over and they said, 'Well, what would you like to go into? What branch of the service?'

The Coast Guard during wartime is part of the Navy. So I said, 'I'd like to go into the Navy.' And he said, 'Okay,' and they stamped my papers.

I went down with thirty-three men to the Naval District Office on Church Street. And they read off thirty-two names and they didn't read my name off. So, I went up to the fella and I said, 'Look, what am I, an orphan? I'd like to know why my name wasn't called.'

He said, 'Well, what's your name?' So we went in to see the officer of the day, and the officer of the day said, 'You're no longer fit for naval duty.'

I said, 'Well, what do I do?'

He said, 'Well, I guess you have to go back to your draft board.' So, I went back to my draft board again, and I couldn't get a job because I had a 1-A classification. But in the meantime, I got another letter, 'Greetings from Uncle Sam,' and I went down to Grand Central again. And this time there was no question as to what branch of the service I would like. So they stamped it 'Accepted Army' and that's how I was drafted into the Army.

I went to basic training in Camp Blanding, Florida. That's an infantry training camp for fourteen weeks and my designation was as a rifleman. And while down there, we were out on bivouac and we were notified that we had a hurricane coming, and they had to pull 17,000 men off the field because of that hurricane threat.

Shortly thereafter, I had an interview with a major down there who was J-2, which is Intelligence in the Army, and we had a discussion. And he said, 'I understand you're a German.'

I said, 'Yes, I am.'

So he said to me, 'What would you do, if we send you when the first wave goes?'

I said, 'Well, there's not much I can do, I'd have to defend myself, but I'd rather not be sent to Germany.' [See,] I passed the interpretation test. They wanted to have me go to Germany, but I didn't want to because I had relatives there, so on and so forth. So they sent me to the Pacific—just two of us out of those 17,000 men that I trained with. The other men all went into the Battle of the Bulge, but this Chinese fella and I were sent to the Pacific. And we went on a long troopship, and we went all the way down to New Guinea because the islands had not been taken at that time. We took a very slow trip, and we had no escort; we were alone and we would inch our way up. And finally, we landed on the island of Leyte, which was still not declared secured.

The 77th Division

I was put into what they call 'replacement depot' there on February 2, which was my birthday. And about three or four days later, I was assigned to a company in the 77th Division because they had just come down from the mountains after the operation; they had been on Guam before that. They had taken the island of Guam and then they were assigned to go into Leyte. I'd be of the 307th Infantry in the 77th Division.

The 77th Division had gone through many different kinds of training. They went through mountain training, they went through desert training, they went through, I don't know, just about any kind of training that they could possibly have, because it was like an experimental division, they had a lot of older men in it, up to the middle 40s, I think. But they began to weed them out, so by the time they went overseas, they were pretty well prepared for anything, you know, and they were called a 'hot' division.

Our commanding general was General Andrew D. Bruce. And we were known over in the Pacific as Bruce's Butchers, most of us coming from the New York-New Jersey-Connecticut area. The officers were mostly southern, but the enlisted men were mostly from the New York metropolitan and tri-state area.

Leyte

On Leyte, I was shot at a couple of times by Japanese who had gone into the hills and stayed there. What happened on Leyte, they were building like recreation rooms and mess halls out of bamboo for us. And we engaged the local natives to go up into the mountains and cut bamboo. We loaned them our six-wheeler trucks and they went up there and they cut the bamboo. But they were being sniped at by the Japanese [hiding up there], so they wanted protection. So they sent a couple of us GIs up there with rifles, but we didn't know that there were any Japanese up there. We would put our rifles by the truck, and we'd wander off into the neighborhood someplace. So I was shot at a couple of times.

The Run-Up to Okinawa

At that point already, they start to prepare for the Okinawa invasion. That was almost a 24-hour deal, unloading ships, loading ships. I loaded the great big 155 mm artillery shells, they were heavy. I came back with a hernia, incidentally. I don't know whether it was from that, or the fact that I carried a flamethrower for one day where I had to take it and throw it on my shoulder, but I came back with a hernia, and that's why I'm getting a slight pension, 10% pension.

That was about a month's time. In that time, we were preparing, and we also went out and we did a little bit of what they call amphibious training. [We were] climbing down the rope nets into the troop carriers, the landing craft, and it got a little bit rough out there sometimes, then we [actually] boarded the ships. I don't remember what day it was that we left, because we were assigned to take five little, small islands to the southwest in the China Sea before the initial invasion began of Okinawa, so we arrived there on the 26th of March and the invasion began on April 1.

My regiment took these five small islands, the Kerama Islands. I was not sent ashore, my company happened to be a reserve, so we did not go in. And then we went back onboard ship and every night the whole division would pull away from the islands, except for the people who remained on the island after they were taken for [garrison duty].

The Kamikazes

We went back into the China Sea and at that point, we got very heavily bombarded by kamikaze planes. The ship to the right of us was hit; this plane went right into the bridge, and I think about 72 officers and men were killed just by that one plane. One of the wounded happened to be Winthrop Rockefeller, who became the governor of Arkansas later on. I had quite a few interesting episodes with him, we used to go beer drinking together.

The ship on the left also was hit. And one evening, we had an alert and we were told to go below. I was reading a book from Bob Hope, and I was sitting on the railing, and I couldn't see myself going down below so fast, so I stayed up there and I looked up. And as I'm looking up, I see this plane coming directly towards us. The gunnery crew of that ship was not very accurate, they were not very good trying to hit the sleeve of that target plane in training back in the Philippines.

'Wow, this is going to be something,' I thought. At that point, I froze; this plane was coming directly in, but all of a sudden, there was a terrific explosion and the 5-inch gun on the tail end of the ship had hit that kamikaze plane directly on the nose and it just disintegrated—the pieces fell on the deck around me. It was headed right towards me!

Hacksaw Ridge-The Maeda Escarpment

The Japanese plan on Okinawa was to let the Americans come ashore and move towards the south and then clobber them, surround them and then do them in. And we got ashore, we were finally committed because the 96th Division was so badly decimated that the generals began to ask themselves, why are they not advancing; they had lost an awful lot of men. So we were finally committed, and it was my first experience getting up to the front lines.

They had advanced to this escarpment, which was a high elevation of rock and coral that ran most of the way across the center of the island. And the Japanese were using that as an artillery observation outpost, and they had the natives dig a network of caves and tunnels, three stories deep, in that thing. And that's why we could not cross it. Every time fellas got to the top, [the Japanese] had machine gun crossfire up there, and they just mowed them down.

I came ashore early in the morning and I saw six litters lying there, with the ponchos covering them, [glistening from the] moisture from during the night. They were just beginning to steam up from the sunshine, and I thought to myself, 'Oh, for heaven's sake, what am I doing here?'

But it took us nine days to take that position. First of all, we got these cargo nets from the ships from the Navy, and we tied them up there. And this fellow Doss was instrumental in helping to tie them up. Having been in the Coast Guard, they called on me as well to tie these cargo nets up to the top, so the soldiers could climb up there with their equipment and try to storm these positions up on top.

Well, like I said, took us nine days. Every time we went up there, we had over 80 percent casualties, in my company as well.

One night we were up there with my squad, and we were in three foxholes. I was in the middle foxhole and three other fellas were in the foxhole to my right and the squad leader was in the foxhole to my left. The sun was going down, and the mailman came up and he gave me a whole stack of letters from Ursula, my wife. I started to read them because there was a little bit of a cutout on the side of this escarpment, and we had piled a couple of rocks up on the edge [for cover], to make it a little bit higher.

He came up and he said, 'You have anything else you'd like?'

I said, 'Yeah, I'd like you to bring me a pair of dry socks.'

He came back a little bit later, he brought some dry socks, and he also brought a couple of doughnuts, I remember. And then I sat there, and I was reading the letters. I must have gotten about 25 or 30 letters at one time.

'Help Me!'

Now it got dark, and they threw up flares, and we would look out all the time. And all of a sudden, there was an explosion in the foxhole next to me; they had thrown a hand grenade in there. And while I'm looking—I'm looking out over Buckner Bay up there, I could see the ships out there—I see this form in the ground crawling up to me. And he saw me, and he said, 'Huneken, help me, help me, help me!'

It was our BAR man, Mike Revak. And he had taken a hand grenade almost on his lap and his leg was shattered, it was really turned around. He was a big guy, he was about six foot, and I couldn't pick him up, I couldn't lift him. So I took him by the belt, and I pulled him into where we were able to evacuate him that night. I cut open his pants leg and I sprinkled some sulfanilamide on him, but he lost the leg anyway. I never saw him again after that. I found out later that he lost all his genitals and lost the leg.

We were told to consolidate our position where the squad leader was. We had two Japanese wooden ladders that were tied together, two 24-foot ladders, and they went to the top, because this whole thing was a sheer cliff of forty feet that we had to go up on the cargo nets and on ropes. Then we consolidated our opposition to that; we waited, and we waited, and it was pretty dark already by now, must have been about eleven o'clock.

Japanese Infiltrators

My squad leader, his name was Harvey Gilliam, tapped me on the shoulder and he said, 'Huneken, get down and get a little bit of rest.' He says, 'Twelve o'clock, come back up and relieve us.'

I said fine. I went down, my foot was on the top rung of that ladder already, because we had a feeling that they were crawling up on us, which they were, and which is what finally happened.

I had just gotten down, about 11:15, something like that, when all hell broke loose up on top and they raided, you know. The Japs wore split-toe sneakers. The Japs, they just crawled; it took them almost four hours to crawl that distance. When the flares went up, we would look out and we'd watch every stone, every rock, and if the stone moved, we knew it was a human being. If it wasn't a rock, it had moved, that's the only way you could make out the figures. Anyway, they raided, they charged with bayonets attached to the bamboo poles, and they got Gilliam in the stomach, and it cut him open. And he just dropped, and I think there were five guys that were left up there. One of them was a New Mexican fella who spoke Spanish, and I can't remember his name. Anyway, he came at me out of a cave, or a cut in the rocks, down below, and I had my rifle at the ready—I was going to pull the trigger and he said, 'Amigo, amigo!' He said, 'Don't shoot, it's me!' So that's how his life was spared. It was just a matter of a split-second, okay?

And then we all scooted around to a great big rock, there were about seven of us. We had a medic, I can't remember his name, but it was not Doss; Doss was in the company command post [at that time]. Anyway, [this medic] stayed with us and he gave my squad leader, Harvey Gilliam, morphine shots all night long. Which kept him quiet, and he didn't utter a sound, because if he had made a sound, the Japanese would have known where we were. We had left everything up there. All the hand grenades, everything that we pulled up all day long and used all day long, they would have thrown down on us, but nobody knew where we were exactly.

'Burn Them Out'

Another incident on the escarpment, how we finally took this position knowing that it was three stories down. We had a V-shaped trough built about 20 feet long, up to a hole, because they're coming out of these holes all the time, up on the top. We poured five-gallon cans of gasoline in it, and it would go down into the hole, then somebody would have to crawl up and throw a phosphorus grenade in there and blow the whole thing up. That's what we did several times. But they came right back up out of those holes again because they just went off into the side passages, and they would come right back up out of them again. This one time, my captain, Captain Vernon, refused an order from the colonel [via] radio contact with the regimental command post.

He said, 'I found a cave.'

And the colonel said, 'Blow it.'

The captain said, 'I can't; I don't know what's under there.'

So he refused the command, and the colonel said, 'I want you to blow it.'

He says, 'No, sir. I'm sorry, I refuse,' because we all would have gone up.

Later on, the colonel came up, and the way they finally took this position is, they took flame-throwing tanks coming around from the front, from the other side. [It had a steep slope], it went down to a 40-foot precipice, and then they finally shot flamethrowers into the holes and everything, which finally burned them out. And then we were slowly able to advance. We were pulled back off the line at that point to about fifteen miles back, where the giant 155mm guns were the gun emplacements, and they put us right in front of those things, and every time they went off, we jump two feet high, for heaven's sake. Because your nerves get a little bit tight, you know.

Then we got replacements, because we had quite a few losses. We got one young kid, 17, 18 years old, right fresh out of high school, and then we were sent back up on the line again. We don't even have a chance to train with them or anything. We were sent back up on the line because they were trying to advance towards Shuri [Castle]; the city was Naha that was off towards the right. On both sides of this, we had another division; on the operation of Okinawa, there were four divisions of infantry and two divisions of Marines. Now, the Marines seem to have gotten most of the credit for that operation, which bothered us all through the years, but they have a good PR system, the Marines.

'Fix Bayonets, No Round in the Chamber'

So we never got our due, although the second time that we were put on the line, we advanced, and we were given the orders. We are going to make a night attack deep into the Japanese territory. And the orders, the way they came down to us were, 'You'll fix bayonets and there will be no round in the chamber.' In other words, they didn't want any noise in that night attack because that was unheard of. Nope, I don't think any American infantry outfit has ever made a night attack like that. But we did, we had two companies, I was in Company B, and Company E. For that we got a Bronze Star, every member of the company. For the escarpment, we got a presidential citation. Those are the medals that I earned over there.

After that, the whole Okinawa campaign was over at the end of June. That was three months, March, April, May—no, that's almost four months, because we were taken off the line about the middle of June and sent back into a rest area. And from there we went back to the Philippines.

Desmond Doss

Desmond Doss became the first conscientious objector to be awarded the Medal of Honor. As a medic assigned in 1944 to 2nd Platoon, Company B, 1st Battalion, 307th Infantry, 77th Infantry Division, he was first awarded two Bronze Stars with a 'V' designation 'for exceptional valor in aiding wounded soldiers under fire on Guam and the Philippines.'

Desmond Doss, on top of the Maeda Escarpment,
Battle of Okinawa, May 4, 1945. US Army photo, public domain.

Desmond Doss was a conscientious objector, and he was a medic. And little by little—see, his Sabbath is Saturday, according to his religion. So, while in training, he had shoes thrown at him, he was berated, he was called down because he wouldn't work, he refused to work on a Saturday, he wanted to go to church. He was a Seventh-day Adventist. He was taken out of the company several times, but he liked the fellas in the company, even though they were not too pleasant to him, so he kept coming back. And when they went to the island of Guam, they began to realize how conscientious

this fellow was in performing his duty as a medic. He would go under all kinds of adverse conditions of pulling these fellas and attend
to them, you know, in combat.

And the same thing happened on Leyte; by that time, they were
pretty well convinced that he was the right guy.

And when it came to Okinawa, he and I were the main ones that
tied up these cargo nets up on the top that enabled the fellas to get
up there. And for the nine days that we were there, I went six days
and six nights without sleep there when we were in that operation
because if you fell asleep, you were dead. You could maybe get a
five- or ten-minute catnap, that was about the extent of it. Anyway,
Desmond Doss very often would go up the rope ladders and go out
where fellas were hit, sometimes very badly. And he would pull
them in, pull them in right under the machine gun fire and everything. He had nothing, he had no fear. That was his belief in God.
So he saved quite a few guys' lives, that's what his Medal of Honor
citation states, that he's saved 75 men's lives.[22]

----

[22] *he's saved 75 men's lives*- Desmond Doss's [1919-2006] Medal of Honor
citation, personally presented at the White House by President Harry S. Truman on October 12, 1945, reads:
"Private First Class Desmond T. Doss, United States Army, Medical Detachment, 307th Infantry, 77th Infantry Division. Near Urasoe-Mura, Okinawa,
Ryukyu Islands, 29 April – 21 May 1945. He was a company aid man when
the 1st Battalion assaulted a jagged escarpment 400 feet high. As our troops
gained the summit, a heavy concentration of artillery, mortar and ma-
chinegun fire crashed into them, inflicting approximately 75 casualties and
driving the others back. Private First Class Doss refused to seek cover and remained in the fire-swept area with the many stricken, carrying them one by
one to the edge of the escarpment and there lowering them on a rope-sup-
ported litter down the face of a cliff to friendly hands. On 2 May, he exposed
himself to heavy rifle and mortar fire in rescuing a wounded man 200 yards
forward of the lines on the same escarpment; and two days later he treated
four men who had been cut down while assaulting a strongly defended cave,
advancing through a shower of grenades to within eight yards of enemy
forces in a cave's mouth, where he dressed his comrades' wounds before

Every once in a while, he got a fella down like that, he would tie ropes under their arms and lower them down. When we got them down below, they would ask for volunteers; we needed four men to carry a litter, and I volunteered quite often because it meant getting back to the base hospital and staying off the line for maybe half an hour, an hour. And you'd have to, of course, go back again, but that little rest there was so helpful sometimes.

After the night attack, let me see if I can recall this, he went out and he tried to get a couple of guys in, and a mortar round struck right close by him and shattered his arm. So he took a carbine, and took the stock out of it, and made himself a splint out of that, to

making four separate trips under fire to evacuate them to safety. On 5 May, he unhesitatingly braved enemy shelling and small arms fire to assist an artillery officer. He applied bandages, moved his patient to a spot that offered protection from small-arms fire and, while artillery and mortar shells fell close by, painstakingly administered plasma. Later that day, when an American was severely wounded by fire from a cave, Private First Class Doss crawled to him where he had fallen 25 feet from the enemy position, rendered aid, and carried him 100 yards to safety while continually exposed to enemy fire. On 21 May, in a night attack on high ground near Shuri, he remained in exposed territory while the rest of his company took cover, fearlessly risking the chance that he would be mistaken for an infiltrating Japanese and giving aid to the injured until he was himself seriously wounded in the legs by the explosion of a grenade. Rather than call another aid man from cover, he cared for his own injuries and waited five hours before litter bearers reached him and started carrying him to cover. The trio was caught in an enemy tank attack and Private First Class Doss, seeing a more critically wounded man nearby, crawled off the litter and directed the bearers to give their first attention to the other man. Awaiting the litter bearers' return, he was again struck, this time suffering a compound fracture of one arm. With magnificent fortitude he bound a rifle stock to his shattered arm as a splint and then crawled 300 yards over rough terrain to the aid station. Through his outstanding bravery and unflinching determination in the face of desperately dangerous conditions Private First Class Doss saved the lives of many soldiers. His name became a symbol throughout the 77th Infantry Division for outstanding gallantry far above and beyond the call of duty."

hold his arm straight. Then they wanted to evacuate him, and they put him on a litter. I wasn't there at that time, [but] while he was [being made] ready to be evacuated, they brought another [hurt soldier] in and the guy seemed to be pretty well wounded. Doss looked up at the medic, who was tending to both of them. And he said, 'Look, I'll roll off, and you take him back on it.' And they took him, he rolled off the litter, and they put the more heavily wounded guy on it. This is the kind of guy he was. And that's why he was recommended for the medal.

More Losses on the Escarpment

I remember one time we were on the escarpment where Colonel Hamilton came up. We were walking out, and they had just poured the gasoline down there, and there was a young lieutenant that came up early in the morning, just up from stateside. He just got off the ship and came down—he was a demolition expert. And they had poured the gasoline in, then I was up there with the fella by the name of LaPrade, who was a French Canadian who came from Maine, and we were close enough to rub elbows. And all of a sudden, before the lieutenant was even at the edge to throw his phosphorus grenade in there, there was a tremendous explosion, the dust and everything flying all over the place. And all of a sudden, this guy [who had been] next to me was missing. He was [found] lying on the ground, he died of a concussion; I saw the blood coming out of his nose and out of his ears. He was dead [but the blast] didn't affect me [then], but I still can't hear that well to this day.

Our captain was killed too, Captain Vernon. After we made this night attack, we kept advancing south towards the Shuri Castle, and he was in a foxhole. And we told him he should move his foxhole because the Japanese knew that he would have had a command post there, and they were [probably] zeroing in on it with knee mortars.

Now, the knee mortars are not something that you put on your knee, they put it on the ground, and they could put those things on a dime. When they pull that cord, you just knew that was going to come. And we told him to move his position, and he said, 'No, everybody knows I'm here and the company...'

He wanted to stay there, and he took one right on the head. A young fellow, 26 years old, the nicest guy I've ever met, Captain Vernon. And the executive officer who was with him, he was killed too, and also in the same foxhole was Captain Vernon's orderly, Samuel Dolce; he came from Rochester. I saw him many years afterward. Well, he was pretty well burned. He was pretty well scarred up.

I also kept a diary, which I never did get back from the guys that were doing this story on Desmond Doss, but that was pretty much the end of the operations on Okinawa—like I say, it took three months.

'Old People and Children'

We went on a little bit of patrol duty, I don't want to go into that [too much], because it involves some things that we're not very proud of, although it had to be done.

I was interested in photography, though I had no film. One of those lieutenants in my company had film and he had a camera, and he asked me to go along with the patrol to take some pictures of the countryside, of the houses, and whatnot. So, I went along, and I came across some brushwork at the side of the road, and I saw a little footprint in the mud there—by that time we had gotten the rainy season, it was really rainy and very nasty—I saw this little footprint and all this brushwork in front of us.

I didn't know it was a hole. I went back to the lieutenant that was leading the patrol and I said, 'I found these footprints.'

I said, 'What do you want to do about it?'

He said, 'Blow the hole.' So they put a satchel charge in, and then they blew the hole, but in there were nothing but old people and children.

But [who's to know]? The Okinawan people were used by the Japanese to bring supplies up to the front lines to them. They used them to carry ammunition, they used them to carry food. So that's why we didn't take any chances. There were no prisoners, very few prisoners were taken on the island of Okinawa. It was either you or I—I mean, that's the way it was, and the Okinawan people even were told that we're going to rape them and this and that. They were taking their children and throwing them off cliffs, and they would jump after them. It happened quite a bit.

Ernie Pyle

Ernie Pyle was with my regiment when he was killed. That affected us more than when we were notified of the death of President Roosevelt. We just said then, 'Well, let's get this all over with.' But when Ernie Pyle was killed, that really affected us because Ernie Pyle indirectly was responsible for the Combat Infantry Badge, and $10 a month extra for combat infantrymen. Yeah, we really felt bad when [he was killed]—he's buried in Hawaii, and I went to see his grave with my wife. He had gone all through Africa, Italy, Europe, always on the front lines with the GIs, always, and he comes to my regiment and is shot right through the head by a sniper. He was like the curious young fellas from high school, they raise their head, they looked around, and quite a few of them were hit by snipers right between the eyes.

At that time of [the atomic bombs], I was back in the Philippines. It was August, I believe. Well, we thought that's the end of the war. It's got to be, because these people, they can't put up with something like that, and it was a good thing that it did happen, because the 77th Division was slated to go right into Tokyo. And the Japanese would not have given up, the women, as well as the men, they were preparing to put up a very stiff fight.

Return to Okinawa

When we left the island of Okinawa, I think there were about 200,000 people living on the island. When I went back in 1981, there were a million and a half people on the island of Okinawa. The Japanese have turned it into a regular resort, because of the beaches and so on, and they travel it quite extensively. But unfortunately, [when we were back as part of a documentary film on Desmond Doss][23], we were not able to do much traveling. We went back to the escarpment, and they filmed up there and they filmed with Doss, showed exactly [where things happened]. And at the final day of filming, they sat us on four chairs up on the escarpment facing north. And all of a sudden, the director of the film said to the four of us GIs, he said, 'Turn around.'

We didn't know what to expect. We turned around, and there were these seven little Japanese [men] coming up the draw, in civilian clothes, naturally. Our hearts almost fell, you know, because to see these [guys]... two of them were ones that had been right on the escarpment, and the others were just veterans from other areas.

We had a dinner that night, or a couple of nights later, where they all attended. And it was supposed to be in our honor, but we sat and ate at the back of the room. Anyway, the Japanese were there [with us], we had a chance to talk to them through interpreters, and it was quite interesting to hear them talk about what they went through there, too. Yeah, they had a rough time, too. They

---

[23] *documentary film on Desmond Doss-The Conscientious Objector*, which in turn inspired the film *Hacksaw Ridge* [2016].

had about 150,000 troops, and we had about 150,000 troops. It was pretty equal as far as that goes.

After I left Okinawa, we went back to the Philippines, back to Cebu, which is an island right next to Leyte. And it was at that point that I was transferred to IX Corps. So I went from the 77th Division to IX Corps, because I had been to business school and I typed, I took shorthand, so they made me a company clerk. With IX Corps, I went up to the island of Hokkaido, to the city of Sapporo. And I was up there for four months, as part of the Army of Occupation.

Psychologically, the war affected me throughout my life because I had many sleepless nights with it. You know, these things come back to you. I've had many sleepless nights to this day. As a matter of fact, as I got older, they became more prevalent. But I feel that I'm as normal [as the next guy].

Henry Huneken became a salesman, cabinetmaker, carpenter, and building inspector after the war. He passed in 2019 at the age of 97.

CHAPTER FIFTEEN

The Navy Corpsman

He sits in a chair before his interviewers in a darkened room two days before Thanksgiving, summoning forth memories that have clearly haunted him on some level from nearly sixty years in the past. Steve Jordan came to the 22nd Marine Regiment [22nd Marines] of the 6th Division as a corpsman in the Pacific—the same outfit that Joe Fiore [*The Pineapple Kid, Volume I*] was a part of—although not of his own choosing, having picked the Navy over the Army when it was time to enlist. Later, in the reserves, he was called up for Korea, and here he also recounts his participation in the subzero Battle of the Chosin Reservoir.

He gave this interview in 2003.

Steve T. Jordan

I was born in Schenectady, New York, October 13, 1924. I just got through freshman year in high school, and then I quit because the war started, and I enlisted at age eighteen. I was in school, but I had no idea where Pearl Harbor was. Most people didn't. We were all going to leave school and enlist, and I guess three or four of us did.

I don't know [why I picked the Navy], I just didn't want the Army, and I thought the Navy would be good. You know, get on a ship and it would be a pretty clean life, that kind of thing. I went through boot camp up in Sampson, New York, early in November 1942. There was a lot of construction going on, and it was in the wintertime, and it was cold and muddy, you know. It was all new to everyone, so it wasn't just me that was walking around, 'wow,' you know, just amazed; it was everyone. We had a couple of boats, but we didn't do much in them, because the winter came quick, and it was a bad one. When on a range, we fired .22s. I had never seen a rifle like it before. It looked like a pipe on the end of a stick, you know. And we were taught how to tie knots and this kind of thing. And that's about the only equipment [training] we did, [besides] some splicing and fitting pins and stuff like that. That's normal seamanship, you forget right after you've done it. [*Laughs*]

Hospital Corps School

I went in there in November, and I got out of there, I think, the end of December. They were pushing us right through. What they did is, they put us in a drill hall, and they said, you know, 'this gang over here, and this middle gang, and another gang, over there.' They said, 'You guys are staying here, and you're going to cooks' and bakers' school.' The next bunch was going to Little Creek, Virginia, they went into the armed guards. The third bunch, they said, 'You guys are going to Portsmouth, Virginia,' and that was the group I was in. I had no idea what it was, you know, until we got to Portsmouth, Virginia, and it was Hospital Corps school! I had to think that one over, I didn't know if I wanted to do that or not. I guess I made up my mind, and I got up the nerve to go to the old man and say, 'Look, I want out of this thing,' and he so much as told me, 'Hey kid, you're in it, and the only way out of it is in a wooden overcoat, so make the best of it!'

So that's what we had to do. It was all the medical stuff. Medical therapeutics, and nursing and first aid, and all that kind of stuff. Doing splints, and carrying people, and all this. And when you got a rate, you were a pharmacist's mate, and to me it didn't relate at all because we didn't do anything with, you know, we gave pills, but a doctor said, 'Here, you give these pills.' We never figured it out ourselves.

We trained there for about eight weeks; I had more training after that. I got out of Hospital Corps school, I went to Norfolk, Virginia, the naval operating base; there was a hospital there and I did a lot of medical work. I handed out tennis balls, and [archery equipment], bow and arrows, and all that kind of stuff; golfing equipment, you know, I had a shed, and all the stuff was in it, and I'd get the patient's name, you know, and that's what I did. But every once in a while, I had to stand watch in some ward where someone was really sick or something. They would give you a rundown of what you had to do, okay. But somewhere along the line, I goofed up because I got shanghaied out of there and I was sent to Camp Lejeune, North Carolina. And there was quite a few of us that went to that, where we went through field medical training school, which was doing what we knew how to do, what we were taught to do in Corps school, [but] out in the field under combat conditions.

I could get a carbine, or a .45, and I chose a carbine until I found out after that it shoots curves—you don't get good distance with it. Later on, I picked up a Garand and that's what I carried.

It's hard to remember how long I was there. It wasn't very long, because we went through all the training, from the infiltration course to the rifle range a couple of times, and all the medical stuff, and then we had classes where you sat in a hot metal building and some Marine officer would give you the history of the Marine Corps and the rocks and shoals, that kind of stuff. It was very boring, you know. He would even fall asleep as he was giving us this stuff, but it was a requirement, you know. But when you think about it, it was good, you know. And the [instructor] who did it was a WWI veteran; he was a major, I think.

After Lejeune I went aboard ship, the *USS Clay*, it was a transport, an APA, and it was a shakedown cruise, and I went aboard as a troop. We were in a replacement battalion; we were in the 39th Replacement Battalion. We rode a train from Lejeune to Norfolk, and then got on the ship, and we went through the Panama Canal and went to Pearl Harbor. We were in a convoy, but they were dragging a target, and there were planes shooting at the back of the target; they were doing a lot of training on the way over. It was a nice ship, it was brand new, but it had a lot of things wrong with it. We didn't realize it, but the crew did.

[When we arrived in Hawaii], we went into some kind of a 'repo depot' where everyone came in, and if they needed a machine gunner, or a cook, or something like that, they would pull them out because it was a mixture of corpsmen and Marines and all that. So then I was told I had to go aboard this ship with some other guys, and we got on this transport, and we took off and we went out into the Pacific, out into the islands. We went to this island that had just been attacked before we got over there, and it was in the Marshall group. I believe it was Roi-Namur. We joined an outfit there, the 22nd Marines there, and I stayed with them for the whole of World War II.

[We dressed in Marine fatigues but wore a Navy rate on the arm.] When I first went there, it was just a red cross, and we wore it down low; that signified we were a corpsman. At the beginning, I was a hospital apprentice, 2nd class, which is equal to a corporal.

So I wore a corporal's stripes, but just on my left arm, and we wore the red cross below it.

At first, [we were not treated by the regular Marines so well], it was nothing but arguments and fights and ridicule, you know, 'swabbie' this and that and the other thing. But we had a couple of sailors that beat up a few Marines, and the old man [had it out for us]; he said, 'I got to find this sailor who beat up four of my Marines!' He was a tough guy. But after we were with him a while and went into training with him, we became friends.

The Invasion of Guam

Our first landing was on Guam. Guam, we were on it for fifty-eight days; [before that], we floated around. See, there is Saipan, Tinian, and Guam. And we were going to hit Guam, but Saipan was having a hard time, so they kept us on reserve. So, we floated around the Pacific for [quite a while]. We got attacked by some Bettys; they came in and they carried a torpedo. Me and this other guy were playing cards, sitting on a spud locker, you know, and this thing came and flew right between our LST and the one right next to us, and [the torpedo] was just skipping the top of the water. And I said, 'Wow, what the hell was that?', and then we see the meatballs on the wings. [It was close]. Phew, I tell you, you can't dig in out there! But we were lucky, we got through it all right. They shot it down, and another came back the next day and raised some more hell.

Then Saipan started to go pretty well, so we went to some other island, I don't remember which one it was. We got some mail, and we got some beer, stayed there overnight, and then a couple days later, we made the landing. First, I was on a transport, and then we transferred from the transport to an LST. We had to sleep topside because there wasn't enough room for everyone. Well, we went to the tank deck and got in the amphibious tractor; I got on this amphibious vehicle. You were assigned to which one, and I was assigned to go in this one that was [commanded] by a major, and he had a jeep on it. I was assigned to him, and he was killed there.

Well anyhow, we started off, you know, we got our wave to go. And we were between, I think, the second wave and the next one. We got out and we made a turn, and all this amphibious tractor does is go round in circles because one of the wheels wasn't working! You know they run on those tracks, even turn in the water, so we were just going around in circles. So now they had to transfer us from that one to another, but the jeep stayed in that one; I mean, we ended up without a jeep. But anyhow, by the time we got on the beach it must have been the third or fourth wave was hitting. And there were a lot of casualties, there were a lot of amphibious tractors that were hit, there were a lot of guys that were in the water, and we were busy taking care of them for the longest time. But then they had another outfit come in, some more corpsmen, and some more Marines came in. The ones that made the initial landing, which included us, we had to start moving; we had to catch up with our troops and move. Well, the major had what we call the 'OP' party, it was the observation party, so we'd have to get up and see what the Japs were doing. You know it was maybe fifteen, sometimes there was twenty-five in a group. He was a pretty gung-ho character, I'll tell you. We took a hell of a beating at a place called 'Road Junction 15' in Guam, and that was on the way to what was left of the Marine Corps barracks. We had a lot of guys killed.

At that Road Junction 15, it was just one of those things we walked right into. They had crossfires set up, and boy, they slaughtered us. [*Pauses, folds arms across chest, looks down in silence for a few seconds, composes himself*].

After we got to the Marine barracks and took over, I got sick—I had the chills and all this business. See, like I said, we were out floating around for fifty-eight days, and we ran out of Atebrin. And there was a lot of malaria and a lot of dengue fever and crap like that, that affected all of us. So I got sent down to the beach and they put a tag on me, they said, 'Go on down to the beach and get some juice and get some rest and then come back when you're feeling better.' You know, the old man told me that, so I said, okay.

I went down to the beach and there was a hospital there, there was a second separate hospital. See we were a bastard [unit] off of the 22nd Marines, we weren't in a division, we were just a regiment. We were with the 4th Marines and the 11th Marines, so we were a brigade, the 1st Provisional Marine Brigade. So anyhow, the hospital was a second separate hospital, and I was staying there. So they gave me a can of juice and they started me on a regimen of Atebrin and right about then the Japs pulled a counterattack; they were knocking off the hospitals on the beach. So they evacuated us all out to the ocean, you know, we got aboard ships. And I got on this ship, well it was an APA. All I remember is that Cesar Romero was a chief on there, it was a Coast Guard thing, I think. I never saw him, but that's what they said, 'Cesar Romero,' and I said, 'Boy, that's great.'[24] But anyhow I ended up back in Pearl Harbor, because we went here, and we went there. Every ship we went to looked down and said, 'We'll take him, him, and him,' and they'd lift you up, lift the litter up off the boat we were in, and they'd pick out who they were going to take, because they were doing triage there.

---

[24] *Cesar Romero*-Cesar Romero [1907-1994] was the self-proclaimed 'Latin from Manhattan' Cuban-descended actor perhaps best known by his shipmates for his role as the Cisco Kid in six westerns in the years leading up to his enlistment in 1942 in the US Coast Guard, eventually serving aboard the assault transport *USS Cavalier* as an apprentice seaman in the invasions of Tinian and Saipan, finishing his enlistment with the rating of chief petty officer.

Well, I looked bad, because I had a lot of blood on me—but it wasn't mine, it was everybody else's. So I got picked on one ship [first] and it was that Cesar Romero's ship. So they were doing operations there, and this doctor said, 'You sit there on the floor,' on the deck, it was in the mess hall, and they were working on everybody, you know. And that's the first time I ever saw that operation [aboard a ship]. I've seen it in the field, the aid station, but never on a ship. So finally this doctor says, 'So where were you hit?'

And I said, 'I wasn't hit,' you know, and he's calling this other doctor saying, 'Look it, he's got blood in his ears.'

He said, 'It's a sign of a concussion.'

I said, 'Wait a minute, I'm a corpsman.' I said, 'This is other people's blood, I wasn't hit!' I got that blood on me somehow, from my hands or whatever.

They stuck me in a ward, and they gave me a shot, and that was the end of it for a while, and I ended up back in Pearl, which was all right. So while I was there, I said, 'Hell, I've got nothing else to do,' my appendix started bothering me, so they took it out. Just one of those things, where the doctor had said, 'You're going to work today,' you know, I'd been there a while. So I get out there to work in a tomato patch, you know, we were hoeing the plants up. Jeez, I got this pain in the gut. So I go see the doctor, and he says, 'You're goofing off.'

I said, 'No, I'm not, I really got a pain!' So he checked me out and he took a blood test, and that's what it was. I had appendicitis. So they took it out, and I took it easy for a while.

Then I got back to the 22nd. They had gone to Guadalcanal, that was our home base where we would set up. So I caught a ride on a ship, and I hitchhiked. I had my records—I carried my own records. They said, 'Get on whatever ship you can, and they'll take you there,' eventually. So it took a while, but I ended up on the Canal, and I ended up in 3rd Battalion and I didn't like that because I was in 2nd

Battalion. Finally I got that squared away and got back to where I belonged.

Okinawa

Then we trained for the next operation. We didn't know what it was, but it was Okinawa, and we landed there. That was April 1. Easter Sunday, April Fools' Day, and it was the whole nine yards, that whole same day—we had an unopposed landing, I think they sucked us right in—and it was easy, and then we went up north. We went the hell up north; we went to the northern tip of Okinawa and we were like 350 miles from the southern tip of Japan, and with nobody on our left flank. So we stayed up there for a while, and then, I guess it was the 27th or the 25th Army Division was having a problem down south. The 1st Marine Division was also down south, and these guys were tied in next to them. So they got the word to us, and they loaded us on trucks and down we went, and we replaced the 1st Marine Division. Man for man, hole for hole. They moved over, and they took out the 27th and gave them a break. And that's when we started getting into a lot of combat. We ran into Sugar Loaf Hill, and that was a mess. And that's when the major got killed.

'He Was Left There to Die'

A couple of days before he was killed, we were on a hill. We were OP'ing it up, 'snooping and booping'; we were watching the Japs and this and that, and all of a sudden, some Jap appeared on top of this hill. It was all rocks and coral, and he had a satchel charge, you know, it was a wooden box with a detonator on it. And he threw that, and it came down and luckily it landed right in between all these rocks. But it blew up, [and for us] it was all concussion—it didn't have any shrapnel, or anything like that, but it blew the shit out of all of us. You know, we were all dopey and crummy there for a while. When it blew this coral, the major got hit in the leg, I think it was the left leg, so I had to take care of that for him. I had put a 12-inch battle dressing on him because he was hit in about four different places. Like I said, he was a gung-ho son of a bitch.

'That's too much of a battle dressing!' He said, 'I can't move around with that, I got to be able to move around!'

So I said, 'All right, okay,' and I pulled some of the stuffing out of it; you know, I did what I could. I got him fixed up and then he was all right.

It was like two or three days later and we hit Sugar Loaf Hill [again], and the first group of the 22nd went up and got kicked right off of it. There was a lot of casualties. I think it was that night or the next night, there was a lot of action going on and we were at the foot of this thing. And the major took volunteers, you know. So we were all there, and I was going to go with him.

He says, 'You go back and stay at the bottom of the hill, I don't want you coming up the hill with us.' [*Arches forward quickly in his seat, looks down, gets briefly emotional...*] He was killed up there... [*Snaps back into composure*] He was a good Marine, [but] I didn't like that man. I'll tell you why I didn't like him. There was one of the guys that we all knew, he was a good guy, and he got the left cheek of his ass blown off. And there he was, lying there, and they had gauze over him, you know, to keep the flies and crap off him, the blowflies. A lot of his insides were sticking out, he'd had it, and they just had him lying there.

They had him pretty well doped up and everyone there would lie to him, you know, [he'd ask], 'How bad is it?'

'Oh, you're all right, you're gonna be okay.' [*Pauses, looks down again briefly*] He was left there to die.

But [the major] comes over, and he picks up the gauze and he says, 'Jesus Christ, you bought the farm!' And you know, that got to me, and I got in some trouble.

I said, 'You're an asshole!' and I yelled at him—I never got any more rate after that, you know, I [had] made second class, but that was the end of it. I don't know whether he had anything to do with it, [because] he was dead a short while after that. Maybe it's my imagination, because I didn't like the man for that reason, I figured, hey, this is a well-educated guy, a major, and he's acting like, well, just what I called him, an asshole.

*

'A Long Trip Home'

Anyhow, we stayed on Okinawa a hundred and ten days and then we got sent back. We went to Guam and that was our home base. It was a year to the day from the time we invaded Guam to the time we came back. So it was quite a celebration. You know, they had the booze out, you know everyone was there to welcome us. So we stayed there, and then I had enough time to come home. See, by then, there were just no ships going home, and then the war ended, so we were sitting there and then this one morning this guy calls me. And he's like, 'Hey, Greek, look down in the bay!'

Great big flattop [is sitting there] [*spreads arms apart*]; it was the *Bonhomme Richard* and they put us on it. [Now it was going to be used] as a ferry boat to bring the guys home, and this was the first trip it made. Jeez, they threw away airplanes and ammunition, they were throwing them over the side, you know, because the war was over! And we were running with lights on, and it was great.

We did everything by alphabetical order, so I slept in the J section, down in the hangar deck, in a square that was marked off with a white J in the middle. In the morning when I got up, I'd fold up that cot and go to another spot where there was another J and stow my gear there. So we had to do that every day, and the rest of the day, we did all kinds of stuff. We chipped paint, you know, we hung around. There wasn't much to do, and it was a long trip home because we took a long route. We got to Treasure Island, in San Francisco, and we came under the bridge, and some of those planes took off from the *Bonhomme* and flew under the bridge upside down! Anyhow we got a little liberty, and I came home and got discharged.

The Reserves

I was in the reserves, I joined the 1st Engineer Company in Albany. It was a Marine Corps engineer company, and some of the guys that I had been in the 22nd Marines with were in it [with me]. So I figured, well, we'll go play cards together and we'll drink a few beers and have some fun; we'll go to Camp Lejeune in the summertime and all this. And we did this, up until August [1950]; I forget what day it was. We were activated, they activated the unit. We marched down New Scotland Avenue [in Albany]; we had been in the Christian Brothers Academy high school rifle range there, that was our home base, and we marched from there all the way down to the train station. The mayor from Schenectady was there, and the city manager, and [Albany] Mayor Corning was there; all the dignitaries were there to see us off. And I remember every one of them, they all took turns saying, 'These men are not going overseas, they're going over there to Camp Pendleton to train those Marines that are going to go overseas.' Yeah, you believe that one, and well, I'll tell you another one.

So we got to Pendleton, and we went right into training again. So I told you before that in 1943, I went through that school at Camp Lejeune and became a field medical technician. Now, a Sergeant Crow was in charge of us. He was a good guy.

He said, 'How many of you guys went through field medical training school?' And I'm thinking to myself, I'm not going to tell him I went through it, you know, let him find that out, and I can get some more training, which I thought I should have.

We started through that stuff again, but halfway through that training, we were at the rifle range and Crow comes down and he said, 'You fall out,' and he called a couple other guys who were pulling the same thing I was. So we were told that we had to go on the next draft because we had already had that training.

He said, 'I know what you were doing,' and he said, 'That's okay,' and he agreed with us.

So anyhow, we went overseas. We got to Japan. We got kids that had snuck through; they were going to go to Christian Brothers Academy [high school], that's how young they were. I was 24, almost 25, when I got recalled, but some of these kids had never been through boot camp! All they knew was what they were taught at the [school] rifle range. Some of them snuck through; they did a pretty good job, they got most of them through boot camp, so they did get the basic training, and I'm happy for that because you had to have it. I strongly believe if you don't have that, then you don't belong out in combat.

On to Korea

So anyhow, we got to Japan, and they outfitted us out. Everybody went out and got drunk and did their thing, and then a couple of days later we were on a ship that took us to Korea. I got there November 12, 1950, and joined the Dog Medical Company. Now this is altogether a different life than I had had with the Marine Corps before.

Before, I was in a company, I was part of a group. Now I'm with a rear echelon kind of an outfit that moves in two sections. One section moves up, and then the other one moves up, and you set up a hospital. I got assigned to that and we were in this place called Chipyong-ni. We were just across from the 38th Parallel. That was after the Wonsan landing, it was a little north of the Wonsan harbor, and then the winter started coming in. And we didn't have any winter gear other than sweaters and some long underwear—stuff like that, and your greens—we didn't have any parkas or gloves, or anything like that. So they had to scrounge up stuff like that for everybody. And we got those shoepacks, they called them Italian mountain boots. They were an awful thing, they were big. If you wore a size ten shoe, or a nine, you were [now] a size twelve shoe, and it had a great big felt insole in it. So you got two pairs of insoles; one pair you kept inside your shirt, next to your body, and a pair of socks, heavy socks. The other pair was in your shoes, so when you changed, you just changed those socks. Well after about a week, you start smelling like hell. Anyhow, those things were always wet. You marched, your feet got wet, and there was no way to get them out of there. You had to dry them somehow. So you had to go through this ritual every night to dry your stuff. That's what caused most of the guys to get frostbite and get their feet screwed up. Mine are screwed up [due to diabetic complications], but they're not bad, there are a lot of guys worse off than me. You know how I feel? I can get along without [the VA doctors], really. There are guys that should be taken care of and thank God most of those guys are being taken care of. So I don't need that, I can take care of myself.

So anyhow, we started off on November 12 and we started going north, and we'd go in like two sections: I was in section one. We'd get on these trucks, on the six-by-sixes, and the tents were on there, and the 55-gallon drums of fuel oil. You know, everything you needed was in there. And you would go up and the first thing you did was put up a hospital tent. And that was 100 feet long, the first one, and then you would add to it as you go on. Then we would put up the pyramidal tents, you could put six guys in them. We put up those for the doctors and the officers, then finally we would get a chance to put our own up. And then a couple of days later the next group would come up with the remainders. Most of the tents were heated; where you had a lot of guys, you had the little tin stove. It could either run on oil or it could run on wood, or coal, or whatever you had, but it got so cold up there we were mixing gasoline with the oil and that was taboo and that was bad. A few tents burned up, but you had to do something. It was really cold up there.

The Chosen Reservoir

On November 27, 1950, Mao Zedong ordered a Chinese force of 120,000 to attack and annihilate 30,000 United Nations troops in North Korea. The surprise attack began a seventeen-day battle in subzero temperatures. A fortuitous UN breakout and withdrawal followed to the port of Hungnam, and the United Nations pulled back completely out of North Korea after inflicting heavy casualties.

We were always moving. The first group would move out and you may be at a place for a couple of days, you may be there a week. When we got up to the reservoir, up to the Chosen Reservoir, we were there a long time, I think it was maybe two weeks, I don't know. We didn't have it as bad as the guys up in there.

So our division went up there, and the 7th Marines were at Yudam-ni, which was northwest, I guess, from us. Then north from us was Hagaru-ri, and the 5th Marines were there and some of the 7th Marines, they were moving around. And some of the 1st Marines went up there, cause we traveled with the 1st Marine Regiment. So we set up at Kodari, which was, I think, twelve miles down the road from Hagaru-ri, and that's where we were. And a couple of times I went up to Hagaru-ri, me and another guy, with a jeep and a trailer because there was a water point up there. We didn't have a water point where we were, and we needed water for the chow lines. So a lot of times when you went up to Hagaru-ri, you had to stay there at night because they didn't want you on the road at night by yourself.

So we stayed, and a few nights we got hit. I think around the 27th of November, all hell broke loose, the old crap hit the fan that night. It was bad all over. And we started getting casualties and you couldn't believe it, the way they were coming in, my God! My job was, I worked outside, and when these guys would come in, we would bring them into the receiving tent and then somebody would take over from there. I didn't do any first aid to anybody there—I was just a pair of hands, and I had a gang that worked with me. Anyhow, that was my job, to unload these guys and then when they were going out, if they were leaving, I had the book. As we put a guy or two guys on a Bell & Howell helicopter, you know, the glass bubble above the skids, where you had half of a Stokes stretcher that had fabric on it to keep the guy warm, and it had a cover for it. So you put two guys on, one on each skid, and they had a little glass [window] where they could look out; they could see the rotors going around or something. But anyhow we would load these guys on, and then I would get their names, make sure that I had everything, and then they would take off.

I stayed there until we got out of the reservoir; we walked out. I don't know how far that was from where we were. It was quite a ways; we had to walk from Kodari to the railhead. What happened was the 7th Marines came from Yudam-ni to Hagaru-ri, and then they came down to Kodari, and then they started on down to go to Hungnam, the seaport, because that's where the ships were that were going to take us out. Then the 5th Marines came through us and went on down and then the 1st Marines fought the rear action on the way down. But the 5th Marines and the 7th were up on the ridges, and they kept the main supply route open so we could get out of there. Anyhow, they said, once you get down to the railhead, you can probably ride on a truck but until that time we had to walk.

It was a long walk, and it was cold; it was like twenty, thirty below zero. As long as you were moving, it didn't bother you. So by eleven o'clock at night, we get down to the railhead.

They said, 'Okay, you can get on the trucks now,' so we got on the trucks, and we started out. I don't think we went two or three miles and the truck in front of us got hit. It was carrying ammunition, so, oh boy, everything was cartwheels coming out of there, you know, all these explosives going off. So we got the hell off of the truck we were on, and it was a good thing we did, because there was 55-gallon drums of aviation fuel on that truck, and we didn't know it, but there were only three of us on the back of that truck.

Anyhow, they ambushed us, and we were lying in this ditch all night until the next morning. That's when my feet really frosted up, because my feet and my socks became wet. The next morning we got going again and we ended up down in Hungnam. They gave us something to eat and then we went aboard the ship.

Then we ended up down in Pusan. That was something, they just kept feeding us breakfast. All the time we were on that ship, all we were getting was breakfast, but it was good.

Chesty

You've heard of Chesty Puller? Well, Chesty had the 1st Marines, and he was right with us most of the time, you know. I knew who he was, you know, you would see him every day and say, 'Good morning, General,' or something, but I didn't shoot the shit with him or anything. But I was out on the strip there, where we had

TBFs or these Navy fighter bombers that would come in and they would take casualties out and I think you could get around six or eight people on them as long as they weren't stretcher cases; as long as they were ambulatory, you could stuff them in there. So we had those, we had some Piper Cubs, where you could put one guy in it, and we had the Bell helicopters that you could put two guys on. If they come in with a Sikorsky, that meant one stretcher case. You had to stick them in through one window and they stuck out the other side, and then you could have some guys go in there that were ambulatory. So anyhow, I worked for Doctor Adams, the guy who was in charge of all the moving of the patients and getting them out to the ships and stuff. This one day, we were out on the field, and he called me and there was a guy with him. So I went over, and it was Chesty Puller. Chesty said, 'Did Captain Barber go out?' So I look in the book, and I said, 'Yeah, we got him out yesterday. I put him on a Sikorsky, he was one of those guys that was jammed in.' Now we had the book and I had initialed it where I put him down, because it was important that you did those things.

So Chesty says, 'Thanks, Aspirin, now I believe it.' And I found out what had happened. He had asked Doctor Adams—of course I got the book, so Adams doesn't know. And he said, did Captain Barber go out? Adams said, 'Yeah, I think so,' and Chesty says, 'I don't care what you think, did he go out?'

The Stolen Cigars

I always had a lot of respect for Chesty. He was a good guy. I'll tell you an incident that happened one time. We had some real thieves in the medical company. Some of these corpsmen, they could get anything you wanted. They went out and they took a jeep, and they went to some Army place, and they got this big cardboard box and they brought it up to Dog Med and we opened it up, and it was full of boxes of cigars! And these were boxes of fifties, so everybody had cigars, everybody; they didn't charge anybody anything. So somehow the Army got ahold of the numbers that were on the jeep, wherever the hell they stole the cigars from.

This colonel and a couple of captains come up and they were at the 1st Marines, raising hell, and they wanted to find out who the hell stole their cigars. So Chesty didn't want to have anything to do with this kind of crap, he's sitting at his desk, with his shirt pocket full of cigars, the hot loot. I had to bring these two corpsmen, because they worked for me, I had to bring them down there, you know. So I go down and Chesty says to these two, 'Okay, I'm going to take care of everything.'

So this colonel keeps saying, 'Well, what are you going to do, are you going to take some kind of action?'

Chesty says, 'This is my command; I'm going to take the action I see fit.'

So here we are, in the asshole of the world, and he tells this Army colonel, he says, 'These men are restricted,' and that was the only punishment. But Jesus, there he is sitting with those cigars in his pocket, and he didn't smoke cigars! He would cut them up and put them in his pipe, then he would light them and smoke them that way. [*Chuckles*]

The Greek Air Force

After we got down from the Chosin, we started out again in the spring. I don't remember, it might have been around this place called Inje. I'm not sure, I lost track of where we were. Doctor Adams, the guy that I worked for, he knew I was Greek, see, and he said, 'We got the Greek Air Force coming in and they got a C-47 and they're going to come in.' Now, we don't have any communications with them, but we'll lay out panels. I had myself, and a black kid; there was an Army outfit there now and they were all blacks. And they had these very good ambulances, boy, they were better than anything we had. They had good heaters in them, and they could really hold a lot of people. So we had this black kid, and come to find out he was from Troy, New York. So he and I became friends. So we go out to the airstrip in the morning, and we lay out the panels and then we would wait there. These Greeks would come around, they would do a loop, they would fly around, and when they would see the orange panels lying out, they would land. When they made that loop, we would radio back and say, 'Okay, start moving the casualties,' because they were like twenty miles away, maybe twenty-five. So they'd start them out in those good ambulances that were well heated, and they would line up and they could take something like forty-something and put them on those C-47s.

And they were stacked in there, man, they had the straps hanging down, you know, and the stretchers would go in. Then they would take off with them.

Those Greeks would always say, 'Come with us, come with us!'

'What do you mean come on with you?'

'We are going to [a couple other places], then we end up in Japan and then we come back and do this route again.'

I said, 'Look, I'm not going with you guys. I mean, one of these days, somebody's going to come looking for me and I'm not going to be around, and then my wife's going to get a letter, "Your Steve is gone," or whatever.'

They finally understood, but they would bring me back a bottle of whiskey or something from Japan. They were good guys. You know what's funny about it? Most of them could speak English. They could speak English so well they had the limey accent, because that's where they were trained.

The Chinese on the Mountain

So it was a good job, I enjoyed it. But one day we got out there and it was me and the black kid and a guy named Gunther, we used to call him 'Gunny.' And somebody else, I forget who the other guy was, but we went out there and were laying our panels out and these Chinese opened up on us. They were up on the side of the hill, in the woods there. They opened up on us, there were only four or five of us out there, whatever the hell it was. Then this other guy came with a jeep, he was going to help. He gets out of the jeep, and we were trying to yell to him, but he was quite a ways away from us. And Jesus, didn't he get shot. He gets hit right in the head, aw, man, it killed him just like that.

We had already radioed back and then they sent a squad of Marines down, and they went up and they went through, and they cleaned those guys out. But that was the only time we really got harassed on the airstrip like that. Most of the time we were all right.

When we were at Kodari, we could see the Chinese up on the mountain there. Now, the only way you could see them is if they turned around and faced you, because then you would see that their faces were dark. They were wearing white parkas and their rifles were white, everything was white. And you couldn't see them, they would move around up there, and you wouldn't see them until they turned around and faced you and then you could see a dark face. And it was a game of, you know, 'Don't bother us and we won't bother you,' and that's the way it went for the longest time. But every once in a while, we would get up in the morning and there would be three or four Chinese sitting outside of our tents there at Kodari, and their feet would be huge. They were wearing those goddamn sneakers. We had trouble with the shoes we were wearing, but these guys were wearing sneakers and their feet were just frozen solid. And they were in bad shape, and they couldn't take that cold any better than we could.

I don't care what anybody says, a lot of guys would say, 'Oh, they're tougher than us or they can withstand that cold, and we can't.' You know, that's a lot of bull. I don't know. And a lot of times they would turn our prisoners loose. When the going got too rough for them, and the Marines were on hot pursuit of their butts, they would turn our guys loose; they would shag ass but leave the Marines there. And that's how we got them back, and they hadn't been too bad to them. In most cases, they were pretty good to them. They gave them rice to eat; you had to eat what they did. They would have a big sock hanging around their neck full of rice. How the hell they ate that stuff, I don't know.

Blood

In Korea, there was more whole blood [available]. In World War II, it was mostly plasma, I never saw much blood. Of course, I wasn't in the rear. We carried plasma. We carried two units; one was the dry unit, and the other was the water unit, and you had to mix them together. Luckily, I always had some Marine that would carry one of my units and I would carry the other one. We would put it together when necessary. It was tough because when a guy is wounded, all his veins, they flatten out, and it's hard to get one. The kits that they had in World War II, the needle they had, it was like an eight-penny nail, for Christ's sake, it was big. And it wasn't very sharp, and you had to stick a guy three or four times to finally get it into him. In the Korean War, I think the needles were better than what we had in World War II. But there was the whole blood, and that was a problem when it was cold, it would stiffen up. What you had to do was put mineral oil on the tygon tubing, and you would hook the guy up, and then you would have to have some guy strip it, like you're milking a cow, to push the blood through, otherwise it would congeal. I don't know, I heard some of the doctors say, 'Thank God there was this freezing,' because wounds would freeze up and there wasn't as much loss of blood as there was in World War II.

'The Chosin Few'

Anyhow, that was a hundred years ago, as far as I'm concerned. I belong to the 'Chosin Few,' and it's a lot of good guys, but there are a lot of these guys, that's all they have in life, is that [time]. I feel sorry for them, really; I mean, that's all they do. I've got one guy, he constantly calls me up [to talk about it]. And I keep thinking, 'Jesus, don't you have another life?' Two weeks out of your life was up there in the Chosin, and that's all the hell you got left?

'You Play the Hand You're Dealt'

I don't know, thank God I was not wounded. Somehow, I got through two wars without being wounded, though I did come close a few times. I think [my time in the service] put me behind quite a bit. Not so much during World War II, because I didn't have anything else to do, okay? But during the Korean War, I was married, I had a two-year-old kid. I was working for the Knolls Atomic Power Laboratory, and I went and I told them, 'Hey, my reserve unit got called and I'm going to have to go.' We were on active duty as of August 7, I guess it was. This guy, I can't remember what his name was, he's all, 'Oh, you can't go!' I was on a fire department, we had this special training, you know, because we were the first people in a situation where we might find a fire, or where there was radioactive material, you know, stuff like that. And we were being trained for all this, so we had kind of an important job to do. So this guy says, 'They can't take you.'

I said, 'Fine, one way or the other.'

Then he comes up and he says, 'You got to go.'

He said, 'I thought I could get you out of it.'

I said, 'Well, you thought wrong, Uncle Sam is thinking different.' And my attitude was, hey, I signed up for this. I was free, white, and twenty-one, and I knew what I was signing. I knew what I was getting into, and if I had to go, I had to go, and I would make the best of it.

You play the hand you're dealt.

Steve T. Jordan was 89 when he passed on May 5, 2014.

CHAPTER SIXTEEN

The Invasion Radioman III

Paul Elisha

Okinawa

We were told it was going to be a rough one. First of all, it was going to be different than any of the other islands. It was the northern Pacific. The Japanese had a long time to prepare. I personally landed with the 2nd Marine Division; we were attached to them for the landing. Some of my units went with [another] infantry division, which also landed with a pincer movement. They were landing on different parts of the island.

There, the landing was a really tough landing because, for one thing, it's a very mountainous island. The Japanese really dug in caves. They also had the heaviest artillery we'd ever come up against, 220 caliber guns, and they were on the sides of the opposite mountain. They'd shoot over the mountains at you.

Humor gets pretty dark with each passing campaign. You're making jokes, toward the end, about life and death. I can't remember any specifics, but I know of this. You know when the humor would really get going toward the end like when we were going into Okinawa, which was really a rough landing. As you'd hit the line of demarcation where the landing craft would speed up and streak for the beach, we would be down and the guys would say, 'Hey, you're got yourself soiled. You got your diapers on?' and stuff like that. Guys would josh back and forth with all kinds of black humor, so to speak. You did it because you were scared shitless, mostly. You never got over that feeling. That last dash to the beach, you do it with your heart in your mouth always because once that ramp is down, there's nowhere to go but straight ahead.

They let us come ashore, but almost immediately after landing, they opened up with everything they had. So the beach was really messy. Mortars as I recall, 220 caliber shells, and a lot of machine-gun fire. It was rough to get off the beach. We did our usual thing. We found a fairly sheltered area, dug in, set up the radio, and began sending messages back for fire support for whatever was needed. Eventually, they did get off the beach and we stayed with that.

It was a tough day, the toughest of any that I recall. I know I read one official account that said that it wasn't so bad, that they let [us] land, but it was a bad landing. They were all bad landings, but they were good if you could walk away from them.

Meeting Ernie Pyle

I was on Okinawa for, I would say, a couple of weeks. After I was there a few days and we got pulled back for rest and a hot meal, I had an interesting experience because I was also serving in a dual capacity for the unit. I had been asked to be a combat correspondent for *Yank Magazine*.

When we had gotten pulled back, I got called to the CO's office and he said, 'I'm going to need you for a couple of days.'

I said, 'What for?'

He said, 'Seems there's this guy, this reporter. What's his name, Pyle? Ernie Pyle is here. They need somebody to take him around to the different units around the island and for interviews. So, while he's on this side of the island, you're it.'

Next thing I know, they introduced me to this little guy and it's Ernie Pyle—*the* Ernie Pyle.

He was great. I spent two days with him, we got to talk a lot. Of course, I took him to some of the different outfits. We had a jeep and a driver, and he interviewed them, and as a matter of fact, I was with him when he got on the boat. You know, they sent a small party over to this small island called Ie Shima, which was just off of Okinawa. And he thought that would be an interesting thing to go on, because they told him it was just going to be a small operation. They didn't even know how many [Japanese troops there were], or if there was anybody over there. They were just a few people going to mop it up, and a sniper killed him.

Oh, he was so much like an ordinary GI. First of all, he hated being everywhere he went. He really didn't like it at all, but he did it. He did this because he had to, you know, and he rarely did it unless it was in the context of setting the stage for what he was doing. He talked to officers, but he was really the enlisted man's journalist. He talked to ordinary dog faces, you know? And they loved him for it because he told it like it was. [He was a good reporter] basically because he got all the facts straight. He did not accept handouts from the brass. He would talk only to the enlisted people, very rarely talked to some brass; there had to be people with them, the enlisted people. He got the unvarnished facts from the GIs. He also knew how to find the human interest in every story, but I literally was one of the people that sort of walked with him down [to them]. They were loading up to go to Ie Shima, which was going to be a clean-up operation, just a couple of patrols really and he went with them. I helped put his gear aboard the landing craft. That's the last I saw of him.

*

I remember one of the treks when I was taking him from one place to another. We got to talking, and he asked, 'What are you going to do when you get out of here?' You know, when this is over.

I said, 'I don't know, I'll probably go on with my writing and stuff.'

He said, 'Check out Indiana University. Great school', he said, 'it's really good.'

Well, as it turned out, when I got out of the service, I sent four letters of application: one to Northwestern, one to the University of Kentucky, one to NYU, and one to Indiana. And they accepted me, Indiana accepted me, so I ended up there. I was the first recipient of the Sigma Delta Chi Ernie Pyle Memorial Award for reporting at IU. I sat at his desk at the Indiana University *Daily Student* in my senior year. And so there's an eerie connection that I have with Ernie Pyle.

*

We idolized [FDR]. I was on Okinawa when Roosevelt died. By the way, that was a strange situation because it's just about—I'm trying to remember the juxtaposition, I can't remember if it was just before or just after, but Simon Bolivar Buckner Jr., the [Commander] of the Tenth Army, the general who ran that operation in Okinawa, was killed on Okinawa... And so that was an eerie feeling, and for me even more so... [because] you had Buckner, Roosevelt, and Ernie Pyle.[25] It was almost as if everyone died all at once. Great grief. I witnessed men openly crying, and for us, especially in the 75th JASCO, we were particularly moved because while we were in Hawaii, before we went off between the Makin and Kwajalein assaults, Roosevelt came to Hawaii to meet with MacArthur and

---

[25] *Buckner, Roosevelt, and Ernie Pyle*-FDR died on April 12. Ernie Pyle was killed by a sniper on April 18. Buckner was killed on June 18 when a Japanese artillery shell landed nearby, and fragments struck him in the chest.

Nimitz, and one of the things that occurred there was that we were the honor guard.[26] We were chosen as the honor guard, and they did a special thing where his open car was pulled up for a review, and we were the honor guard for that, and he gave us a presidential unit citation for what we had done up to that point, and it's one of the medals I never collected.

GI Reporter

If you were a GI and you were a reporter, it wasn't like being a [civilian] correspondent like those other people were. You still have to do what you have to do, and as a matter of fact, some of the officers looked on it as, you know, you're looking to get something extra special. 'You, who do you think you are?' You know, that sort of thing. I got a byline and I still somewhere have my letter of commendation when it was over saying, 'you guys have done a great job and we thank you for it' and et cetera.

We were censored. We had received a set of instructions on how-to, you know, what not to write, and you were supposed to follow them. We pretty much did. You know, we weren't out to scoop the US Army in those days and there were some differences, really strong differences compared to what would come later. Let's say [as opposed to] Vietnam and those wars, everybody really believed in this, in that war, and you didn't want to do anything to foul it up. You know, you did what you had to do. And I think that,

---

[26] *Roosevelt came to Hawaii to meet with MacArthur and Nimitz-* Pacific Strategy Conference, July 1944. Admiral Leahy and General MacArthur were also present. "MacArthur decided to upstage Roosevelt by arriving in a long open limousine with elaborate motorcycle escort, accepting the welcome from the cheering crowd. Even before he arrived at Hawaii, he was already unhappy for being forced to leave his troops to attend this 'picture-taking junket,' as he commented." Source: Pacific Strategy Conference, World War II Database, ww2db.com/battle_spec.php?battle_id=75.

even among correspondents, that was pretty much the rule. I got to meet some of them, but, you know, they're very hazy right now. You have to understand that there wasn't a great deal to see. This was the thing with Ernie Pyle. He sought out enlisted men to talk to; the average war correspondent during WWII went with the brass, they got their briefings on things. They weren't allowed that close to the action, really. I would say D-Day was probably the most participatory action they got into.

[As a reporter for *Yank*] we weren't able to tell anything ahead of time, but after the fact, you could write it up. You could interview people, you could write up events that took place in any of the campaigns you were on, and then you would submit them, of course, to the *Yank* people, who would run them through the censor. Then they'd end up in *Yank Magazine*. It was like *Stars and Stripes*, except instead of a newspaper, it was a magazine format. I enjoyed it because it gave me a chance to write. I did it until I went home.

Pushing the Odds

The Japanese soldier was tough as nails. Committed, literally committed. The only time I recall seeing any prisoners at all was after Kwajalein, I think there were five or six that were taken, and that's because they were wounded and hadn't the resources to kill themselves. Everywhere else they would fight until they were beaten and then they would die. On Okinawa, for instance, when we finally isolated them at the far end of the island, we had bullhorns and translators who tried to tell them. By the way, in Okinawa, there were also Japanese civilians who were sent there to colonize the place and they were with the troops. We tried to coax them to give themselves up. Some of them killed themselves with hand grenades and others went to a cliff at the end of the island and just jumped down on the rocks and were killed. Mothers with little children in their arms did that. So they were really committed people.

*

We were pretty lucky; I'd say we had about somewhere between thirty and forty percent casualties, but many of those I found out later; you'd see a guy taken away and you wouldn't know what became of him. I later found out that not as many were fatal as many other units were. We were lucky. By rights, if you look at the odds, going into that many landings, we had had eight combat landings, and a number of us like myself were literally in the first wave of every landing. We would talk about it. The last couple I remember we were saying, 'You know, if we come out of this one, it's a miracle,' because we were pushing the odds.

Mr. Elisha's story will continue in the final section.

PART FIVE

FINAL THOUGHTS

"I think that a commander is faced with a decision of what must be done at that given moment to achieve an objective and end that battle or that war. You cannot expect him to think, 'Well, we're going to kill all those people,' when he's looking at his own people being killed at the same time. I mean, what's a good killing, and what's a bad killing?
We should have thought of all that before we began at all."

—US Army Radioman, World War II

CHAPTER SEVENTEEN

Occupation Duty

We are gathered here, representatives of the major warring powers, to conclude a solemn agreement whereby peace may be restored.

The issues involving divergent ideals and ideologies have been determined on the battlefields of the world, and hence are not for our discussion or debate.

Nor is it for us here to meet, representing as we do a majority of the peoples of the earth, in a spirit of distrust, malice, or hatred.

But rather it is for us, both victors and vanquished, to rise to that higher dignity which alone befits the sacred purposes we are about to serve, committing all of our peoples unreservedly to faithful compliance with the undertakings they are here formally to assume.

It is my earnest hope, and indeed the hope of all mankind, that from this solemn occasion a better world shall emerge out of the blood and carnage of the past—a world founded upon faith and understanding, a world dedicated to the dignity of man and the fulfillment of his most cherished wish for freedom, tolerance, and justice.

—REMARKS BY GENERAL DOUGLAS MACARTHUR, SURRENDER CEREMONY

On September 2, 1945, Admiral "Bull" Halsey's flagship *USS Missouri* was in Tokyo Bay awaiting the arrival of the Japanese delegation with General MacArthur and Admiral Nimitz aboard, positioned in the exact spot where Commodore Matthew C. Perry had anchored on his first visit to Japan in 1853, and flying his original 31-star flag. The Japanese delegation was escorted promptly aboard at 9:00 a.m. and at MacArthur's invitation, signed the terms of surrender. In the United States and Europe, it was six years to the day that the bloodiest conflict in human history had begun.

Mitchell Morse was just fifteen years of age when the United States declared war on Japan. He enlisted in the spring of 1944, after an earlier admission into the Army Specialized Training Reserve Program, which he did not like. Still, he found himself an officer in Japan just as the fighting ended, as part of the Army of Occupation. A free spirit, he relates his experiences commanding an all-Black detachment, the racism his soldiers encountered, and his opinion of the now-conquered people of Japan, including a tearful reunion four decades later with the Japanese teenager who served him as a houseboy.

Mitchell Morse

I was born March 10, 1926, in the infamous place, Brooklyn, New York. I was with a friend in Brooklyn [when I heard about

Pearl Harbor]. We both used to breed tropical fish, and we were waiting on one of his fancy guppies to give birth. And we were sitting looking into his fish tank when we heard it come over the radio; it seemed like total insanity to me. Totally unexpected and a real shocker.

I was in college at the time, at age fifteen. I went into the Army Specialized Training Reserve Program, and I spent three months in Princeton. I had a lousy record there since it was mostly science, which was not my bag. And from there I went into basic training on April 9, 1944, at Fort Bragg, North Carolina.

It was pretty awful. Aside from the physical rigors, which I was not used to, I couldn't get used to the attitude southerners had towards anybody who was not from the South. And my biggest shock was when one of the guys who I was taking basic training with, apparently, he had owned a dry-cleaning store, and he enthusiastically told us the great joy he had when some black guy came in and wanted to know where his clothing was, and it wasn't ready. And the man said something about it, and he took such a great pleasure in physically throwing him out. And then, going into bus stations, and seeing the isolated restrooms. And the way it was, just quite a culture shock for somebody from New York.

During basic, I decided it was much better to be an officer than an enlisted man, so I applied for OCS. Before that, the government had started a new program whereby they were taking ten people from throughout the services, all over the country, into West Point, directly, without the usual senatorial approval and recommendations and so on. I applied for that. I figured that's even better, four years in college, by then the war will be over, and I'll spend a couple of extra years in the Army and be on my way.

Training to be an Officer

Well, I almost got through to it; I was narrowed down to the last handful in Fort Bragg, and then, probably because I was a smartass in those days, I was not accepted. So the next best thing was to get to be an officer another way. So I applied for OCS and was accepted; I went to Fort Benning, Georgia, Benning School for Boys. That was tough physically, very rigorous; I think I was eighteen at the time. Most of the guys had been in the Army for some time. A lot of them had been in combat overseas as enlisted men, then came back to try to get a commission. I was, if not the youngest, one of the youngest in the entire class. We started the class with 300 and graduated with a class of 150.

[The training was] exceptional. The physical training was excellent, and whatever training you can get for leadership was excellent too, although I don't think that's something you can [really] train somebody for—either it's within or it's not.

I spent a year in Camp Gordon, Georgia. That was a lot of hard work, but that turned out to be fun; I enjoyed that a great deal. Giving classes in hand-to-hand combat, I weighed about 135 pounds and one of my good buddies was 6' 3", much larger. He used to attack me from the rear with a knife and I would flip [him] in moving my shoulder, much to the surprise of all the trainees, and much to my surprise as well. I used to take a particular delight [in that].

'An Education Beyond Belief'

[After that training], the war was still on in the Far East and the islands, and I received orders to go overseas to fight in these various godawful island battles. I got to Fort Ord in California, and they give you a last-minute physical inspection before you ship. I'd had my shipping orders already, but they discovered I had a hernia, maybe from carrying a footlocker in one hand and a duffle bag over the other, whatever the reason was. So they pulled me out, stuck me in the hospital, operated on me, and by the time I was out of the hospital, the war was over.

Instead of going into combat, I spent about ten or eleven months in Japan [as part of the occupation force]. That was an experience, an education beyond belief. First of all, to discover that the Japanese were not the horrible people, that the everyday man in the street was not the horrible person we were trained to believe. We went over there, obviously, 'to civilize them.' That's what we were trained to do, to go over there and teach them what the world was all about. But the average Japanese [person] was a very kind, gentle soul. And I liked most of them, and I had a very close feeling for the country at large and the culture at large. Being a believer in reincarnation, I kind of figured well, maybe I'd been here in a previous lifetime.

I was a second lieutenant. I didn't get to be first lieutenant until they kicked me out of the Army, well, not kicked me out, but finally got out of the Army.[27] I never got promoted while I was in Japan because I was a bit of a cut-up, so when I was due to be promoted, the colonel and I didn't get along too well, so he always passed me by.

'They Thought I was Sent from Heaven'

At first, I was a company commander of an infantry platoon in the 34th Regiment of the 24th Infantry Division. And being where we were, in order to facilitate the cleaning of the men's clothes, there was a Quartermaster Mobile Laundry Detachment which used to service the entire regiment, clean the clothes and so on.

---

[27] *got out of the Army-* Mr. Morse served in the Army Reserve until 1983.

Well, the lieutenant in charge of the quartermaster detachment had to go home on emergency furlough. His mother was in a hospital, severely ill, so they needed somebody to take over temporarily. Being in the infantry, hearing 'quartermaster,' I immediately volunteered, and being the most recent arrival to the regiment, I was put in charge. I stayed right on the same base, and I was put in charge. And the name of this, to give you an idea of the time, was the "354th Quartermaster Mobile Laundry Detachment 'parentheses' Colored". That was part of the official designation. So here I was, commanding officer of a laundry detachment with all black guys, I guess, no, I don't know what you'd say nowadays. In those days it was 'Colored,' now it's 'Black' or 'Afro-American.' In any event, I had this crew with whom I got along famously; I used to play poker with them. Officers had a liquor ration, and I got a certain amount of beer and a bottle of booze every once in a while, which I gave to my guys, because I didn't drink, so they thought I was sent from heaven. [*Laughs*] Used to shoot craps with them too. I forgot all the terminology but some of the [craps vernacular] was just great, for when you 'speak to the dice.' That was an experience unto itself, a total education.

When they were by themselves doing their job, [morale was] terrific, but we were attached to a Southern regiment. And we used to get monthly rations, so many candy bars, so many cans of beer, so many soap, this and that. And when the rations came in, everybody would get in a long line; it would snake tail all the way out. I forget who was in charge of the PX, some major from down South. And no matter how long the line was, how early they got there, he always made my guys get at the end of the line. So if there were a hundred of my guys there, and they got on a line, then another hundred [white soldiers] came, [this major would] make my guys get to the very tail end of the line. It reached the point to where I got into a fist fight with him over this. Which you're not supposed to

do with [your superior officer], I hate to use the term 'superior officer,' he was [downright] inferior; he just happened to be a higher-
ranking officer.

Of course, my guys then felt like I was family. 'Hey, Lieutenant,
do you want us to get him for you?' You know, they'd have left him
lying somewhere; nobody had ever fought their battles for them before. So their morale was pretty good. As I said before, I gave them
my liquor ration and beer ration, whatever it was, used to play
poker with them.

The Japanese Houseboy

I was nineteen at the time, and I acquired my Japanese houseboy,
Yukihiro Miada. He was sixteen, I was nineteen, but I was the big
honcho. He drove me crazy, though. He'd shine my shoes, he'd hold
my shirt while I dressed, and I almost dropped him a couple of times
because when I got out of the shower, he insisted upon toweling me
down. This was just too much, I couldn't stand it. But he was absolutely adamant about it.

During that period of time, a good buddy of mine who was still
with the infantry regiment I had been with, he and I were at a track
meet at a nearby town, meeting with another regimental track
team. We arrived there by train, and in the train station there were
a number of Japanese war orphans, just sort of living in the station,
waifs with distended stomachs from not eating enough, and so on.
So when we arrived, all we had with us was some chewing gum and
candy, which we gave to these little boys. Two days later, we came
back, and there they were, chewing on the same chewing gum. So,
through an interpreter, we found out that they had no parents, that
they were lost during the war, so we took [two little boys] back with

us, and they lived with us for many months until we both came back to the States.

When we got them, they were all scruffy with distended stomachs, and then we fattened them up, had little suits made for them by the local tailor, and they lived with us for a while. That was an exciting experience. And Miada San, we gave him the nickname of Jacko. Jacko not only took care of me, but he also took care of the two little boys. So that was an experience unto itself.

An Extended Stay

Under the point system then you got rotated based on the number of points. About a month or two before I was supposed to come home, the colonel in charge of the regiment called me up and said, 'Morse, you're short on training officers, I want you to train [more guys].'

I said, 'I'm sorry, Colonel, can't do that, I'm responsible for $500,000 worth of equipment,' and I gave them all the excuses why I couldn't do it. Well, there had been a Seabee outfit not too far away, and when they were disbanded and all went home, they left a lot of vehicles around. So I picked up a jeep, and the motor pool, painted it OD for me, and put 354th Quartermaster Mobile Laundry Detachment [logo] on it. So I had my own vehicle, but all of a sudden that jeep, which I had acquired several months before, [became a problem]. The colonel was going to bring me up on court-martial charges for stealing a jeep, which I'd been using for months and months; it was common knowledge. And with officers, it's a general court-martial, so it's serious stuff. So, I had my choice of a general court-martial or spending thirty days confined to officers' quarters or barracks; the thirty days went past the time I was supposed to come home. So I had to stay there an extra three weeks because he was going to teach me a lesson, which he did.

Transitioning to Home

Anyhow, I'd already registered to go back [to school], because I had finished two years of college before I enlisted. I was one of those precocious kids, I got into college at 15. So by the time I enlisted, just before I was eighteen, I'd finished two years of college. So when I went back, I got discharged in Fort Dix. I went back to school because of the two years before, I accumulated enough credits for one more year while having gotten the credits from Princeton University and then for OCS and they gave you credits for various things. So I only had one year and an extra course to go to graduate, which I did. And I got a job and married a year later at the age of 21, married to the same beautiful lady who came in [today] with me. That was fifty-three years ago. So, at the age of 21, I had been working for a year, and graduated from college and spent 33 months in the Army. So, it was a very busy youth that I spent, very productive.

When I started out in college, I was majoring in accounting. Which, for me, was kind of strange, but in those days, you majored in what you thought you could make a living at. So after much discussion with my parents, we decided, well, accountants always make a living; even during the Depression, accountants made a living. So I started out majoring in accounting. While I was in the Army, I realized that was not for me. So I went back to school, I switched to foreign trade, graduating with a BBA, bachelor of business administration, majoring in foreign trade. I got a job with an import-export company, spent six years with this company and somewhere along the way decided that was not the way I wanted to spend the rest of my life, either.

Then I had this revolutionary idea, revolutionary for a Depression baby. What would you like to do? Well, what I'd like to do is be a sculptor. Yeah, but you're not good enough to make a living being a sculptor. Well, what's next? A painter? No, you're not good enough to be a painter. So I did the next best thing. I decided if I couldn't sell my own paintings and sculptures, I'd try to sell somebody else's.

In 1953, I started the first traveling art gallery in the United States on wheels. I bought a brand-new station wagon—it was a Chevy, three thousand bucks—and I went around to the different artists in Greenwich Village and I got art on consignment. [At that time], after the war, there was a lot of construction going on all over Long Island, nearby Connecticut, nearby New Jersey, so I made flyers on a mimeograph machine and I went around myself to all these new developments, and on foot I stuck a flyer in every mailbox. I would get calls from people, and I would go to the house, and assuming for your house you needed a painting in the living room, I'd run in and out 10-20 times, holding paintings up over the sofa until you saw something you liked. Through this, I got recommendations, now I picked up a couple of interior designer accounts. Now I was steady with repeat business; by this time the station wagon was so full you could barely see out the back, and we had two infants only eighteen months apart. We'd drive around, Ellie was next to me, I'd be driving, she'd be in the front seat, and we took the two kids with us with all these racks of paintings bouncing around; once we stopped for a traffic light, and things kept sliding over the top, and hit one of us in the back of the head.

We started getting worried about the kids in the car so we said, 'Well, it's time, we're gonna have to plant roots somewhere,' so we picked what we considered to be an affluent town where I'd done a lot of business, a general area where we opened up a retail shop [specializing in what] was called 'wall décor,' all kinds of things for [the home, and it all grew from then on].

'From Smart-Ass Boy to A Man'

[My World War II experience] turned me from a smart-ass boy into a man. It was miserable, and it was horribly rotten, but very beneficial. It was very positive, absolutely. Japanese people are different, and I have the same opinion today—the average Japanese, the man on the street, is a kind, gentle, considerate soul, but it's the upper echelon corruption there that makes everyone here seem like they're amateurs. In Japan, everything is, you know, one hand washes the other, and they take care of each other, and the average person has no say, but they keep voting for the same political group for over fifty years now. Everything is done for the protection of the entrepreneur, the big businessman, and that's why it's been so difficult for our companies and European companies to open anything up over there; they place so many restrictions, so many barriers, that it makes it impossible.

Reunion

Forty-one years [after the war], my daughter became a member of what the Japanese call the JET program, Japanese-English Teachers. She had been teaching English as a second language in Manhattan, in the World Trade Towers. And she found out about this opportunity to go over there. They were recruiting teachers from all over the world, but they wanted native-speaking English, so that the children could learn the vernacular—not just the stiff formal textbook English—which most of the teachers taught and spoke themselves. They got them from the United States, England, New Zealand, Australia, all the English-speaking countries. So she'd been over there about a year at the time when we decided to go over and visit.

We were touring here and there, and I arranged the schedule so we could go to the old town where I had been when Jacko was my houseboy. And I remembered his address from then, because for several years after I came back, we had corresponded, though of course with time we lost track of one another. I remembered that and I still remember the address to this day, 569 Yushiro [Street]. So we took a detour to Himeji, and we had a Japanese interpreter. We went to the town hall to try to find him, a really remote possibility.

[The dwelling at] 569 Yushiro Street had burnt to the ground years ago, and now there was a gasoline station there. But the people at the home office in Himeji were incredible. The chief of the whole village hall, the town clerk or whatever he was, he had three people going through all the old records. They tracked down everybody who had lived on that block at that time, called them all up, and served us tea in between, fussed all over us. About two hours later, one of them located where Jacko's brother lived. He gave us the phone number. We left there and we were really excited about the possibility of finding him, but we couldn't get through to the brother for some time. I don't know, the family must have been out working.

Finally, late in the day, about three, four o'clock, we got through, using the interpreter, of course. We spoke to Jacko's sister-in-law and got his telephone number. Hurray, my God, it looks like we're getting close to finding him, forty-two years later. So, we left a message with his sister-in-law [giving her] the hotel we were staying at, which I think was in Osaka, and to please call us there; I had to leave the following morning, and I didn't want to be this close without seeing him! We don't hear from him all afternoon. Then, lo and behold, we're in our room getting dressed to go down and have dinner, and the phone rings; he called up! I'm jumping up and down with joy; I get all teary just thinking about it. It turns out he was downstairs in the lobby, with his wife. [*Gets emotional, asks for the camera to be turned off momentarily so he can compose himself*]

So, we went downstairs and had a fantastic reunion, we had dinner together, and his English, although not perfect, was excellent. And he had been from—I found out later on—a well-established family. His father had been a Japanese military officer. His older brother had gone to the military academy and Jacko had been destined to go to the military academy, but the war ended, and he ended up with me instead.

After that, we were in touch with him on a regular basis, and a year later, my daughter married a Japanese high school English teacher. And if anybody would have told me when I was there earlier that I would have a Japanese son-in-law, and two Japanese grandchildren, I'd have had them committed in a straitjacket. Remember I went over there to 'civilize' those people, me and everybody else [in the Army of Occupation].

Jacko came to the wedding; he was part of our side of the family. I don't know if you know it, but Japanese weddings, even if they have 500 people, for the actual ceremony, there are only fifteen people from each side of the family, maximum of thirty people, no matter how many people are waiting outside. So Ellie and I were there, my son was there, a Japanese art dealer friend with whom I was doing business with in New York. Jacko was there with his daughter and wife, from our side of the family. We went back the following year, for the birth of our first grandson, and Jacko was there again, bouncing my grandson on his knee, and like an uncle, perhaps. So that story had a very happy ending.

Of course, ever since then, we've been going back. See, in the past twelve years, we've been there about sixteen times. Totally unexpected, as I say, when I was there, and if anybody would have suggested the possibility to me, of what would have happened years later, I would have had myself or them committed.

CHAPTER EIGHTEEN

The Invasion Radioman IV

Paul Elisha

After Okinawa, we went back to Luzon, which is actually outside of Manila. They put us in a tent encampment there and we were waiting for orders. And as a matter of fact, we had begun map readings, so we were restricted to the encampment. They covered this with barbed wire and sent MPs to guard the area. Well, once you started looking at the maps of the next place you were going to go, that became sensitive. Literally, I remember the day that they dropped the bomb on Hiroshima. We were reading maps of Tokyo Harbor when the bomb was dropped.

We knew—the word went like wildfire, you know. But particularly for us, we were again going to be in the first wave to land and we were going to be the communications people for that landing. We would have gone right into Tokyo Harbor; we began to get orientation for what would have been the landing on Japanese soil itself. I don't think many of us would have come back from that.

*

[We had known the war was winding down]. You hear reports, you know it. For instance, we knew VE Day came when we were up to our eyeballs in battle on Okinawa. In some ways, you get more apprehensive because you're this close to what you think could be the end, and what you say is, 'Shit, if I get it now...' That's really miserable. It's a funny thing. I've thought about this, and I have no idea what it's like now in combat. But one of the things I can never remember is the people I was with not doing 150% of the job they were sent there to do on every single operation. I mean, you would go beyond. You would rack your brain on how to get it done better, how to do it better. For me, I have to say this, as you can tell I have a great affection for the man who was the sergeant of my unit. He said an interesting thing. I don't know how he got this wisdom because he'd never been in combat before. He'd been in the service because he was a National Guardsman who got mobilized.

He said, 'Look, Elisha. Let me tell you something. You keep your mind on what the job we got to get done here is and that'll get you through. Don't think about all the other stuff, what might happen. This is what's got to happen. Stick with me.' He was hell for leather, by the way. He got rid of his carbine, he got himself a Thompson submachine gun which he always carried into battle. He was always in the thick of where the fighting was, and I was like within a foot of him at all times. After a while, there are like, what would you call it, talismans? For some reason, he was my immortal sergeant. My talisman. I felt as long as I stuck with Elmer, I'd make it back. Now, we both made it back, but what I would do largely, at the moment of greatest fear, is to concentrate on the job having to be done, and it worked.

[Our biggest motivation in combat] was getting it over with. The other thing our lieutenant used to say was, 'Just remember, the quicker we get these guys out of here, the quicker we beat them and take this place, the quicker we can go home.' He would say that before every landing. If you kept that in mind, that was your motivation.

[You depended on your buddies a lot.] We worked in teams, always. At night, especially in the initial stages of the campaign, we would set up our perimeters and they were all foxholes. Either you were singly very close together or you were two people and two people and two people. So, you've learned to work together. The other thing was on most of the ones in Attu, Kiska, Makin, Kwajalein, and Aitape. When we landed, the first couple of nights silence was the rule and you did not use your weapon. The order was, 'You do not use your weapon unless you absolutely must as a last resort.' You had a knife which you were to use, or you were to use the butt of the weapon, but you didn't shoot because that could set off a whole bunch of stuff and nobody would know where anybody was. Anyway, so not being able to use conventional methods, you had to rely on all sorts of things, which meant you relied on each other, whatever signals you set up, whatever code you set up.

'The Style of the Times'

In my unit, I was one of four people who were Jewish. There were guys that I literally went through hell with. We would share foxholes, we would repel banzai charges together. When it was all over, they call me 'Jew boy.' Oh, yeah. 'Hey, Jew boy. You're going to town tonight?' It was discrimination, tinged with some camaraderie. But for instance, after Okinawa, I can remember back when we went back to the Philippines, and we were waiting to see if we were going to go to Japan or not. We were in a big tent, and I can remember a poker game started. One of the staff sergeants by the name of Noyer, who was one of the Jews with me, was in that poker game and they began to talk about going home and getting civilian clothes. One of them said, 'We'll go to one of those sheeny shops in Brooklyn,' because Noyer was from Brooklyn, 'and see if we can get a good deal, jew him down on a suit of clothes.' Then they began talking about different experiences of how they were gypped by Jews. A fight broke out in which I was a party, and there were like two or three of us against twenty. My sergeant, Elmer Kaminski, came in and knocked some heads together and told them off, in effect saying, 'These guys saved your ass not too long ago! What the hell's the matter with you assholes?'

Those things did happen. By the way, we had with us two Navajo Indian radio operators also. Code talkers. They were great. They would talk back and forth in their language. So that way, we knew that we weren't going to be intercepted. I got to know one of them pretty well largely because several times, I helped him home when we were still in the States and when we were in Hawaii. We used to help each other a lot that way. If somebody had a little too much to drink or something, we'd see that they all got home okay. They were both called 'Chief,' naturally. One of them was fairly garrulous and he got along fairly well. But you know, it was the same kind of bigoted camaraderie that I had to put up with. 'Damn Indians, can never hold your liquor,' and stuff like that. 'Dumb Indian.' Things of that sort went on. Thinking about it now, we had some Polish guys that they call 'polacks' and 'square heads.' But you know what? These things went on between groups in the whole outfit. It was almost like a style of the times; these were the times, let's put it that way. There were those times, but then there were other times when the hell was so hellish, you shared it, and religion, [race], had nothing to do with it anymore.

Home

We were put aboard ship. Well, by the time we got aboard the ship, we were waiting to hear. They use the points system. Of course, we had been in so many combat landings. Our officers told us we'd get back among the first and we did. I think I forget how many points you needed but I had like 141 points or something like that.[28] So then they took us down to the harbor. They put us aboard the ship, we went blackout and in convoy from Manila to Hawaii. At Honolulu, they put us aboard a ship that had been a cruise ship. It had lights strung from stern to bow and all the lights aboard went up, and we went from Honolulu to San Francisco.

[Arriving in San Francisco], I remember we went ashore, and we met a cab driver. We were taken to an area where they said, 'You're going to be here for a few days,' and they gave us passes, clean uniforms, got us all our combat ribbons and we went into town. I remember the cab driver at the gate at the Presidio, one of us said, 'We got to get some money. We haven't been paid.' The cab

---

[28] *Adjusted Service Rating Score point system*-Witnessing the frustration incumbent with the Army's failed demobilization efforts at the end of World War I (where entire divisions were sent home at once, rather than individuals based on merit/time served) as General Pershing's Chief of Staff, General George C. Marshall ordered up a study for a more objective, timely methodology for getting the troops home in late 1943. It called for the following:
One point for each month of Army service
One point for each month in service abroad
Five points for each campaign
Five points for a medal for merit/valor
Five points for a Purple Heart
Twelve points for each dependent child (up to three)
Source: Bamford, Tyler. *The Points Were All That Mattered: The US Army's Demobilization After World War II.* National WWII Museum, August 27, 2020. www.nationalww2museum.org/war/articles/points-system-us-armys-demobilization

driver said, 'Are you kidding? You guys won't be able to buy a drink.'

He was right. That city was wide open waiting for us. I remember I wanted to sit at a table because we had eaten so much on the ground and out of cans. I wanted to sit at a table. I remember I wanted to sit at a bar and order a drink and look around. So all the way across the Pacific we kept saying, 'When I get back, I'm going to the Top of the Mark and have a drink in the bar.' And we did. We went to the end of this bar, and it was just gorgeous.

Then they took us to the outside of LA by truck after a few days. We waited there a week and you'd wait for your number to come up. We were near an airfield and what they were doing was, they had a bunch of old C-47s with bucket seats. As Air Force guys were being mustered out, they give them a plane to fly back to the East Coast. They load forty guys aboard. That's how they sent you back. We went back to New York that way. By the way, it took 21 hours on a C-47. We went from LA to Denver to Kansas City to New York.

Believe it or not, I was with several other guys who got mustered out on the same day. We were from the same unit and one of them was from Brooklyn, the other one was from Rochester, New York. They said, 'Hell, we're not going home right away. We're going to New York City and tie one on!' So I joined them and actually went to New York City for two days and had a ball and then we went our separate ways. I went home to Asbury Park, New Jersey.

Adjusting to Civilian Life

Separation, for me, was kind of hard. There was a bond that took place, and, you know, you thought that you were suddenly in a different world.

I called my parents. I told my father I had a stop to make first. Didn't quite tell him where, [but it was to celebrate with my buddies in New York]; I told him when I'd be home. By the time I got home, there was a huge party, get-together in my hometown, and that was it.

I had trouble with my mother who didn't understand who I was yet, who thought it would be just like the day before I went away. There was some difficulty there. Well, they wouldn't leave you alone and they wouldn't allow—they didn't realize that you had a [different] life for three years, making literally life-and-death decisions. And now, you didn't want anybody to tell you where to go, and what to do, when to do it, when not to do it, and everything else. They were just being who they were, but she didn't realize that I'd gone far beyond that.

My father realized this because he had been in combat in World War I. He pretty much left me alone. He took me out for a drink a couple of times. Just the two of us, man to man. So I had difficulty with my mother, and with many civilians who didn't understand. I got in big trouble with a cousin of mine. I still remember, he gave a party in New York City, which I went to. I haven't even bought a civilian suit yet. I had my ruptured duck insignia on. And there was this guy who had been a 4-F, a lawyer. Here was this apartment down at University Place in New York and jammed with people. Great cocktail party.

This guy came up to me and looked at all the ribbons and everything and he says, 'I guess you had a pretty rough time, didn't you?'

I said, 'Well, yeah.' Like this, I didn't really want to talk to anybody about it.

He said, 'Why do you think you had it rough? You know, we couldn't get a can of Bumblebee salmon for three years.'

Something just hit me, and I came up from the floor, literally. I decked him. Of course, he was a good friend of my cousin. Everybody sort of looked and said, 'See, that's what they're coming back like.'

I could see these people talking. 'Look at him. Look at him.'

I left the party. I went a few doors down the block to where there was a bar and saw a couple of GIs in there. I went in like, you know, to be at home.

I still remember I embarrassed my father terribly. I lived in the small town of Bradley Beach, about a mile from Asbury Park. My father was in a store there where he worked. I came to have lunch with him, and we were coming out of this store to go across to a luncheonette. Then just about that time, a car backfired, and I did a full splat right down like that. In the middle of the street. It was a reflex. I heard this *Bam!* and I just went down. I hit the dirt and he looked around.

'What the hell's the matter with you like that?'

'What do you mean what the hell's the matter with me?' I was embarrassed as hell but...

I had gotten out in September, joined what they call the 52-20 Club, [began to] get my bearings, and began writing letters to colleges. Then by January, I'd gotten an acceptance to Indiana University. I went out there for the January term. I graduated from IU in August of '48 on the GI Bill, and I worked on the side as a tutor and did odd jobs or whatever to help. You got 75 bucks a month. You know? And I got to sit at Ernie Pyle's desk at the Indiana *Daily Student* in my senior year. The Sigma Delta Chi was giving a prize and they decided to name it the Ernie Pyle Memorial Prize, and I was the first winner. So now you know it was just good to be back to see it all. You know that you had a feeling, that's what you were fighting for. You get back and just enjoy it all.

'I'm Not Going to Be A Part of It'

I found out that it was not easy to be a working musician in New York. So I took a job in a newspaper on Long Island, and then a friend of mine said, 'You were in the Signal Corps; you're a writer.' They're looking for people from Fort Monmouth, and I became a civilian public information officer attached to the signal school in 1950 at Fort Monmouth. I stayed for four years. I was there during the McCarthy-Army fiasco. That, in some ways, bothered me more than the war did. Well, I had pride during the war. [Now], I sat in a lot of strategy sessions, where, you know, I said, 'Well, what are we going to do now?' [The feeling was], you know, 'Let's man the guns. Let's go to work on this,' and I don't know, 'We have to co-operate in every way.' You felt like you were helping him ferret out all these Reds, but there weren't any, you know, not really. They never brought anybody to trial or anything like that. They ruined a lot of lives, and [McCarthy came here] with Roy Cohn and held a lot of public meetings and [went around to] high schools around Fort Monmouth with everything but the 'Sieg Heil' afterward, you know, and I was really upset about it. And finally, I went in to see the CO of the unit. I was with the Reserve Officers Training School. That was my public information job, and I said, 'You know, I can't handle this. I just can't be a part of it."

He said, 'Well, our hands are tied, there's nothing we can do.'

So I tendered a letter of resignation. My parents were beside themselves because they thought it would seem as if I had resigned at the time that it would look like I had been one of those ferreted out, so I said, 'No, I'm not going to be part of it.' I went in, I got a letter of commendation going out. No repercussions, ever. I had done too much good work. [*Chuckles*]

Lessons of War

I don't think there was a person in my unit who would have ar-
gued with [Truman's decision]. You know? I have always believed,
along with Harry Truman, that in many ways, he felt that he was
saving more lives than were expended. And if, in a war of that kind,
you had to choose between whose lives you were going to save, you
would choose your own. The other thing is, if you think about it,
the Japanese started that war. We didn't go attack Tokyo, they attacked us. I don't feel glad about the death of anyone, whether they
be Japanese or German or anyone else. I think that war is senseless
and death by war is probably the worst possible kind of death for
anyone, and we should look for every way we can to keep it from
happening.

[Today], I have a great sense about it, and I know all the arguments about us. What we did to Dresden, for instance, and the fire
bombings and what we did to Hiroshima and the other Japanese
city, Nagasaki. But wartime, once the war has begun, I think split-
ting hairs over so-called ethical questions is an exercise in futility.
Largely because we didn't start the war. Nobody talked about ethics
when Hitler leveled the city of Amsterdam and Rotterdam with
Stuka dive bombers. All of these things, the Japanese—just look at
what happened on the Death March to Bataan. I think that a commander [in chief], and even the commander of a small unit, has a
horrendous decision to make. He's faced with a decision of what
must be done at that given moment to achieve an objective and end
that battle or that war. You cannot expect him to think, 'Well, we're
going to kill all those people,' when he's looking at his own people
being killed at the same time. I mean, what's a good killing, and
what's a bad killing? We should have thought of all that before we
began at all.

Someone could say, 'Well, the real culprits are the people who allowed Hitler to become what he was, and Hirohito and Tojo to become what they were.' But it was done. I think that's the lesson that for me is the strongest. When I see lessons not being learned today, and I don't give a damn about whether or not there's a stable government in Iraq, but when I see the war [end] and [victory declared while leaving] the mechanism in place for the next war as with Saddam Hussein, I mean that's unconscionable. Because somebody else is going to have to go clean up that mess, and that means other Americans will someday have to fight and die, which is exactly what happened.

I'm hoping that somebody in Afghanistan or wherever it is, we will take note right now of all these lessons that we learned in a war and do something to make certain it doesn't happen again. But once it's happening, for a person to stop and say, 'Well, you shouldn't do this because that's unethical,' but this is okay because that's a 'clean killing' [is not relevant anymore]. Like we talk [now] about 'clean' and 'dirty' bombs.

'You Have to Have Been There'

World War was an experience. Well, I can understand what Hemingway meant when he said that for most men, it's an experience unlike none other that they will ever have in their lifetime. He was absolutely right. No matter what your experience is, it's nothing quite like it. It's almost difficult to really explain it so that someone else can feel it. You have to have been there. It's the only way I know. I can understand the attitudes of many people who have not. I can also not understand some attitudes of people who have, and still haven't learned the lessons. Having gone through it now, I wouldn't take anything for what I gained from it. I would have to

346 | THE INVASION RADIOMAN IV

say that if necessary if the time came, I would probably do it again for my country under the same kinds of circumstances.

My perspective now is interesting to me because I've had such a long history as a political writer, a student, and an observer of politics. Looking back, men in war don't think a great deal about politics; as they say, for the ordinary infantryman, his entire scope is fifty feet in front of his foxhole, and back then, you really had that sense and thinking. Thinking back about it, that sergeant of ours I mentioned so much, Elmer Kaminsky, when you used to ask him for opinions, he would say, 'You know, I don't think too much about it. They got higher-paid folks than me making those decisions.' I'm sure all of us that survived have since become a lot more critical, politically, than we were then.

I believe in an enlightened army. I believe in an enlightened populace; I think they fight better for what they believe in, but then it behooves the leadership to make sure that they only have to fight for things that are deeply believed in and at critical times, and all other times, if they are adventures, we should stay the hell out of them.

The 'Greatest Generation'

I don't know if [we were] the 'Greatest Generation' or not, having been a part of it. I think about it. I've done a lot of reading about the Civil War, and I wonder if they weren't the greatest generation or if they didn't think of themselves as that, and rightly so when you think about it, and I've done a lot of reading about the Revolutionary War. When you think of what those people went up against, to establish an idea, which became a nation, I'm wondering if *they* weren't the greatest generation. So I think it may be a bit presumptuous. Yes, I think the world was on the brink of near extinction, at least civilization as we knew it was, and in many ways, we were a great generation, and I was proud to be part of that. But I'm not so sure I would say we were the 'greatest.' I don't know.

Looking back, one of the things that I've come to believe is that wars—maybe Napoleon was right, that the victor is the one that makes the least mistakes—war is really a series of mistakes; that's how you get into them, and looking back on some of the operations I went through, it's amazing that we got through them and that we won, which more and more brings me back to the fact that so much of war depends on ordinary soldiers, sailors, Marines, and airmen. Yes, you need brilliant people to lead them, but God, when I think of some of the things that happened because ordinary people just did the impossible, or the near impossible... That's really what I think about war and why we need to do everything we can to keep from getting into them. But one of the things I have to say is that I have the greatest respect for the people who give their lives to military service. In this democracy, we couldn't maintain a democracy without it. I know there are people who believe, you know, we could do without the military. No, you couldn't.

You need to always be there for whatever the needs of that democracy are with the military, just as the ordinary citizen has to be there. But I do believe that because of our history as a participatory democracy, and the whole idea of the citizen army and citizen soldier, we don't have enough respect for the people who fill those roles. I think you come to have, you know, those in the professional military. I understand they have an elitist feeling about what they do, but I still believe that we need to maintain proper respect for the people who drop everything and come when their country calls.

I was proud to do it and I'd probably do it again.

Paul Elisha passed away at the age of 92 on August 16, 2015.

"New York Army National Guard Lt. Col. William O'Brien, commander of the 1st Battalion, 105th Infantry Regiment, leads his unit in the relief of another outfit during the battle of Saipan, June 18, 1944. O'Brien would receive the Medal of Honor posthumously for his leadership and actions during the largest Japanese suicide charge of the Pacific Theater July 6-7, 1944." Credit: New York State Military History Museum. National Guard, Public Domain.

EPILOGUE

The Resting Place

With many casualties and ammunition running low, Lt. Col. O'Brien refused to leave the front lines. Striding up and down the lines, he fired at the enemy with a pistol in each hand and his presence there bolstered the spirits of the men, encouraged them in their fight and sustained them in their heroic stand.

Even after he was seriously wounded, Lt. Col. O'Brien refused to be evacuated and after his pistol ammunition was exhausted, he manned a .50-caliber machine gun, mounted on a Jeep, and continued firing.

When last seen alive he was standing upright firing into the Japanese hordes that were enveloping him. Sometime later his body was found surrounded by enemy he had killed.

— MEDAL OF HONOR CITATION

The late spring sun was setting in the idyllic cemetery I had passed so many times without stopping before. I kept looking for the resting place of this lieutenant colonel I had read about. In the end, I had to refer to GPS coordinates and photographs on the internet of a past military remembrance ceremony at his grave to find it.

Back in Section 7, Lot 23, after 20 minutes of searching, I finally found a simple brass marker embedded flat to the ground, no formal headstone or memorial other than a simple homemade wooden cross painted white, and two small American flags rippling in the breeze, side by side. No wonder I missed it.

WILLIAM J O'BRIEN
MEDAL OF HONOR
LT COL US ARMY
WORLD WAR II

The Congressional Medal of Honor Society notes:

"O'Brien joined the Army from his birth city of Troy, New York, and by June 20, 1944, was serving as a lieutenant colonel in the 1st Battalion, 105th Infantry Regiment, 27th Infantry Division. On that day, on Saipan in the Mariana Islands, he braved enemy fire to reach several American tanks which were unknowingly firing on their own troops. The next week, on June 28, he oversaw and personally led an attack on a Japanese-held ridge. On July 7 his battalion came under attack from a much larger enemy force, the largest banzai charge of the Pacific War. He refused to leave the front lines even after being wounded and continued to rally his men until being overrun and killed. He was posthumously awarded the Medal of Honor on May 9, 1945, for his actions throughout the battle for Saipan."[29]

---

[29] William J. O'Brien's (1899-1944) full Medal of Honor citation reads as follows: "For conspicuous gallantry and intrepidity at the risk of his life above and beyond the call of duty at Saipan, Mariana Islands, from 20 June through 7 July 1944. When assault elements of his platoon were held up by intense enemy fire, Lt. Col. O'Brien ordered 3 tanks to precede the assault companies in an attempt to knock out the strongpoint. Due to direct enemy fire the tanks' turrets were closed, causing the tanks to lose direction and to fire into our own troops. Lt. Col. O'Brien, with complete disregard for his own safety, dashed into full view of the enemy and ran to the leader's tank, and pounded on the tank with his pistol butt to attract 2 of the tank's crew and, mounting the tank fully exposed to enemy fire, Lt. Col. O'Brien personally directed the assault until the enemy strongpoint had been liquidated. On 28 June 1944, while his platoon was attempting to take a bitterly defended high ridge in the vicinity of Donnay, Lt. Col. O'Brien arranged to capture the ridge by a double envelopment movement of 2 large combat battalions. He personally took control of the maneuver. Lt. Col. O'Brien crossed 1,200 yards of sniper-infested underbrush alone to arrive at a point where 1 of his platoons was being held up by the enemy. Leaving some men to contain the enemy he personally led 4 men into a narrow ravine behind, and killed or drove off all the Japanese manning that strongpoint. In this action he captured 5 machine guns and one 77-mm. fieldpiece.

Bill O'Brien was born in 1899. His parents are here. He died in this most horrific banzai charge of World War II, in which the 1st and 2nd Battalions of the 105th Infantry Regiment, 27th Division front line lost 650 killed and wounded, but also took over 4,300 of the enemy to their deaths.[12]

And he was not the only MOH recipient, posthumous, from this town who died on Saipan that day; in Part Two of this book you also learned about the actions of 28-year-old Thomas A. Baker, 'propped up against a tree.' And what of the dentist-turned-combat doctor from Minnesota from this same 105th Infantry Regiment, Captain Ben Lewis Salomon?[30] He was another of the officers killed

---

Lt. Col. O'Brien then organized the 2 platoons for night defense and against repeated counterattacks directed them. Meanwhile he managed to hold ground. On 7 July 1944 his battalion and another battalion were attacked by an overwhelming enemy force estimated at between 3,000 and 5,000 Japanese. With bloody hand-to-hand fighting in progress everywhere, their forward positions were finally overrun by the sheer weight of the enemy numbers. With many casualties and ammunition running low, Lt. Col. O'Brien refused to leave the front lines. Striding up and down the lines, he fired at the enemy with a pistol in each hand and his presence there bolstered the spirits of the men, encouraged them in their fight and sustained them in their heroic stand.

Even after he was seriously wounded, Lt. Col. O'Brien refused to be evacuated and after his pistol ammunition was exhausted, he manned a .50 caliber machine gun, mounted on a jeep, and continued firing. When last seen alive he was standing upright firing into the Japanese hordes that were then enveloping him. Some time later his body was found surrounded by enemy he had killed. His valor was consistent with the highest traditions of the service."

[30] Captain Ben Lewis Salomon's (1914-1944) Medal of Honor Citation reads: "For conspicuous gallantry and intrepidity at the risk of his life above and beyond the call of duty. Captain Ben L. Salomon was serving at Saipan, in the Mariana Islands on July 7, 1944, as the Surgeon for the 2nd Battalion, 105th Infantry Regiment, 27th Infantry Division. The Regiment's 1st and 2nd Battalions were attacked by an overwhelming force estimated between 3,000 and 5,000 Japanese soldiers. It was one of the largest attacks attempted in

in the charge, but not before inflicting perhaps one hundred deaths of the enemy protecting his wounded patients, and posthumously awarded the Medal of Honor in 2002 for his heroic defensive actions.

Three MOH citations, one action, one infantry regiment. That kind of selfless self-sacrifice is rare; in fact, as retired New York Army National Guard Lt. Col. Paul Fanning noted on the seventy-fifth anniversary at the foot of O'Brien's grave, 'There is nothing like this in our Army history, where three men all sacrificed themselves in such a way to save the lives of their fellow soldiers.'[13]

*

---

the Pacific Theater during World War II. Although both units fought furiously, the enemy soon penetrated the Battalions' combined perimeter and inflicted overwhelming casualties. In the first minutes of the attack, approximately 30 wounded soldiers walked, crawled, or were carried into Captain Salomon's aid station, and the small tent soon filled with wounded men. As the perimeter began to be overrun, it became increasingly difficult for Captain Salomon to work on the wounded. He then saw a Japanese soldier bayoneting one of the wounded soldiers lying near the tent. Firing from a squatting position, Captain Salomon quickly killed the enemy soldier. Then, as he turned his attention back to the wounded, two more Japanese soldiers appeared in the front entrance of the tent. As these enemy soldiers were killed, four more crawled under the tent walls. Rushing them, Captain Salomon kicked the knife out of the hand of one, shot another, and bayoneted a third. Captain Salomon butted the fourth enemy soldier in the stomach and a wounded comrade then shot and killed the enemy soldier.
Realizing the gravity of the situation, Captain Salomon ordered the wounded to make their way as best they could back to the regimental aid station, while he attempted to hold off the enemy until they were clear. Captain Salomon then grabbed a rifle from one of the wounded and rushed out of the tent. After four men were killed while manning a machine gun, Captain Salomon took control of it. When his body was later found, 98 dead enemy soldiers were piled in front of his position. Captain Salomon's extraordinary heroism and devotion to duty are in keeping with the highest traditions of military service and reflect great credit upon himself, his unit, and the United States Army."

Today, literally as I string together these last few words to reflect upon these men, the last living World War II Medal of Honor recipient, Iwo Jima Marine veteran Hershel 'Woody' Williams, is lying in state in the US Capitol Rotunda, having recently passed at the age of 98, symbolizing the passing of the World War II Generation's MOH recipients and indeed, the passage of this entire generation of veterans. When he was awarded the medal personally by President Truman, he felt conflicted, which he expressed in an interview later:

'I no longer just represented me. I now represented the Marines who protected me, Marines who sacrificed their lives doing that... If I had written that recommendation for the Medal of Honor—which I didn't, my commanding officer did—I would have never used the word '*alone.*' I sort of resent that word in my citation. It says, '*He went forward alone.*' That's not correct. Four Marines were protecting me, and two of them were killed while they did it. So I have said from the very beginning that it does not belong to me. It belongs to them.'[143][1]

---

[1] Woody Williams' (1923-2022) Medal of Honor citation reads: "*For conspicuous gallantry and intrepidity at the risk of his life above and beyond the call of duty as Demolition Sergeant serving with the First Battalion, Twenty-First Marines, Third Marine Division, in action against enemy Japanese forces on Iwo Jima, Volcano Island, 23 February 1945. Quick to volunteer his services when our tanks were maneuvering vainly to open a lane for the infantry through the network of reinforced concrete pillboxes, buried mines and black, volcanic sands, Corporal Williams daringly went forward alone to attempt the reduction of devastating machine-gun fire from the unyielding positions.*
Covered only by four riflemen, he fought desperately for four hours under terrific enemy small-arms fire and repeatedly returned to his own lines to prepare demolition charges and obtain serviced flame throwers, struggling back, frequently to the rear of hostile emplacements, to wipe out one position after another. On one occasion he daringly mounted a pillbox to insert the nozzle of his flame thrower through the air vent, kill the occupants and silence the gun; on another he grimly charged enemy riflemen who

He also battled the demons that our veterans pick up on the battlefield, the ones that never truly leave them, haunted by the friends he had lost, the men he had killed.

They once walked among us as humble giants of humanity. Some of these survivors, like Woody, a career counselor of veterans, went on to dedicate their lives to others. As I've stated before, they were our neighbors, our teachers and coaches, shopkeepers and carpenters, millworkers and mechanics, nurses and stenographers, lawyers and loggers, draftsmen and doctors, people from every walk of life, high school dropouts and college graduates. They were the World War II Generation, and there was a time after the war when we just simply took them for granted. They were ordinary people who did extraordinary things, on the battlefield, and in their lives that followed. It is my hope that this series brings us closer to this part of the American character that we really can't afford to forget.

Maybe it is presumptuous of me to be quietly disturbed that Bill O'Brien, MOH, has a final resting place that doesn't call attention to the man or his deeds, that a Medal of Honor recipient doesn't even have an upright stone. But maybe that's the way Bill would have wanted it; this generation was like that. Maybe the family felt the same, in their quietly overwhelming private grief. And maybe it's just really none of my business, after all. But I just can't move on

---

attempted to stop him with bayonets and destroyed them with a burst of flame from his weapon.
His unyielding determination and extraordinary heroism in the face of ruthless enemy resistance were directly instrumental in neutralizing one of the most fanatically defended Japanese strong points encountered by his regiment and aided in enabling his company to reach its' [sic] objective. Corporal Williams' aggressive fighting spirit and valiant devotion to duty throughout this fiercely contested action sustain and enhance the highest traditions of the United States Naval Service."

without sharing this story, because it is our story, too, the story of America. Like Woody said, 'I no longer just represented me...'

You don't have to search for the cemeteries or final resting places to learn to appreciate what that generation did. You've taken the time to listen to their stories. Say their names, and the names of their fallen friends, and they will live forever. [32]

---

[32] *and they will live forever-* As this book was going to press, I received an email from a reader of my previous books. It arrived just as I was finishing this chapter, and, with his permission, I would like to share what my reader expressed about his grandfather's pain and trauma, and a grandson's yearning to know him better.

RE: THE THINGS OUR FATHERS SAW

8.1.22

FROM: Dennis M.

"Mr. Rozell, I have always been fascinated by World War II and the history behind it. I am 51 years old, and my grandfather fought in the Pacific, and like most of his generation, he never spoke of it. I know he struggled with PTSD his whole life and I unfortunately learned more about his military career when he passed than I had known when he was alive.

According to my father, my grandfather was a really intelligent man before the war and was well respected in the community that they lived in a small town in western Minnesota. He was my mom's father and from the little bit I was told, he was not a front-line soldier but with all the casualties they suffered in the beginning, he volunteered to be a machine gunner and I know he was wounded five times. Being [as] he grew up in a small town and also where racism was unfortunately more prevalent back then, my mother told me they were raised to look at people the same, no matter what their color was, and the only reason I bring this up [is because] I was told when he was wounded on two of those occasions, Black soldiers helped save him.

He was awarded multiple medals, but unfortunately, *he threw them all overboard on his way home from the war* [*author emphasis*], and no one in the family knew this until after his death. I was only 17 years old when he passed away and I would have loved just to sit down and talked with him

Because dying for freedom isn't the worst that could happen. Being forgotten is.

---

about his military experiences and service, but unfortunately that was never to be.

He was just one [of] million[s] of men drafted and pulled from their lives to go and serve in the military and do their duty until the war ended. My father told me the war changed him for the rest of his life, after it was over, and I often wondered what kind of man he would have been like had he not like millions of other men had to go to war and seeing the horrific experiences of it.

He was unfortunately an alcoholic his whole life after the war and my father said the war is what caused this; although this is going to sound crazy to say, he was a 'good' alcoholic, if there is one, in that he always treated us grand-kids with love and kindness—you rarely knew he was intoxicated, although when you are young and naïve, we could never tell because he was always so good to us.

There were a couple of letters he wrote while he was overseas [that didn't tell much] with how they censored mail back then—and I am sure not to make my grandma worry—but the only time he mentioned anything about fighting in the war [was] where he wrote that at night they never got much sleep, because they always had to worry about the Japanese trying to sneak into their fox holes.

I just wish I would have known more about his military career and what medals he earned while serving overseas. Thank you again for preserving their stories for future generations before all of these great men and women are gone as I love reading the stories that these men and women have shared in a time when everyone from that generation pitched in and did their part for the war effort and unfortunately some of them made the ultimate sacrifice.

Sincerely, Dennis M."

Thank you for reading!

I hope you found this book interesting and informative; I sure learned a lot researching and writing it. If you liked it, you'll love the other books!

***

UPCOMING TITLES

Check Here:

BIT.LY/MRBWWIIBOOKS

THE THINGS OUR FATHERS SAW®

ABOUT THE AUTHOR

Photo Credit: Joan K. Lentini; May 2017.

Matthew Rozell is an award-winning history teacher, author, speaker, and blogger on the topic of the most cataclysmic events in the history of mankind—World War II and the Holocaust. Rozell has been featured as the 'ABC World News Person of the Week' and has had his work as a teacher filmed for the CBS Evening News, NBC Learn, the Israeli Broadcast Authority, the United States Holocaust Memorial Museum, and the New York State United Teachers. He writes on the power of teaching and the importance of the study of history at TeachingHistoryMatters.com, and you can 'Like' his Facebook author page at AuthorMatthewRozell for updates.

Mr. Rozell is a sought-after speaker on World War II, the Holocaust, and history education, motivating and inspiring his audiences with the lessons of the past. Visit MatthewRozell.com for availability/details.

...And if you would like to learn more about our GIs and the Holocaust...

~SOON TO BE A MAJOR FILM~

"What healing this has given to the survivors and military men!"-Reviewer

FROM THE <u>ABC WORLD NEWS 'PERSON OF THE WEEK'</u>

A TRAIN NEAR MAGDEBURG

THE HOLOCAUST, AND THE REUNITING

OF THE SURVIVORS AND SOLDIERS, 70 YEARS ON

–Featuring testimony from 15 American liberators and over 30 Holocaust survivors

–500 pages-extensive notes and bibliographical references

BOOK ONE—THE HOLOCAUST

BOOK TWO—THE AMERICANS

BOOK THREE—LIBERATION

BOOK FOUR—REUNION

THE HOLOCAUST was a watershed event in history. In this book, Matthew Rozell reconstructs a lost chapter—the liberation of a 'death train' deep in the heart of Nazi Germany in the closing days of World War II. Drawing on never-before-published eye-witness accounts, survivor testimony, and wartime reports and letters, Rozell brings to life the incredible true stories behind the iconic 1945 liberation photographs taken by the soldiers who were there. He weaves together a chronology of the Holocaust as it unfolds across Europe, and goes back to literally retrace the steps of the survivors and the American soldiers who freed them. Rozell's work results in joyful reunions on three continents, seven decades later. He offers his unique perspective on the lessons of the Holocaust for future generations, and the impact that one person can make.

A selection of comments left by reviewers:

"**Extraordinary research** into an event which needed to be told. I have read many books about the Holocaust and visited various museums but had not heard reference to this train previously. The fact that people involved were able to connect, support and help heal each other emotionally was amazing."

"**The story of the end of the Holocaust and the Nazi regime** told from a very different and precise angle. First-hand accounts from Jewish survivors and the US soldiers that secured their freedom. Gripping."

"**Mr. Rozell travels 'back to the future'** of people who were not promised a tomorrow; neither the prisoners nor the troops knew what horrors the next moment would bring. He captures the parallel experience of soldiers fighting ruthless Nazism and the ruthless treatment of Jewish prisoners."

"**If you have any trepidation** about reading a book on the Holocaust, this review is for you. [Matthew Rozell] masterfully conveys the individual stories of those featured in the book in a manner that does not leave the reader with a sense of despair, but rather a sense of purpose."

"**Could not put this book down**--I just finished reading *A Train Near Magdeburg*. Tears fell as I read pages and I smiled through others. I wish I could articulate the emotions that accompanied me through the stories of these beautiful people."

"**Everyone should read this book**, detailing the amazing bond that formed between Holocaust survivors likely on their way to death in one last concentration camp as WWII was about to end, and a small number of American soldiers that happened upon the stopped train and liberated the victims. The lifelong friendships that resulted between the survivors and their liberators is a testament to compassion and goodness. It is amazing that the author is not Jewish but a 'reluctant' history teacher who ultimately becomes a Holocaust scholar. This is a great book."

About This Book/
Acknowledgements

*

A note on historiographical style and convention: to enhance accuracy, consistency, and readability, I corrected punctuation and spelling and sometimes even place names, but only after extensive research. I did take the liberty of occasionally condensing the speaker's voice, eliminating side tangents or incidental information not relevant to the matter at hand. Sometimes two or more interviews with the same person were combined for readability and narrative flow. All of the words of the subjects, however, are essentially their own.

Additionally, I chose to utilize footnotes and endnotes where I deemed them appropriate, directing readers who wish to learn more to my sources, notes, and side commentary. I hope that they do not detract from the flow of the narrative.

*

First, I wish to acknowledge the hundreds of students who passed through my classes and who forged the bonds with the World War II generation. I promised you these books someday, and now that many of you are yourselves parents, you can tell your children this book is for them. Who says young people are indifferent to the past? I will continue to argue that it just needs to be presented to them in an engaging manner. We underestimate them sometimes.

I was also happy to be tipped off by former students that Vol. I of *The Things Our Fathers Saw®* series, also on the Pacific and published seven years ago, is quoted a few times in Dan Carlin's popular Hardcore History podcast, *Supernova in the East.* Thanks, Dan, for recognizing the importance of this oral testimony.

The Hudson Falls Central School District and my former colleagues have my deep appreciation for supporting this endeavor and recognizing its significance throughout the years. I also express my appreciation once again to my friends James and Elise Sedore for carving out a therapeutic writing retreat opportunity this year as I began this book, far away from the harsh winter winds of the Northeast, and my wife Laura for her constant support and companionship, and her help in getting the books out the door to you.

Naturally this work would not have been possible had it not been for the willingness of the veterans to share their stories for posterity. All of the veterans who were interviewed for this book had the foresight to complete release forms granting access to their stories, and for us to share the information with the New York State Military Museum's Veterans Oral History Project, where copies of the original interviews reside. Wayne Clarke and Mike Russert of the NYSMMVOP were instrumental in cultivating this relationship with my classes over the years and are responsible for many of the interviews in this book as well; Lt. Col. Robert von Hasseln and Michael Aikey also conducted some of these early NYSMM interviews. Please see the 'Source Notes.'

Cara Quinlan's sharp proofing and suggestions helped to clean up the original manuscript.

*

I also have decided to dedicate this volume to the memory of Tom Vesey, Sr., a Korea veteran, like my own dad. Tom was my father-in-law and recently passed peacefully at the age of 92 in the presence of his daughter, my wife. Hands-down, he was the kindest, sweetest man I have ever known. Like my dad, he was a school-teacher; he and his twin brother Genie taught in side-by-side elementary school classrooms on Long Island, New York. He was a voracious reader until his eyesight began to fail him, but he never complained. He was a fan of this series and appreciated every volume. Tom was the last of twelve children from a family that, like mine, traced its roots back to Ireland. We are better people because of Tom Vesey, and his late wife Shirley, and their generation of Americans, which is now pretty much gone. They left the world a better place. This book is for you, Tom.

I would be remiss if I did not recall the profound influence of my late mother and father, Mary and Tony Rozell, both cutting-edge educators and proud early supporters of my career. To my younger siblings Mary, Ned, Nora, and Drew, all accomplished writers and authors, thank you for your encouragement as well. Final and deepest appreciations go to my wife Laura and our children, Emma, Ned, and Mary. Thank you for indulging the old man as he attempted to bring to life the stories he collected as a young one.

NOTES

Source Notes: **Frank J. Castronovo.** Interviewed by Robert von Hasseln and Wayne Clarke, May 25, 2001. Freeport, NY. Deposited at NYS Military Museum.

Source Notes: **Charles M. Jacobs.** Interviewed by Michael Aikey and Wayne Clarke, August 8, 2001. Latham, NY. Deposited at NYS Military Museum.

Source Notes: **Paul Elisha.** Interviewed by Robert von Hasseln, December 12, 2000. Interviewed by Michael Aikey and Wayne Clarke, July 16, 2001, November 28, 2001. Latham, NY. Deposited at NYS Military Museum.

Source Notes: **James A. Smith, Jr.** Interviewed by Michael Russert and Wayne Clarke, February 20, 2003. Saratoga Springs, NY. Deposited at NYS Military Museum.

Source Notes: **Samuel R. Dinova.** Interviewed by Michael Russert and Wayne Clarke, January 7, 2003. Troy, NY. Deposited at NYS Military Museum.

Source Notes: **Albert J. Harris.** Interviewed by Michael Aikey and Wayne Clarke, July 30, 2001. Latham, NY. Deposited at NYS Military Museum.

Source Notes: **Unknown Japanese Soldier.** Diary entries, July 11, 1944, to July 8, 1944. Saipan. Translated transcription mailed to Matthew Rozell by Terry Barber, Fort Ann, New York, in a letter dated December 12, 2011. It was acquired by him from his wife's aunt, whose deceased husband was a veteran of the Pacific war. The original diary's whereabouts are unknown.

Source Notes: **John H. Kolecki.** Interviewed by Michael Russert and Wayne Clarke, February 22, 2006. Buffalo, NY. Deposited at NYS Military Museum.

Source Notes: **Henry C. Huneken.** Interviewed by Michael Russert and Wayne Clarke, August 5, 2004. South Setauket, NY. Deposited at NYS Military Museum.

Source Notes: **Steve T. Jordan.** Interviewed by Michael Russert and Wayne Clarke, November 25, 2003. Saratoga Springs, NY. Deposited at NYS Military Museum.

Source Notes: **Mitchell Morse.** Interviewed by Michael Aikey and Eric Scott, April 11, 2001. Kingston, NY. Deposited at NYS Military Museum.

[1] Pyle, Ernie. *Back Again.* Wartime Columns of Ernie Pyle, The Media School Indiana University. sites.mediaschool.indiana.edu/erniepyle/1945/02/06/back-again
[2] Lancaster, Marc. *Ernie Pyle killed on Ie Shima.* World War II on Deadline, April 18, 2021. ww2ondeadline.com/2021/04/18/ernie-pyle-killed-ww2-correspondent
[3] Hewett, Frank. *The Battling Bastards of Bataan.* 1942.
[4] Pyle, Ernie. *On Victory in Europe.* Wartime Columns of Ernie Pyle, The Media School Indiana University. sites.mediaschool.indiana.edu/erniepyle/1945/04/18/on-victory-in-europe/
[5] Lancaster, Marc. *Ernie Pyle killed on Ie Shima.* World War II on Deadline, April 18, 2021.

ww2ondeadline.com/2021/04/18/ernie-pyle-killed-ww2-corre-
spondent
[6] Toland, John. *The Rising Sun: The Decline and Fall of the
Japanese Empire 1936-1945*, Random House, 1970. 470.
[7] Chapin, John C. *Marines in World War II Commemorative Series, Breaking the Outer Ring: Marine Landings in the Marshall
Islands*. National Park Service. www.nps.gov/parkhis-
tory/online_books/npswapa/extcontent/usmc/pcn-190-003124-
00/sec2.htm
[8] The Peleliu operation is further discussed and remembered by
veterans in Vol. I of this series, Voices of the Pacific.
[9] Miller, Donald. *The Story of World War II*. New York: Simon
& Schuster, 2001. 416.
[10] Miller, *The Story of World War II*. 458-61.
[11] *Tenth Army*- Source: Battle of Okinawa. wikipe-
dia.org/wiki/Battle_of_Okinawa. Cross-referenced.
[12] Valenza, Andrew, N.Y. Guard Soldiers Remember Medal of
Honor Recipients, New York National Guard. July 9, 2019.
www.nationalguard.mil/News/Article/1898451/ny-guard-sol-
diers-remember-medal-of-honor-recipients
[13] 'There is nothing like this in our Army history'- Paul Fanning,
New York Army National Guard Lt. Col., Ret., quoted in
Valenza, Andrew, N.Y. Guard Soldiers Remember Medal of
Honor Recipients, New York National Guard. July 9, 2019.
www.nationalguard.mil/News/Article/1898451/ny-guard-sol-
diers-remember-medal-of-honor-recipients
[14] *Woody Williams quote*-Tuthill, Matt. *Living Legend: the Story
of Hershel "Woody" Williams*. Chef Irvine.com,
chefirvine.com/magazine/living-legend-the-story-of-hershel-
woody-williams.

Made in the USA
Monee, IL
30 November 2023

47689576R00203